The Wisdom of Will:
365 Days of Shakespeare's Wit

Jill O'Hora

All quotations from Shakespeare's works are taken from the 2001 revised edition of *The Arden Shakespeare Complete Works,* edited by Richard Proudfoot, Ann Thompson, and David Scott Kastan and published by The Arden Shakespeare.

All Celtic images are taken from Marty Noble's *Full-Color Celtic Designs CD-ROM and Book,* published by Dover Publications, Inc. in 2002.

Contact the author at www.thewisdomofwill.com.

First published by Dog Ear Publishing
4010 W. 86th Street, Ste H
Indianapolis, IN 46268
www.dogearpublishing.net

ISBN: 978-1-4575-2304-5

This book is printed on acid-free paper.

Printed in the United States of America

For my sisters,
Judy and Colleen Matria
and
for my sons,
Ben and Nate

Rebirth

JANUARY 1

Shepherd

But look thee
here, boy. Now bless thyself: thou met'st with things
dying, I with things new-born.

The Winter's Tale 3.3.110-12

After discovering a newborn babe, the Shepherd says this to his son the Clown. The Clown has just simultaneously witnessed a shipwreck and the violent death of Antigonus, the man who has placed the babe on the shore.

Shepherd*: But look at this, son. Make the sign of the cross. You encounter things that are dying while I encounter those that are newly born.*

Dawning Consciousness

JANUARY 2

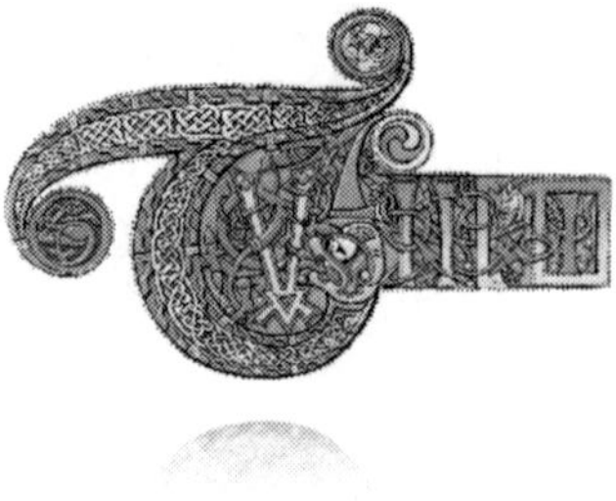

Prospero

Their understanding
Begins to swell, and the approaching tide
Will shortly fill the reasonable shore
That now lies foul and muddy.

The Tempest 5.1.79-82

Prospero, the deposed Duke of Milan, says this to the spirit Ariel about Alonso, the King of Naples. Alonso has just awakened from the spell Prospero has cast upon Alonso and other shipwrecked passengers in order to enact revenge and bring about their repentance.

***Prospero**: Their consciousness is starting to increase, and the rising tide of clarity will before long sweep clean the shore of reason that is now obscured and confused.*

Humor

JANUARY 3

Falstaff

I am not only
witty in myself, but the cause that wit is in other men.

King Henry IV, Part 2 1.2.9-10

Falstaff says this when his page repeats a humorous but mocking message that Falstaff's doctor has sent regarding his patient's urine sample. In his reply Falstaff snatches victory out of the jaws of defeat.

Falstaff*: I am not only clever and inventive in my own right, but also the source of such talent in those around me.*

Ease of Giving Advice

JANUARY 4

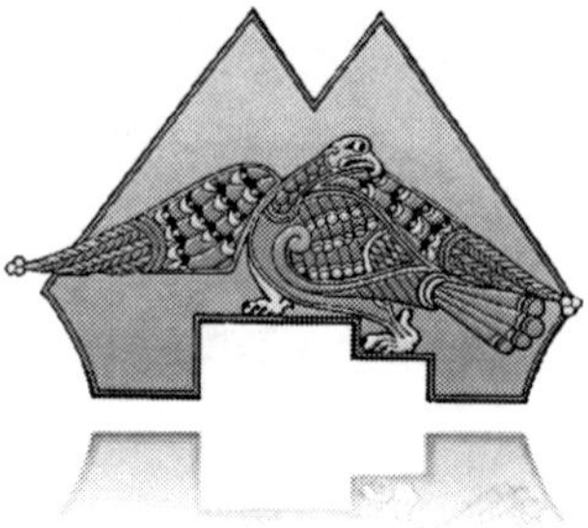

Leonato

for, brother, men
Can counsel and speak comfort to that grief
Which they themselves not feel. . . .

Much Ado About Nothing 5.1.20-22

Leonato, Governor of Messina, says this to his brother Antonio. Leonato believes that his daughter is dead, having been falsely accused of being unfaithful to her fiancé the night before her scheduled wedding.

***Leonato**: Brother, people can easily advise and offer consolation concerning a sorrow that they themselves do not experience.*

Fickle Loyalties

JANUARY 5

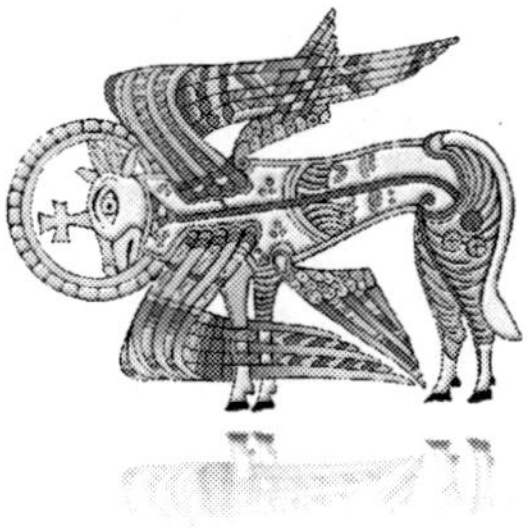

Archbishop

What trust is in these times?
They that, when Richard liv'd, would have him die
Are now become enamour'd on his grave.

King Henry IV, Part 2 1.3.100-02

Speaking to some of the rebels who are trying to regroup after their loss at the Battle of Shrewsbury, the Archbishop of York remarks upon the irony that those who during his lifetime wished the former King Richard II dethroned--and even killed--are now mourning his death.

***Archbishop**: How is it possible to have any faith in the present age? Those people who wanted King Richard dead while he was alive are now passionately embracing his tomb.*

Expression of Love

JANUARY 6

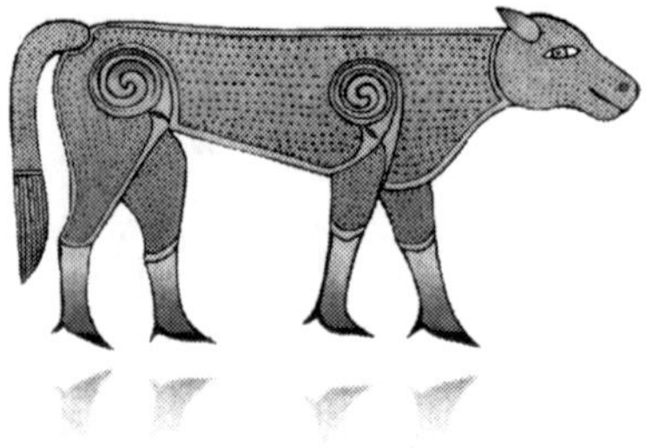

Sonnet 102

My love is strengthened, though more weak in seeming;
I love not less, though less the show appear.
That love is merchandised, whose rich esteeming
The owner's tongue doth publish everywhere.

Lines 1-4

***Sonnet 102**: My quiet demeanor may suggest I love you less; however, my love for you has grown stronger. That love is only cheapened when, claiming to cherish it, the lover proclaims it publicly.*

Intoxication and Desire

JANUARY 7

Porter

Therefore, much drink may be said to be an equivocator with lechery: it makes him, and it mars him; it sets him on, and it takes him off; it persuades him, and disheartens him; makes him stand to, and not stand to: in conclusion, equivocates him in a sleep, and, giving him the lie, leaves him.

Macbeth 2.3.31-36

Returning to Macbeth's castle to waken King Duncan, Macduff and Lennox encounter a porter at the gate who is recovering from a night of intoxication. The Porter tells the two arrivals that drink is a great stimulant. When Macduff asks what things drink provokes, the Porter explains.

***Porter**: Too much alcohol can be said to be a misleader of lust: it creates desire and ruins it; it stimulates lust and dissuades it; it convinces desire and then dampens its spirits. Drinking makes desire take a stand and then fall. To sum up, drunkenness tricks lechery into a sleep and then lays lust out flat.*

Seeking Shelter

JANUARY 8

1 Murderer
The west yet glimmers with some streaks of day;
Now spurs the lated traveller apace,
To gain the timely inn. . . .

***Macbeth* 3.3.5-7**

The first murderer says this as he and another murderer await the arrival of Banquo and his son Fleance. It is ironic that a murderer remarks upon familiar daily cycles.

***1 Murderer**: The western sky still vibrates with remnants of sunlight and prods tardy travelers to find a convenient place to stay for the night.*

Abuse of Power

JANUARY 9

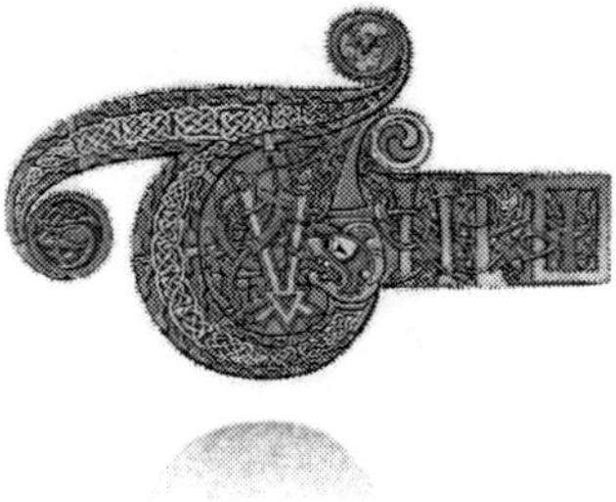

Isabella

O, it is excellent
To have a giant's strength, but it is tyrannous
To use it like a giant.

Measure for Measure 2.2.108-10

Isabella, pleading before Lord Angelo for her brother's life, says this to Angelo as she pleads for his compassion in passing sentence on her brother's act of adultery.

***Isabella**: Oh, it is splendid to have the force of a giant, but it is cruel to wield power like one.*

Riches of Books

JANUARY 10

Prospero

Me, poor man, my library
Was dukedom large enough.

The Tempest 1.2.109-10

Prospero says this to his daughter Miranda as he recounts to her for the first time the violent acts that made him flee from Milan when Miranda was only a babe. Although Prospero was Duke of Milan, he preferred a life of learning to the life at court, and in Prospero's absence, his brother Antonio usurped power.

Prospero: *My room full of books was a kingdom vast enough for me, poor soul.*

Ravages of Aging

JANUARY 11

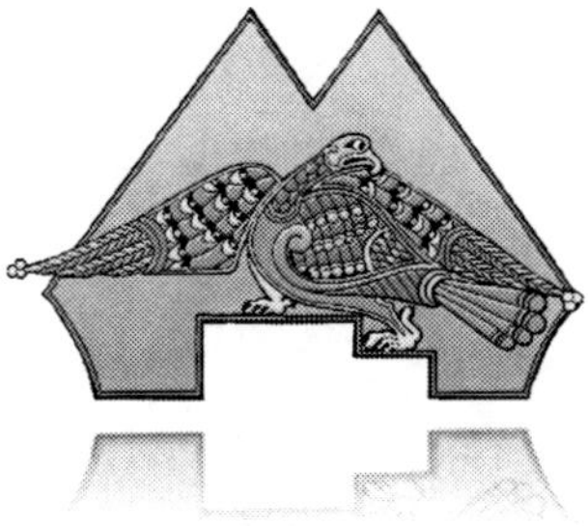

Sonnet 2

When forty winters shall besiege thy brow,
And dig deep trenches in thy beauty's field,
Thy youth's proud livery, so gazed on now,
Will be a tattered weed of small worth held. . . .

Lines 1-4

Sonnet 2*: After forty years have assaulted your forehead and furrowed deep wrinkles in your beautiful face, your youthful appearance, often stared at now, will become a ragged, worthless weed.*

Prayer

JANUARY 12

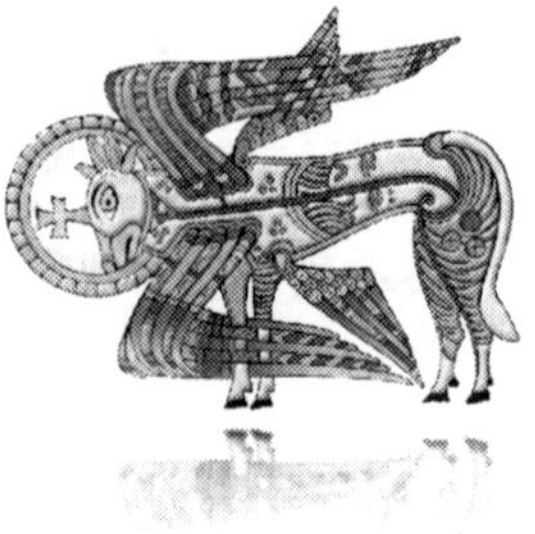

Adam

He that doth the ravens feed,
Yea providently caters for the sparrow,
Be comfort to my age.

As You Like It 2.3.43-45

The faithful old servant Adam says this to his master Orlando whose life has been threatened by the envious Duke Frederick.

Adam: *Oh He who gives food to the ravens and with careful foresight provides for the sparrow, may you bring assistance to my old age.*

Power of Gentleness

JANUARY 13

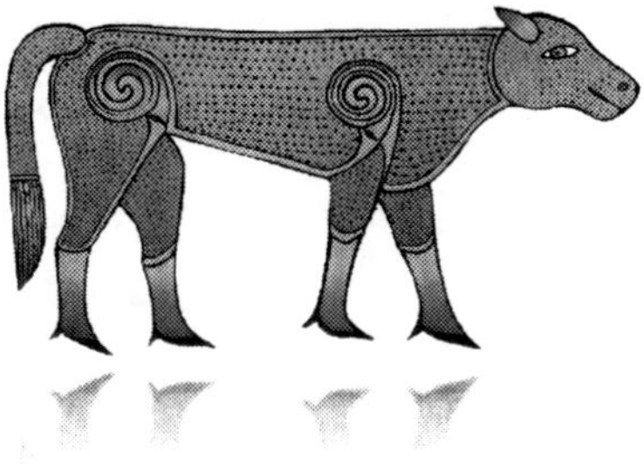

Duke Senior
What would you have? Your gentleness shall force,
More than your force move us to gentleness.
As You Like It 2.7.102-03

Duke Senior, who though exiled is content living in the Forest of Arden, says this to newcomer Orlando. Weak with hunger, Orlando demands food from the strangers he meets in Arden. Orlando seeks food not for himself but in order to revive the failing old servant Adam who lies hidden nearby.

Duke Senior: *What do you want? Your gentleness has more power than your violence does to persuade us to be generous to you.*

Escaping Responsibility

JANUARY 14

Edmund

This is the excellent foppery of the world, that when we are sick in fortune, often the surfeits of our own behaviour, we make guilty of our disasters the sun, the moon and the stars, as if we were villains on necessity, fools by heavenly compulsion, knaves, thieves and treachers by spherical predominance. . . .

King Lear 1.2.119-24

The bastard son Edmund says this, having just duped his father Gloucester into believing the lie that his legitimate son Edgar desires his father's death in order to seize Gloucester's estate.

***Edmund**: Herein lies the unsurpassed foolishness of the world. When our circumstances are shameful, often as a result of the excesses of our own deeds, we blame our misfortunes on the sun, the moon, and the stars as if we were unprincipled scoundrels by constraint, idiots by divine force, and rogues, villains, and cheats due to the position of the planets.*

Impatience of Love
JANUARY 15

Theseus

O, methinks, how slow
This old moon wanes! She lingers my desires,
Like to a step-dame or a dowager
Long withering out a young man's revenue.
A Midsummer Night's Dream 1.1.3-6

Theseus, Duke of Athens, says this to his betrothed, Queen Hippolyta, whom he is due to marry in four days' time.

***Theseus**: Oh, how sluggishly this declining moon progresses. She delays the satisfaction of my longing like an aged stepmother or widow whose long life gradually exhausts a young man's inheritance.*

Process of Creativity

JANUARY 16

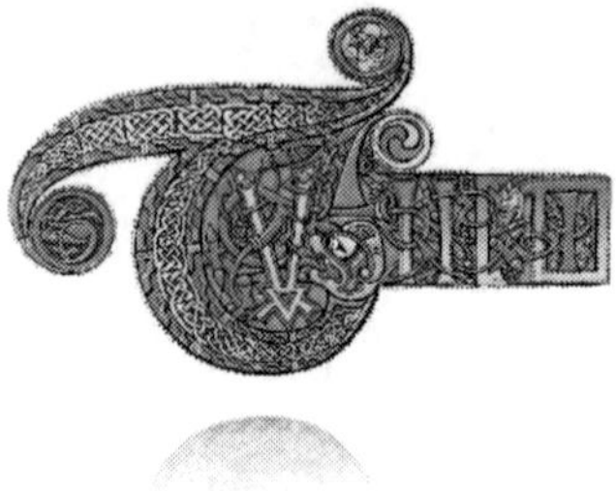

Theseus

as imagination bodies forth
The forms of things unknown, the poet's pen
Turns them to shapes, and gives to airy nothing
A local habitation and a name.

A Midsummer Night's Dream 5.1.14-17

Theseus says this to his wife Hippolyta after he hears the fantastic stories that the young lovers--Helena and Demetrius, Lysander and Hermia--tell of their night of confused love and switched loyalties in the forest.

***Theseus**: As the imagination gives birth to structures of things that are hitherto unexpressed, the poet's pen then transforms them into concrete images, thus giving definition and specific locale to unsubstantial nothingness.*

Vulnerability

JANUARY 17

Lear

Go to, they are not men o'their words: they
told me I was everything; 'tis a lie, I am not ague-proof.

King Lear 4.6.103-04

Having been driven out of home and shelter by his cruel daughters, King Lear discovers the lie concerning his invincibility that his councilors, courtiers, and subjects have perpetrated.

***King Lear**: No way! They are not truthful men. They told me I was all-powerful. But that's a lie. I am not immune to a fever.*

Patience

JANUARY 18

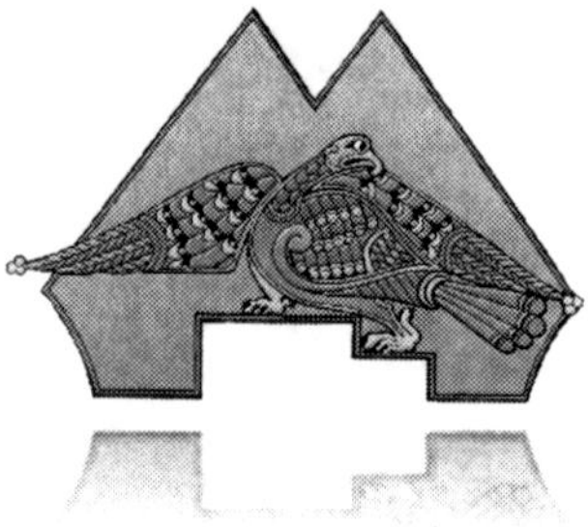

Lear

Thou must be patient. We came crying hither:
Thou knowst the first time that we smell the air
We wawl and cry.

King Lear 4.6.174-76

The mad King Lear says this to the blind Gloucester. In his derangement Lear attempts to offer consolation to the suffering Gloucester.

***King Lear**: You have to be patient. We arrived in this world crying. You know that the first moment we breathe outside the womb we wail and weep.*

Manners

JANUARY 19

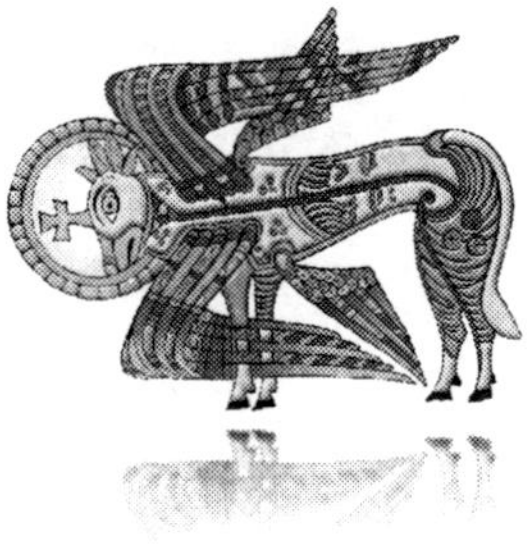

Corin

Those that are good
manners at the court are as ridiculous in the country
as the behaviour of the country is most mockable at the
court.

***As You Like It* 3.2.43-46**

The shepherd Corin says this to the fool Touchstone after Touchstone berates the shepherd for not being sophisticated because Corin never circulated in court society.

***Corin**: Court manners in the country are as ludicrous as country manners are at court.*

Priceless Value of Simple Things

JANUARY 20

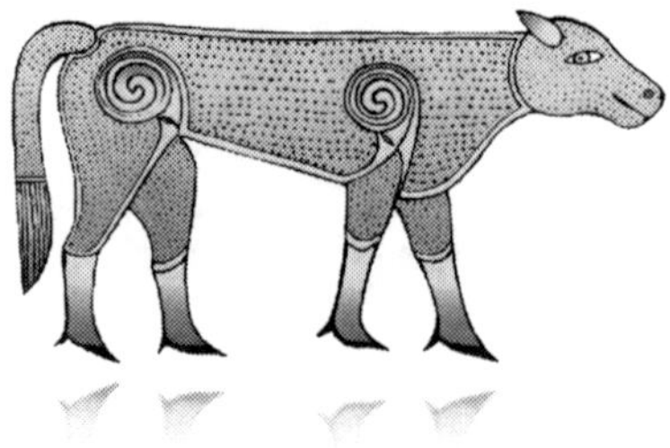

Gonzalo

Now would I give a thousand furlongs of sea
for an acre of barren ground - long heath, brown furze,
anything. The wills above be done, but I would
fain die a dry death.

The Tempest 1.1.65-68

Gonzalo says this in the midst of a ferocious tempest at sea. Unbeknownst to him, Prospero has created the storm with his magic. Frightened, Gonzalo longs to be on dry land.

Gonzalo*: Right now, I would trade ten thousand acres of ocean for one acre of desolate land covered with wild heather, prickly evergreen shrubs, anything. God's will shall be done; however, I would prefer to die dry.*

Transforming Suffering

JANUARY 21

Gaunt

There is no virtue like necessity.
Think not the king did banish thee,
But thou the king. . . .
Look what thy soul holds dear, imagine it
To lie that way thou goest, not whence thou com'st.

King Richard II 1.3.278-280; 286-87

Gaunt here is counseling his son Bolingbroke to bear gracefully the exile from his native England, a sentence which King Richard has just imposed on Bolingbroke.

***Gaunt**: There's no moral training like the constraining power of circumstance. Don't imagine that the king has exiled you, but that you have exiled the king. Consider whatever it is that your soul treasures, and imagine it to reside in the direction to which you are going, not in the place from which you are departing.*

Morning's Beauty

JANUARY 22

Sonnet 33
Full many a glorious morning have I seen
Flatter the mountain tops with sovereign eye,
Kissing with golden face the meadows green,
Gilding pale streams with heavenly alchemy. . . .

Lines 1-4

Sonnet 33*: I have witnessed many brilliant mornings as the sun makes the mountain peaks more beautiful with its regal stare, kissing the verdant meadows with its dazzling face and making dim streams golden with its heavenly chemistry.*

Overconfidence of Old Age

JANUARY 23

Polonius
By heaven, it is as proper to our age
To cast beyond ourselves in our opinions
As it is common for the younger sort
To lack discretion.

Hamlet 2.1.114-17

Polonius reveals to his daughter Ophelia that perhaps he made a mistake in commanding Ophelia to refuse Prince Hamlet's love letters and to forbid Hamlet to have access to her. Hamlet has just made a visit to Ophelia's chamber, disheveled in appearance and temper and apparently quite mad.

***Polonius**: For heaven's sake, it is as characteristic of our age group to overstep ourselves in our convictions as it is typical of youth to lack proper judgment.*

Witty Retorts

JANUARY 24

Rosencrantz
I understand you not, my lord.
Hamlet
I am glad of it. A knavish speech sleeps in a foolish ear.

Hamlet 4.2.21-23

Prince Hamlet has just told his childhood acquaintances Rosencrantz and Guildenstern that Claudius is using them to obtain information about Hamlet and that Claudius will simply squeeze them dry like a sponge. Rosencrantz replies.

Rosencrantz*: I don't understand you, my lord.* ***Hamlet****: I'm glad. The ear of a fool cannot hear an impudent remark.*

Rationalization

JANUARY 25

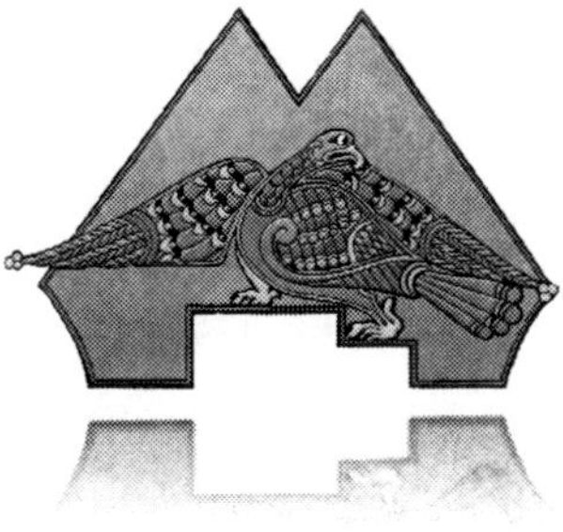

King

And never yet did insurrection want
Such water-colours to impaint his cause,
Nor moody beggars starving for a time
Of pellmell havoc and confusion.

King Henry IV, Part 1 5.1.79-82

After Worchester lists the rebels' grievances against King Henry IV, the King dismisses the arguments as rationalizations intended to justify the rebels' own desires.

____

____

____

____

____

____

***King Henry**: Never in history has rebellion lacked a pallet of watercolors to paint its cause, nor has rebellion ever lacked disgruntled malcontents hungering for a time of chaos and disorder.*

Complaints About Youth

JANUARY 26

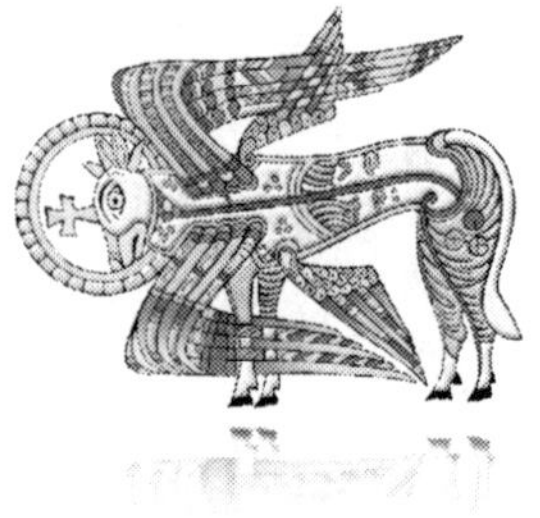

Shepherd

I would there were no age between ten and
three-and-twenty, or that youth would sleep out the rest;
for there is nothing in the between but getting
wenches with child, wronging the ancientry, stealing,
fighting. . . .

The Winter's Tale 3.3.59-63

The crusty old Shepherd says this in frustration after two young men have chased away two of the best sheep in his flock.

Shepherd: *I wish there were no period of life between ages ten and twenty-three or else that young people would simply sleep through this time. Nothing goes on in the meantime except for getting girls pregnant, harming old people, stealing, fighting.*

Subjectivity of Thought

JANUARY 27

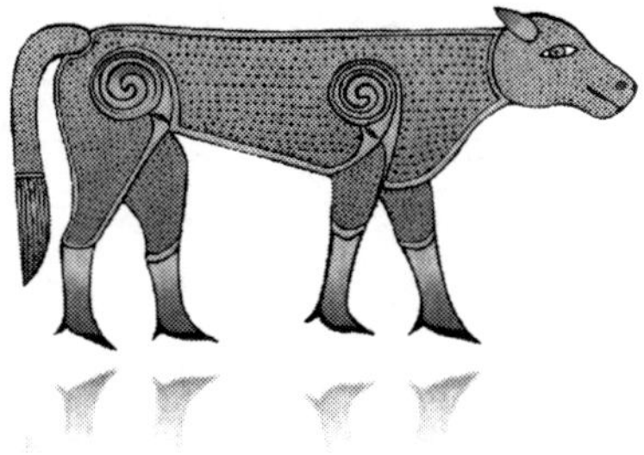

Hamlet

there is nothing
either good or bad but thinking makes it so.

Hamlet 2.2.250-51

Hamlet, Prince of Denmark, says this to Rosencrantz after he has just disagreed with Hamlet's dark statement that Denmark is a prison.

***Hamlet**: Nothing in itself is good or bad; it is thought itself that shapes experience so.*

Self-justification

JANUARY 28

Falstaff

Thou knowest in the
state of innocency Adam fell, and what should poor
Jack Falstaff do in the days of villainy? Thou seest I
have more flesh than another man, and therefore more
frailty.

King Henry IV, Part 1 3.3.165-69

When Falstaff claims that he has been robbed of an expensive ring and a number of bonds at Mistress Quickly's house, Prince Hal calls Falstaff a liar. Hal says that Falstaff's pockets contained only tavern receipts and paraphernalia from local whorehouses. Ever the king of spin, Falstaff here tries to justify his lies.

***Falstaff**: You know that even in the pure state of the Garden of Eden Adam sinned, then what is wretched Jack Falstaff to do in the days of sinfulness? You can see with your own eyes that I have more meat on my bones than the next person and, therefore, more tendency to sin.*

The Appeal of Death

JANUARY 29

Hermione

Now, my liege,
Tell me what blessings I have here alive,
That I should fear to die?

The Winter's Tale 3.2.105-07

Hermione says this to her husband King Leontes who has unjustly accused her of infidelity and who has then ordered their newborn daughter to be killed as well as Hermione herself.

Hermione: *Tell me now, my lord, what gifts of divine favor do I still have existing in this present life that might make me afraid to die?*

Fierceness of Nature

JANUARY 30

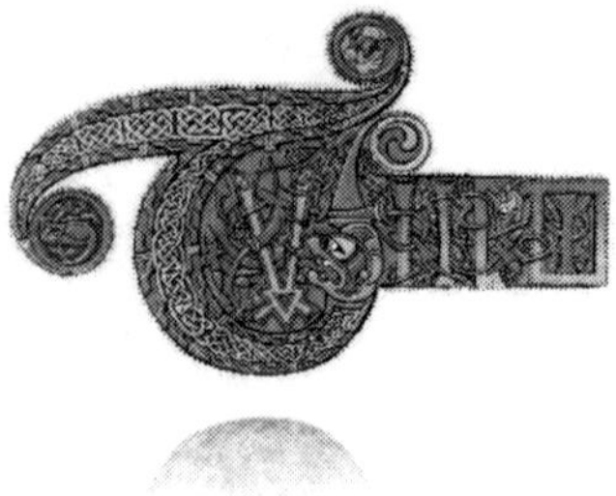

Kent
Such sheets of fire, such bursts of horrid thunder,
Such groans of roaring wind and rain I never
Remember to have heard.

King Lear 3.2.46-48

Kent says this to Lear who is wandering mad on the heath in a tumultuous storm.

Kent: *Such panels of flames, such explosions of terrifying thunder, such lamentable moans of the fierce wind and rain I don't ever recall hearing before now.*

Misinterpreting Events

JANUARY 31

Cicero
Indeed it is a strange-disposed time.
But men may construe things after their fashion
Clean from the purpose of the things themselves.

Julius Caesar 1.3.33-35

Caska reports the unnatural portents he has just witnessed in the streets of Rome, such as a storm that discharges fire. Cicero responds to Caska's news with a caution.

Cicero: *The present is an extraordinary time. Nonetheless, people may interpret events subjectively, entirely removed from the original meaning of the events themselves.*

Sunrise

FEBRUARY 1

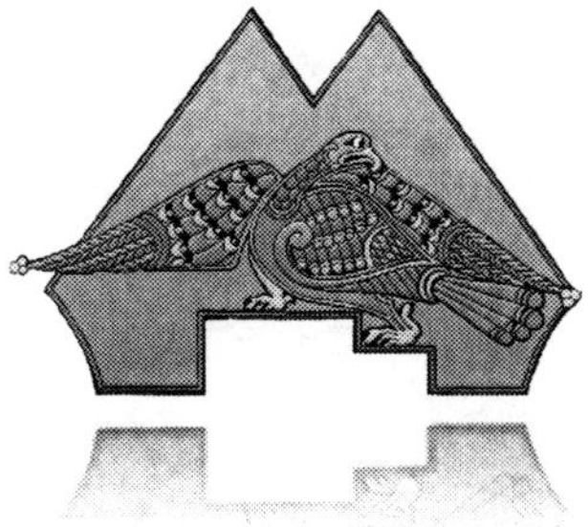

Horatio
But look, the morn in russet mantle clad
Walks o'er the dew of yon high eastward hill.

Hamlet 1.1.171-72

Trying to distract Marcellus from ruminating on the ghost they have just seen, Horatio calls attention to the beautiful sunrise.

Horatio: *Look! The morning sun, clothed like a traveler in a russet cloak, glides over the dew-covered earth on that hill directly east.*

Empathy

FEBRUARY 2

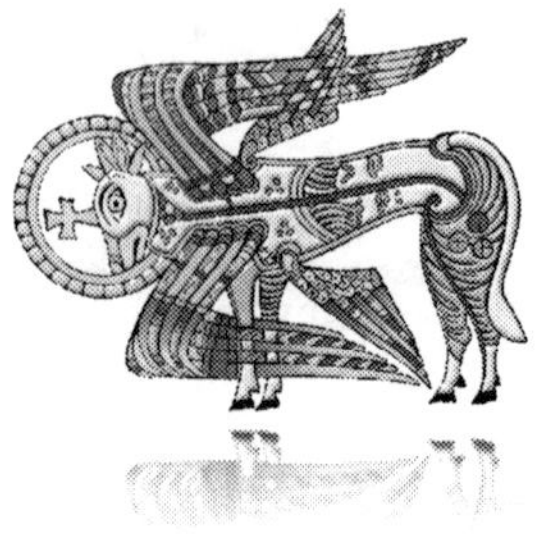

Miranda

O, I have suffered
With those that I saw suffer – a brave vessel
(Who had no doubt some noble creature in her)
Dashed all to pieces. O, the cry did knock
Against my very heart!

The Tempest 1.2.5-9

Miranda says this to her father Prospero as she witnesses a shipwreck that he has created with his magic skills. Although Prospero will assure her that no one has perished, innocent Miranda identifies wholeheartedly with the victims of the storm.

***Miranda:** Oh, I have suffered along with those I saw suffer--a splendid ship that obviously contained admirable people--shattered to bits. The pitiful cries reverberate against the walls of my own heart!*

Battle of the Sexes

FEBRUARY 3

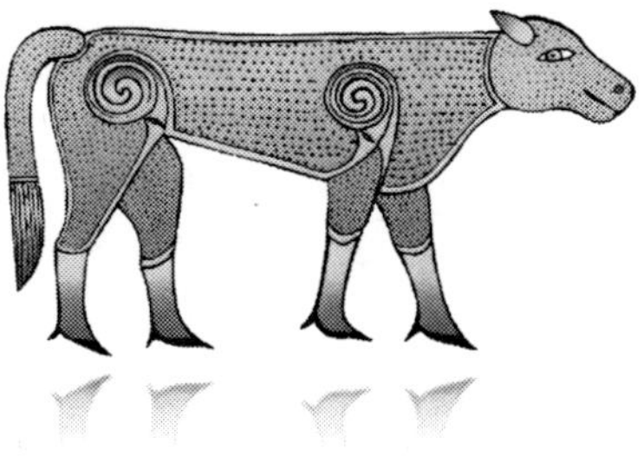

Benedick
What, my dear Lady Disdain! Are you yet living?
Beatrice
Is it possible Disdain should die, while she hath such meet food to feed it as Signior Benedick?

Much Ado About Nothing 1.1.113-16

Beatrice, the niece of the Governor of Messina, speaks to the man she loves to hate, Benedick, a noble from Padua who has just returned from a military campaign. Both Beatrice and Benedick claim to despise romantic love. When Benedick is left alone with Beatrice, he attempts a conversational remark that falls flat after Beatrice tells him that nobody is listening to him.

***Benedick:** Who's this? My dear Lady Disdain? Are you still alive?*
***Beatrice:** Can Disdain ever die when she has such perfect food to nourish herself on as you, Signior Benedick?*

State of the World

FEBRUARY 4

Falstaff

A plague upon it
when thieves cannot be true one to another!

King Henry IV, Part 1 2.2.26-27

Falstaff curses Poins who has hidden Falstaff's horse, forcing Falstaff to plod along on foot with his considerable bulk. Since the two are planning a robbery, Falstaff laments the sad state of the world.

Falstaff: *The times are doomed when one robber can't be loyal to another of his kind.*

Friendship

FEBRUARY 5

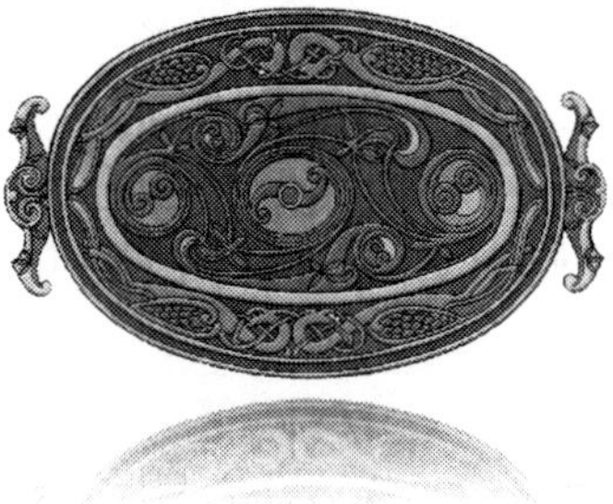

Hamlet
Since my dear soul was mistress of her choice,
And could of men distinguish her election,
Sh'ath seal'd thee for herself. . . .

Hamlet 3.2.64-66

Hamlet, Prince of Denmark, says this to his beloved friend Horatio. In the poisonous atmosphere of Denmark where Hamlet is overcome by the shock of grief, betrayal, and murder, his friendship with Horatio becomes even more precious.

Hamlet: *Ever since I was able to choose for myself and my soul could ferret out her choice of friends, she has stamped you for her very own.*

Triumphing Over Misfortune

FEBRUARY 6

Duke
The robbed that smiles steals something from the thief,
He robs himself that spends a bootless grief.

Othello 1.3.209-10

Signior Brabantio, Desdemona's father, appears before the Venetian Senate to protest the recent marriage of his daughter to the Moor Othello. When Desdemona publicly proclaims that she married Othello out of love rather than because of a witch's spell, Brabantio despairs. The Duke tries to console the despondent father.

Duke: *The robber's victim who still smiles takes something back from the thief. A person steals from himself who exhausts his efforts in useless grief.*

Cultivating Public Affection

FEBRUARY 7

King
By being seldom seen, I could not stir
But like a comet I was wonder'd at,
That men would tell their children, 'This is he!'
King Henry IV, Part 1 3.2.46-48

Henry IV says this to his son Prince Hal who spends most of his time in the pubs of east London, fraternizing with bawds, barkeeps, drunks, and petty criminals. Henry reveals that his own method for earning public respect has been the exact opposite of Prince Hal's habit of familiarity with the common people.

King Henry IV: *By making myself scarce in public, I could not appear before the people without, comet like, being marveled over such that men would exclaim to their children: "This is the one!"*

Slave to Love

FEBRUARY 8

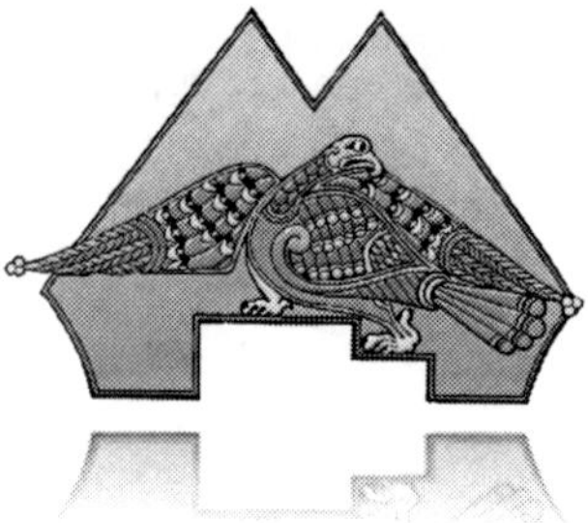

Helena

I am your spaniel; and, Demetrius,
The more you beat me, I will fawn on you.

A Midsummer Night's Dream 2.1.203-04

Rejected by Demetrius, Helena pursues him all the more--even after he tells her he cannot and will not love her.

Helena: *I am your faithful dog, Demetrius. The more you mistreat me, the more I will adore you.*

Selfishness as Unappealing

FEBRUARY 9

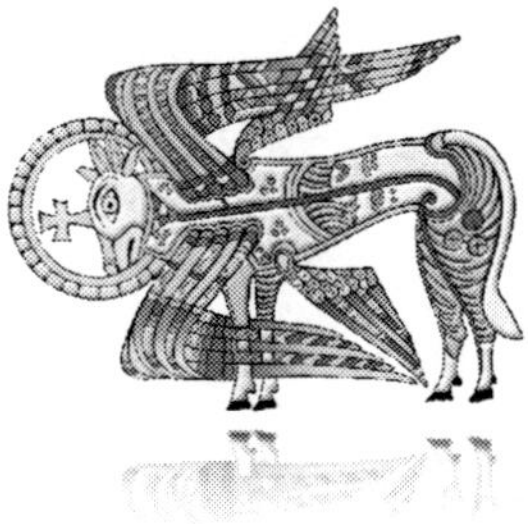

Goneril
I have been worth the whistling.
Albany
O Goneril,
You are not worth the dust which the rude wind
Blows in your face. I fear your disposition;
That nature which contemns its origin
Cannot be bordered certain in itself.

King Lear 4.2.30-34

In a rather dark comic moment, Goneril, cruel daughter of King Lear, expects her kind husband Albany to be fired up by her physical attractiveness. Instead, Albany is disgusted with the woman whose savage mistreatment of her father has driven him insane.

***Goneril:** I used to be worth whistling at. **Albany**: Oh, Goneril, you are worth less than the dust that the wild wind presses against your face. I shudder at your innate nature. That inborn character that despises its parentage cannot be expected to remain within its own human boundaries.*

Necessity Altering Worth

FEBRUARY 10

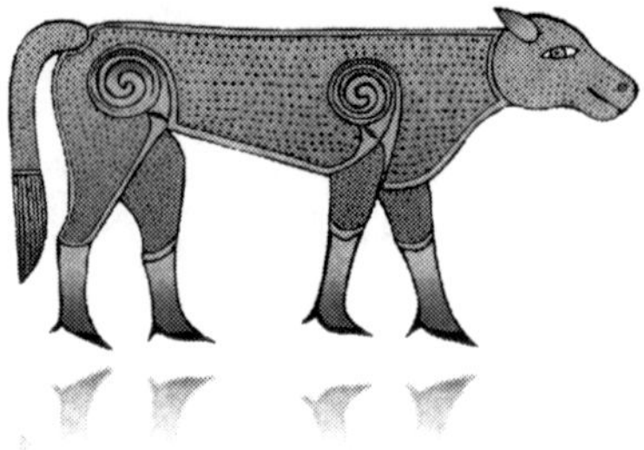

Lear

Where is this straw, my fellow?
The art of our necessities is strange,
And can make vile things precious.

King Lear 3.2.69-71

Locked out of his daughter's lodging, Lear wanders mad on the heath in the middle of a fierce storm. In a moment of sanity, Lear asks the disguised Kent to bring the Fool and Lear himself to a hovel for shelter.

King Lear: *Where is this makeshift bed, my companion? Pressing need functions in an astonishing manner: that which is worthless can be made to be a treasure.*

Curse

FEBRUARY 11

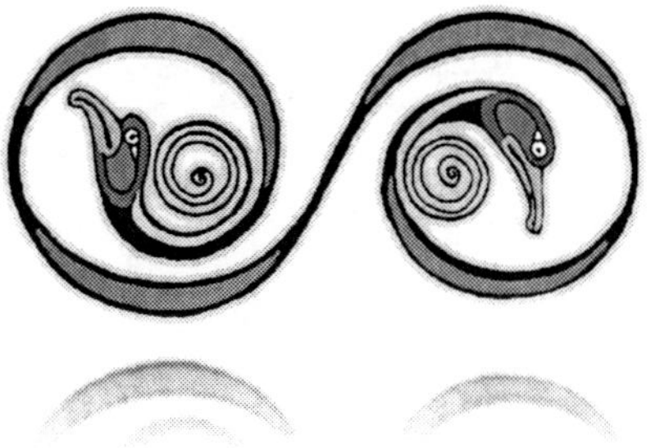

Lysander

Get you gone, you dwarf;
You minimus, of hindering knot-grass made;
You bead, you acorn.

A Midsummer Night's Dream 3.2.328-30

Lysander says this to his beloved Hermia to whom he has been thoroughly devoted only moments before. Now that Puck has mistakenly dropped love juice into Lysander's eyes, Lysander dotes only on Helena and scorns Hermia. Hermia's formerly attractive short stature is now an object of ridicule.

***Lysander:** Go away, you midget, you minuscule creature, made of weeds which stunt your growth.*

Nature's Music

FEBRUARY 12

Caliban

The isle is full of noises,
Sounds and sweet airs that give delight and hurt not.
Sometimes a thousand twangling instruments
Will hum about mine ears. . . .

***The Tempest* 3.2.136-39**

Caliban, the son of the witch Sycorax, is trying to console Stephano who has heard music coming from nowhere and wonders if it is the work of the devil or an unseen human being. Caliban refers here not only to the natural sounds of the island but also to the "unnatural" music created by the magician Prospero. It is, in fact, the spirit Ariel playing a tabor and pipe that Stephano hears.

***Caliban:** This island is bursting with melodious sounds, vibrations, and delicate breezes that bring pleasure, not pain. At times it sounds like a thousand ringing musical instruments vibrating in my ears.*

Inaccessibility of Grief

FEBRUARY 13

Hamlet

I have that within which passes show,
These but the trappings and the suits of woe.

Hamlet 1.2.85-86

Hamlet, Prince of Denmark, says this to his mother after Gertrude asks him to get over mourning the death of his father and get on with his life. Queen Gertrude says she can't understand why, if Hamlet knows that death is common, he is so affected by his father's death.

Hamlet: *There is something within me not visible on the surface. What you see are merely the ornaments and garments of grief.*

The Folly of the Lover

FEBRUARY 14

Silvius
How many actions most ridiculous
Hast thou been drawn to by thy fantasy?
Corin
Into a thousand that I have forgotten.
Silvius
O thou didst then never love so heartily.
If thou remember'st not the slightest folly. . . .

As You Like It 2.4.28-32

The young shepherd Silvius who is in love with the disdainful Phoebe seeks the advice of the old shepherd Corin.

***Silvius:** How many foolish deeds have you been pulled into by your flights of imagination? **Corin:** Into a thousand that I have forgotten. **Silvius:** Oh, then you never really loved passionately. If you can't remember even the tiniest stupidity that love forced you into, then you have never really been in love.*

Majesty of Authority

FEBRUARY 15

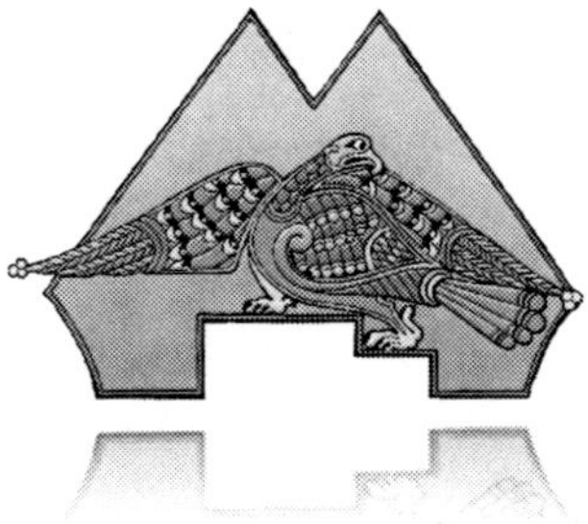

Antony

When Caesar says 'Do this', it is performed.

Julius Caesar 1.2.10

Antony has just been asked by Caesar to strike Caesar's barren wife, Calpurnia, as Antony passes by her during a traditional ritual on the feast of Lupercal. The runners carry goatskin thongs, and those women who are struck are believed to be cured of barrenness. Awestruck by Caesar, Antony responds to Caesar's request.

***Antony:** When Caesar utters a command, it is as good as done.*

Death and Decay as Great Equalizers

FEBRUARY 16

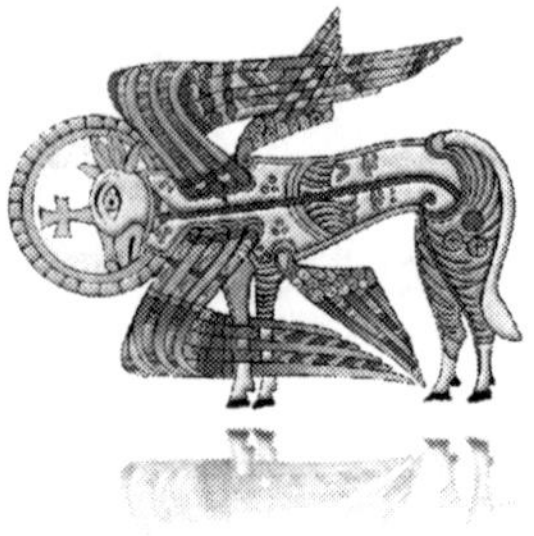

Hamlet

Your worm is your only emperor for diet: we fat all creatures else to fat us, and we fat ourselves for maggots. Your fat king and your lean beggar is but variable service – two dishes, but to one table.

Hamlet 4.3.21-24

The mad Prince Hamlet says this to King Claudius when Claudius asks him where the dead body of Polonius can be found.

Hamlet: *The worm is the only reigning emperor when it comes to eating. We feed all other creatures for the sole purpose of feeding ourselves, and we feed ourselves ultimately only to feed maggots. Your well-fed king and your starving beggar are but different courses at a feast: two dishes going to the same buffet.*

Necessity of Variety

FEBRUARY 17

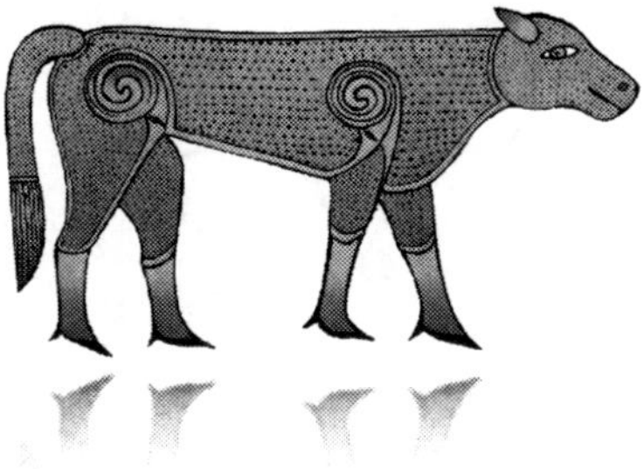

Prince
If all the year were playing holidays,
To sport would be as tedious as to work. . . .
King Henry IV, Part 1 1.2.199-200

Prince Hal says this in soliloquy, justifying his decadent lifestyle in Eastcheap, hanging out in taverns while his father King Henry IV bemoans Hal's absence at court. Hal argues that once he does reform his life, it will appear even more glorious in the public eye because of his earlier tarnished reputation.

Prince Hal: *If every day of the year were a vacation day, relaxing would be as boring as working.*

Death as Sleep
FEBRUARY 18

Duke

Thy best of rest is sleep;
And that thou oft provok'st, yet grossly fear'st
Thy death, which is no more.

Measure for Measure 3.1.17-19

Disguised as a friar, the Duke of Vienna counsels Lord Claudio to prepare for his execution scheduled for the next day. The Duke draws an analogy between sleep and death.

Duke: *The greatest part of repose is sleep, something that you often desire. Yet you are terrified of your death, which is nothing more than sleep.*

Fall From Virtue

FEBRUARY 19

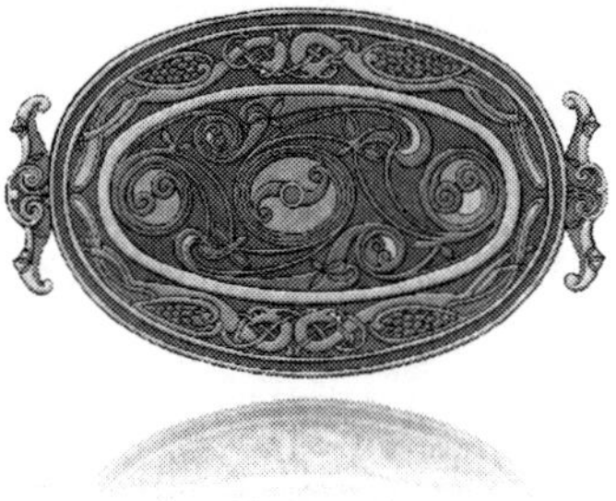

Sonnet 94

For sweetest things turn sourest by their deeds;
Lilies that fester smell far worse than weeds.

Lines 13-14

Sonnet 94: *Those things that are the most precious become the most rotten through corrupt action. Lilies that go bad smell infinitely worse than weeds that decay.*

Greatness

FEBRUARY 20

Hamlet

Rightly to be great
Is not to stir without great argument,
But greatly to find quarrel in a straw
When honour's at the stake.

Hamlet 4.4.53-56

Prince Hamlet says this just after he witnesses Fortinbras, the heir to the Norwegian throne, marching by to fight the Poles over a worthless piece of land. Admiring Fortinbras' decisiveness, Hamlet tries to formulate what greatness means.

Hamlet: *To be truly noble means refusing to act without an important reason for engagement. But greatness also means to find something worth fighting for in a trivial matter when honor is at issue.*

Relative Safety of Nature

FEBRUARY 21

Duke Senior

Are not these woods
More free from peril than the envious court?

As You Like It 2.1.3-4

Duke Senior, who was banished from court by his usurping brother, says this to his lords who have also taken refuge with him in the Forest of Arden.

Duke Senior: *Is it not true that this forest endangers us less than life in the court overrun by envy?*

Self-deception

FEBRUARY 22

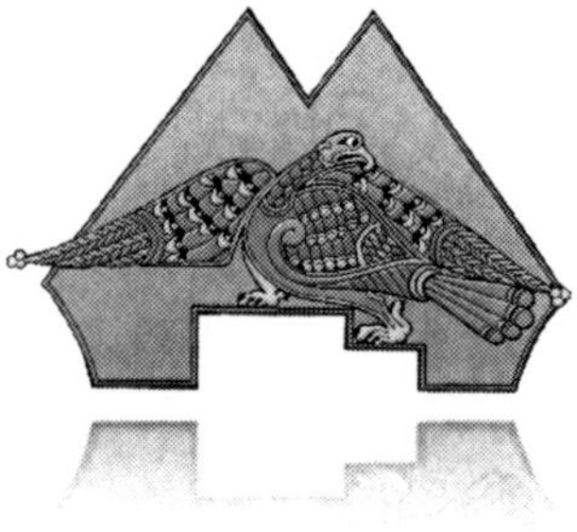

Sonnet 119

What wretched errors hath my heart committed,
Whilst it hath thought itself so blessed never?

Lines 5-6

Sonnet 119: *What dreadful transgressions has my heart engaged in while imagining itself as never having been as pure?*

High Status Masking Sin

FEBRUARY 23

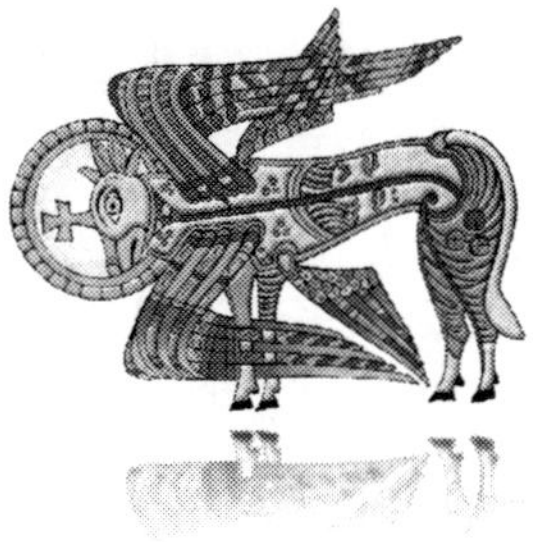

Lear

Through tattered clothes great vices do appear;
Robes and furred gowns hide all.

King Lear 4.6.160-61

The mad King Lear says this to Gloucester as Lear imagines the hypocrisy of justice when a public officer guilty of a greater hidden crime punishes a poor person who commits a minor infraction.

King Lear: *Huge offenses are visible through ragged clothing. Judges' robes and expensive attire conceal everything.*

The Duty to Speak Out

FEBRUARY 24

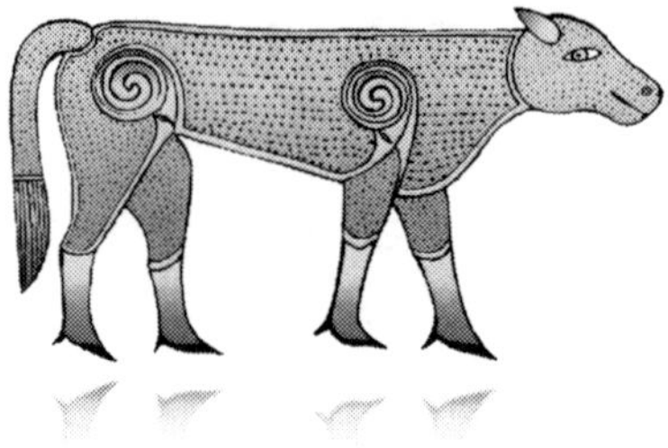

Kent

Think'st thou that duty shall have dread to speak,
When power to flattery bows? To plainness honour's
bound
When majesty falls to folly.

King Lear 1.1.148-50

Kent says this to his master, King Lear, after Lear has just disinherited his favorite daughter, Cordelia. Cordelia's only sin is to refuse to pronounce her love for her father in public as her two calculating sisters have just done.

Kent: *Do you honestly believe that our regard for a superior will make us afraid to speak when those in power succumb to flattery? When those above us fall prey to foolishness, we who are under them are honor bound to speak the simple truth.*

Riches of Love

FEBRUARY 25

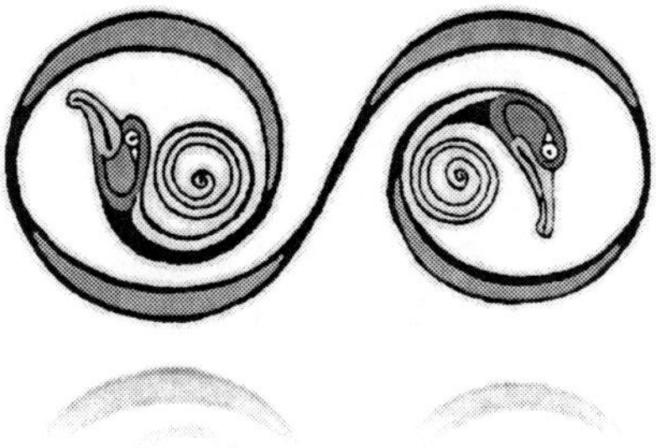

Sonnet 91
Thy love is better than high birth to me,
Richer than wealth, prouder than garment's cost,
Of more delight than hawks or horses be. . . .

Lines 9-11

Sonnet 91: *Your love is worth more to me than aristocratic birth, more precious than riches, more magnificent than exquisite clothes. It brings me greater pleasure than diverting myself with hawks or horses.*

Beauty of Sincerity

FEBRUARY 26

Theseus
For never anything can be amiss
When simpleness and duty tender it.
A Midsummer Night's Dream 5.1.82-83

Theseus says this to Philostrate, who is trying to convince Theseus not to select as his wedding entertainment a play that the mechanicals have cobbled together to celebrate the event. Philostrate argues that the quality is poor. Theseus counters his argument.

Theseus: *Nothing can be wrong with that which is offered out of a spirit of innocence and reverence.*

Emotional Influence

FEBRUARY 27

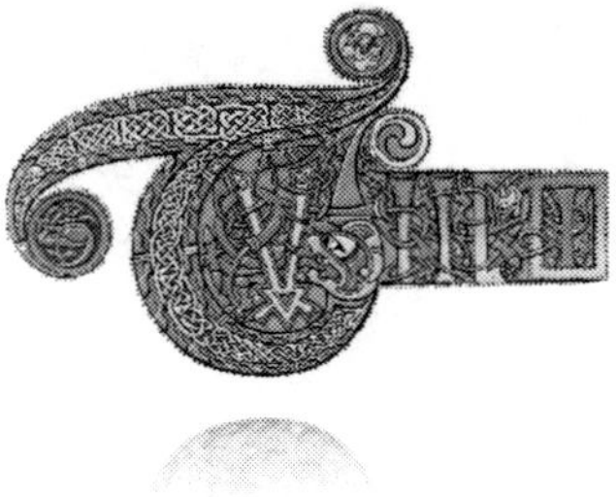

Gonzalo

It is foul weather in us all, good sir,
When you are cloudy.

The Tempest 2.1.142-43

Gonzalo, the faithful councilor, says this to Alonso, King of Naples. Alonso believes he has lost his son Ferdinand in a shipwreck that Prospero, the deposed Duke of Milan, magically conjured as an illusion.

Gonzalo: *All of us experience tempests, dear sir, when you are gloomy.*

Disorder

FEBRUARY 28/29*

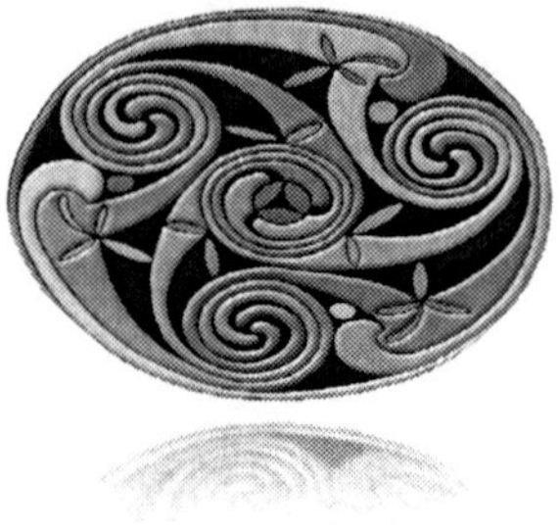

Gloucester

'Tis the time's plague when madmen lead the blind.

King Lear 4.1.49

The blind Gloucester says this as he is led away by the mad beggar Tom o'Bedlam. Gloucester has had his eyes gouged out for giving aid to King Lear against the wishes of Lear's daughter and son-in-law. Unbeknownst to Gloucester, Tom o'Bedlam is Gloucester's own son Edgar who is in disguise because he has been told that his father seeks Edgar's death.

**2016 only*

Gloucester: *It is a sign of the evil of the present age when madmen are compelled to guide those who are blind.*

Prayer

MARCH 1

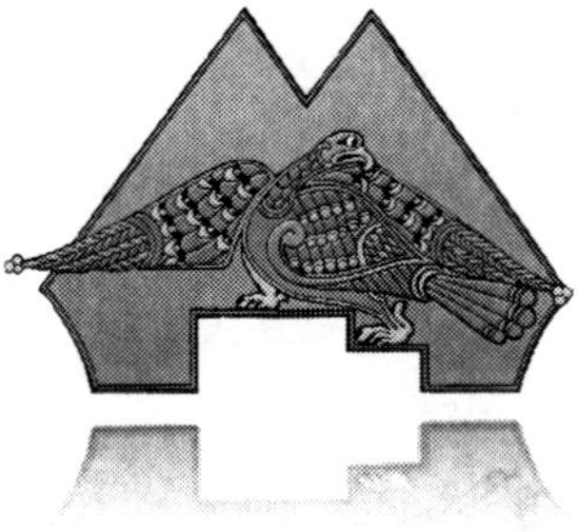

Leontes

The blessed gods
Purge all infection from our air whilst you
Do climate here!

***The Winter's Tale* 5.1.167-69**

Leontes says this to Florizel, the son of his childhood friend Polixenes from whom Leontes has been estranged for sixteen years. Leontes is welcoming Florizel to the kingdom of Sicilia.

Leontes: *May the blissful gods remove all impurities from our atmosphere while you remain here!*

Love's Depths
MARCH 2

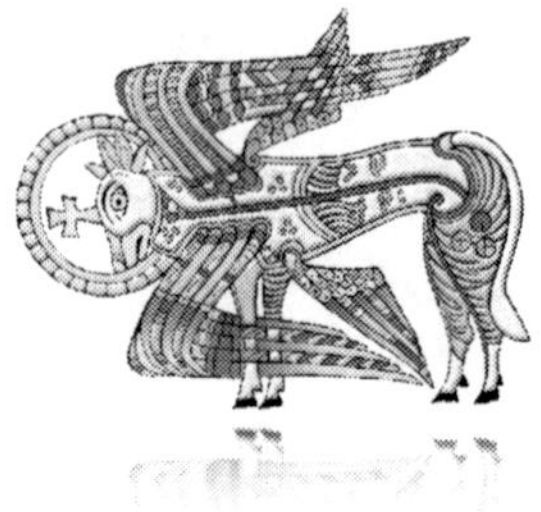

Rosalind

My affection hath an
unknown bottom, like the Bay of Portugal.

As You Like It 4.1.199-200

Talking privately to her cousin Celia, Rosalind admits how deeply in love she is with Orlando even though she will not admit this to Orlando himself.

Rosalind: *My feeling for Orlando has an endless depth, as does the Bay of Portugal.*

Disguising Sorrow

MARCH 3

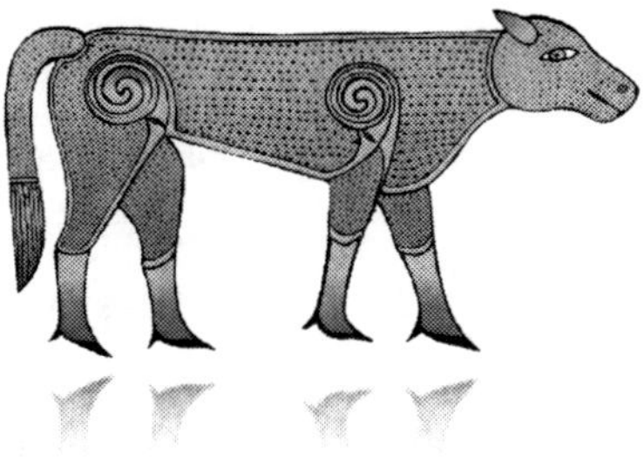

Edgar
Bad is the trade that must play fool to sorrow. . . .
King Lear 4.1.40

On the heath and disguised as Poor Tom (a mad beggar), Edgar encounters his blind father, Gloucester. Unbeknownst to Edgar, his father's eyes have been gouged out by the cruel Cornwall to punish Gloucester for aiding the mad King Lear to escape from his daughters' treachery. Edgar comments.

Edgar: *It is a dire turn of events when one is compelled to act like a jester while overcome by sorrow.*

Love's Folly

MARCH 4

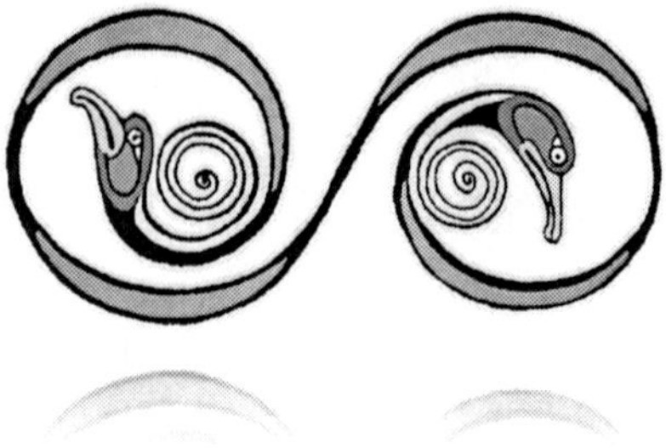

Puck
Lord, what fools these mortals be!
A Midsummer Night's Dream 3.2.115

Puck mistakenly pours love juice on Lysander's eyes, causing Lysander to abandon his love for Hermia and to woo Helena instead. Oberon then drops the love potion on Demetrius' eyes to cause Demetrius to return Helena's love. Puck impishly savors the sight of two men fighting over the same woman.

Puck: *Christ! What morons these humans are!*

Intuition

MARCH 5

Hamlet
O my prophetic soul!

Hamlet 1.5.41

Hamlet, Prince of Denmark, makes this remark after his father's ghost reveals that he was murdered by his own brother Claudius. This news merely confirms the dread that already dwells in Hamlet's heart after the Prince learns that his mother has married Claudius.

Hamlet: *Oh, my intuitive sense!*

Endurance

MARCH 6

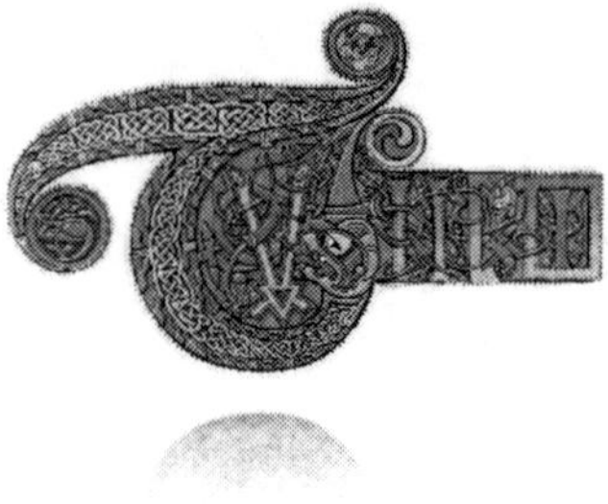

Gloucester

I am tied to the stake and I must stand the course.

King Lear 3.7.53

Gloucester says this to Regan and her husband Cornwall who have viciously bound Gloucester to a chair (and who will eventually gouge out his eyes there). Against their wishes, Gloucester has warned the mad King Lear to flee Dover because Lear's daughters, Goneril and Regan, seek to end his life. Regan is challenging Gloucester to tell her the truth about why Lear is fleeing to Dover.

Gloucester: *Like a bear who is chained to a stake while vicious dogs are set loose to attack me, I am bound to the post, and I must endure the attack.*

False Courtesy
MARCH 7

Horatio
This lapwing runs away with the shell on his
head.
Hamlet
A did comply with his dug before a sucked it.

Hamlet 5.2.186-88

The fawning courtier Osric has just left, and Hamlet, Prince of Denmark, and his friend Horatio laugh at the courtier's foolishness. Osric's inflated language is matched in folly only by his painfully exaggerated desire to please his betters.

______

______

______

______

______

______

***Horatio:** This newly hatched chick is running away with the shell still stuck to its head. **Hamlet:** He undoubtedly thanked his mother's nipple before he nursed from it.*

Deluded Idolatry

MARCH 8

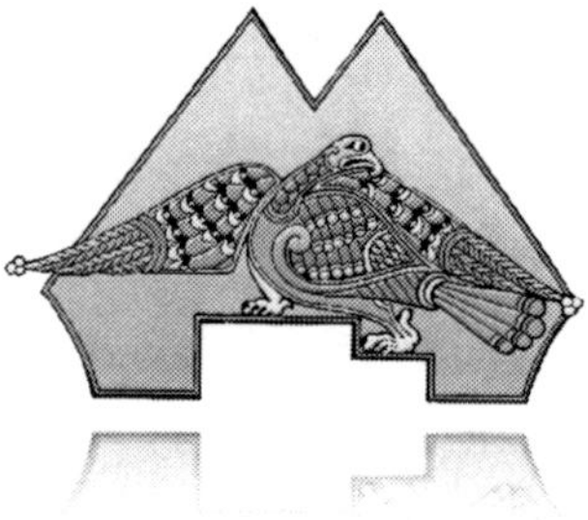

Caliban

What a thrice-double ass
Was I to take this drunkard for a god,
And worship this dull fool!

The Tempest 5.1.297-99

Caliban, the son of the witch Sycorax, berates himself after he realizes that Stephano is a mere drunken servant whereas Caliban had believed him to be an all-powerful creature worthy of adoration.

Caliban: *What a jackass six times over was I to mistake this drunk for a divine being and idolize this brainless nincompoop!*

Awareness of Deception

MARCH 9

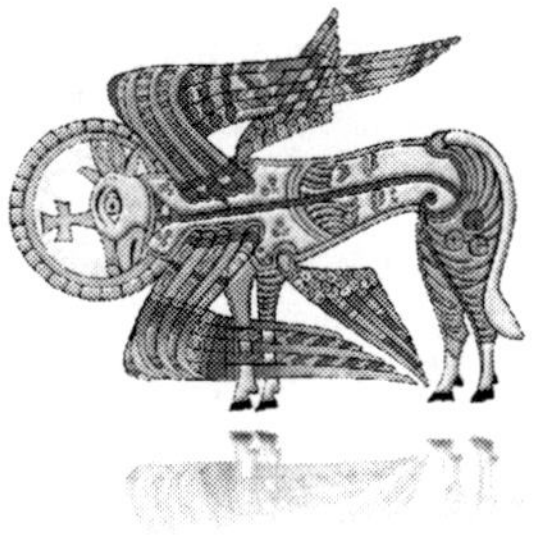

Sonnet 138

When my love swears that she is made of truth,
I do believe her, though I know she lies,
That she might think me some untutored youth
Unlearned in the world's false subtleties.

Lines 1-4

Sonnet 138: *When my beloved insists she is telling me the truth, I accept it as true even though I know she is deceiving me. I play along so that she might view me as an unsophisticated young man who is inexperienced in the treacherous ways of the world.*

Healing Potential of Bad News

MARCH 10

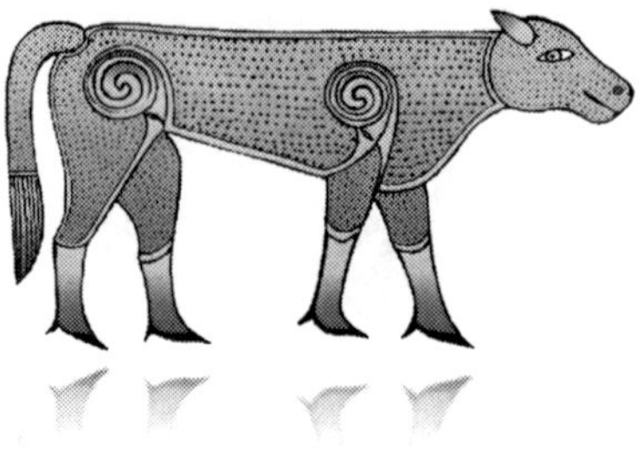

Northumberland
In poison there is physic; and these news,
Having been well, that would have made me sick,
Being sick, have in some measure made me well.
King Henry IV, Part 2 1.1.137-39

The ill Northumberland has just learned that his son Hotspur was killed in the failed rebellion at Shrewsbury. Then Northumberland is told that the King has dispatched troops to seize the sick lord.

Northumberland: *Such toxic news contains a healing dimension. Had I been well, such news would have made me sick at heart. However, being sick already, the news in some sense prompts me to be well, to take action.*

Danger of Unconscious Desires

MARCH 11

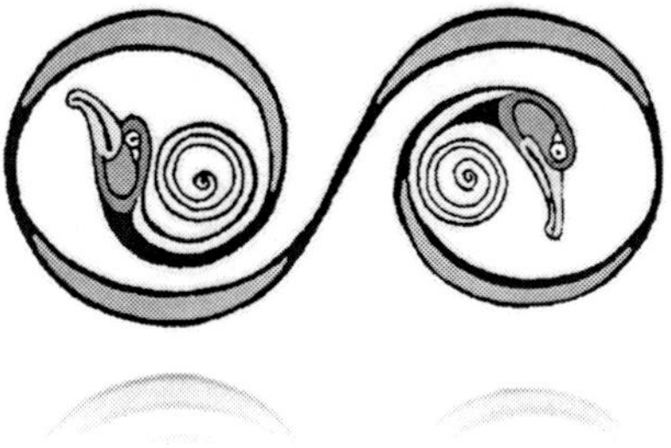

Antony

Thus did I desire it.
What our contempts doth often hurl from us
We wish it ours again.

Antony and Cleopatra 1.2.127-29

Antony says this when he learns of the death of his wife Fulvia. We assume that because of his relationship with the legendary Cleopatra, the Queen of Egypt, he has wished for Fulvia's death as a release from his obligation to his wife.

Antony: *I wished for such a thing. What our disdain often drives away from us, we later wish we still possessed.*

Admiration

MARCH 12

Florizel

Each your doing,
So singular in each particular,
Crowns what you are doing, in the present deeds,
That all your acts are queens.

The Winter's Tale 4.4.143-146

Florizel, Prince of Bohemia, says this of his beloved, the shepherdess Perdita, who, unknown to either of them, is actually the abandoned Princess of Sicilia.

Florizel: *Each of your deeds, so uniquely yours in each detail, dignifies whatever you are presently engaged in. As a result, every action you undertake becomes queenly.*

Humor

MARCH 13

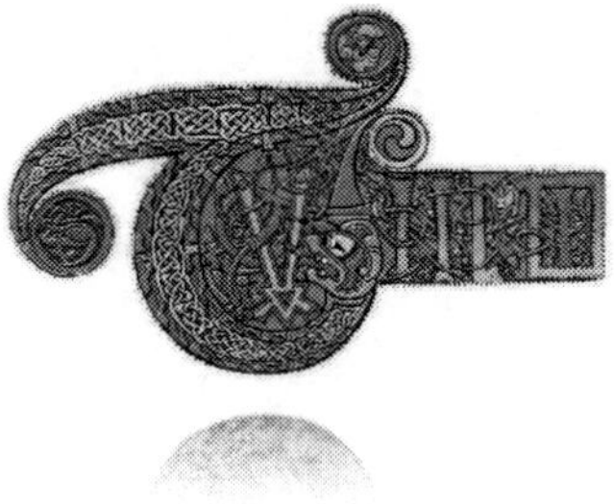

Prince

Why, thou globe of sinful continents, what a life
dost thou lead!

***King Henry IV, Part 2* 2.4.285-86**

Prince Hal says this to Falstaff after Hal and Poins, disguising themselves as bartenders, overhear Falstaff speaking badly about them behind their backs.

Prince: *You rotund mass of corrupted chunks of flesh, what a life you're living!*

Enthusiasm

MARCH 14

Puck
I'll put a girdle round about the earth
In forty minutes.

A Midsummer Night's Dream 2.1.175-76

Puck says this to Titania, Queen of the Fairies, after she asks him to fetch a purple flower for her to concoct a love juice and then to return quickly to her side.

Puck: *I will circle the globe in forty minutes!*

Prophesy

MARCH 15

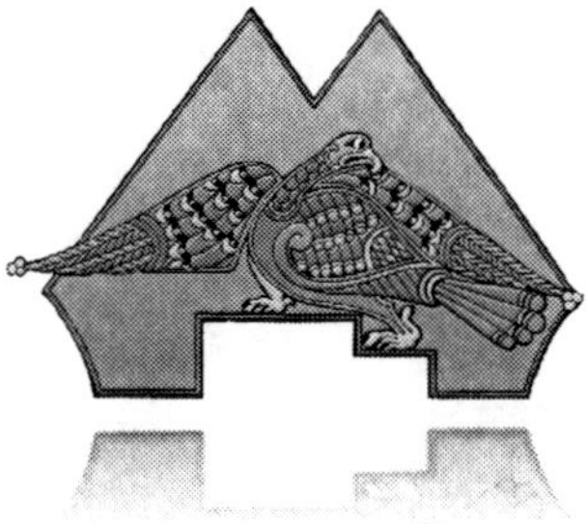

Soothsayer
Beware the Ides of March.

Julius Caesar 1.2.18

The Soothsayer says this to Caesar as he is about to meet his death on the steps of the Capitol.

Soothsayer: *Look out for danger on March 15th, the full moon of the new year.*

Acceptance of Duty

MARCH 16

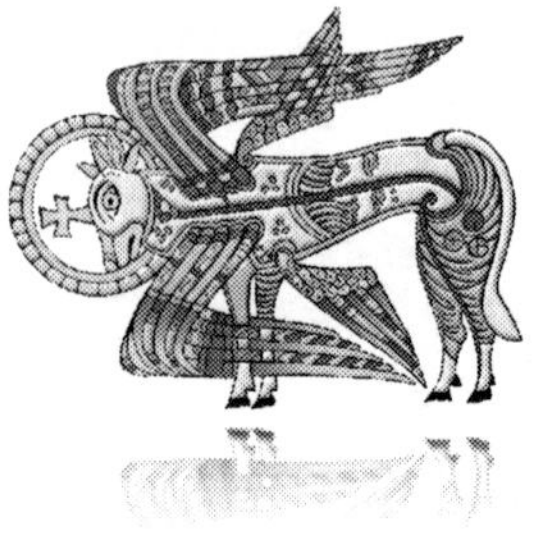

Feeble

By my troth I care not, a man can die but once,
we owe God a death. . . .
No man's too good
to serve's prince, and let it go which way it will, he that
dies this year is quit for the next.

King Henry IV, Part 2 3.2.233-34, 235-37

Feeble, one of the defenseless souls who have been nabbed for conscription to the King's army, watches in silence while Bullcalf and Mouldy bribe Bardolph in order to escape their conscription.

Feeble: *Truly, I don't care. A person dies only once, and each of us owes God one death. No person is too good to serve his leader. Regardless of what happens, the person who dies this year is free of the obligation to die next year.*

Alchemy of Poetry

MARCH 17

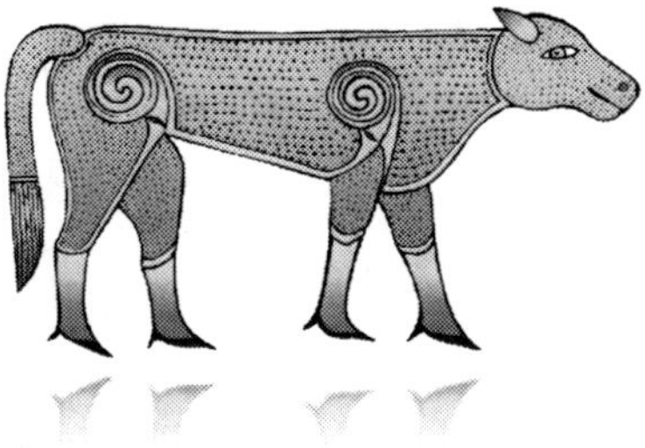

Theseus

Lovers and madmen have such seething brains,
Such shaping fantasies, that apprehend
More than cool reason ever comprehends.
The lunatic, the lover, and the poet
Are of imagination all compact. . . .

A Midsummer Night's Dream 5.1.4-8

Theseus says this to Queen Hippolyta after listening to the young lovers--Hermia and Lysander, Helena and Demetrius--recount their tales of confusion and switched loyalties under the spell of fairy juice in the forest.

____

____

____

____

____

____

Theseus: *Those in love and the insane possess such sizzling, boiling brains, such inventive imaginations, that they conceive more than the detached lens of reason ever grasps. Those in love, the mad, and the poet are all united by their creative faculty.*

Humble Exterior of Honesty

MARCH 18

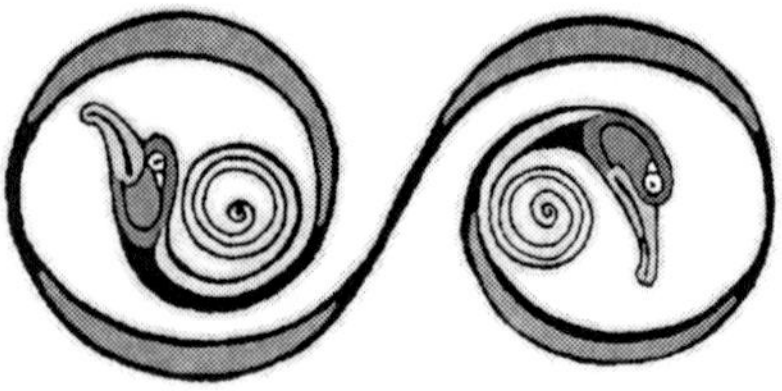

Touchstone

Rich
honesty dwells like a miser sir, in a poor house, as your pearl in your foul oyster.

As You Like It 5.4.58-60

Touchstone says this of the homely goatherd Audrey whom he is about to marry.

Touchstone: *Honesty lives like a wretch, sir, in a shabby dwelling, just as a pearl lives in an unattractive oyster.*

Appeal of Rejection

MARCH 19

Demetrius
I love thee not, therefore pursue me not.
Helena
You draw me, you hard-hearted adamant. . . .
A Midsummer Night's Dream 2.1.188, 195

Helena says this to Demetrius as he dismisses her love, seeking Hermia's love instead.

Demetrius: *I'm not in love with you, so don't follow me.* ***Helena:*** *You pull me toward you, you iron-hearted magnet.*

Unexpected Consolation

MARCH 20

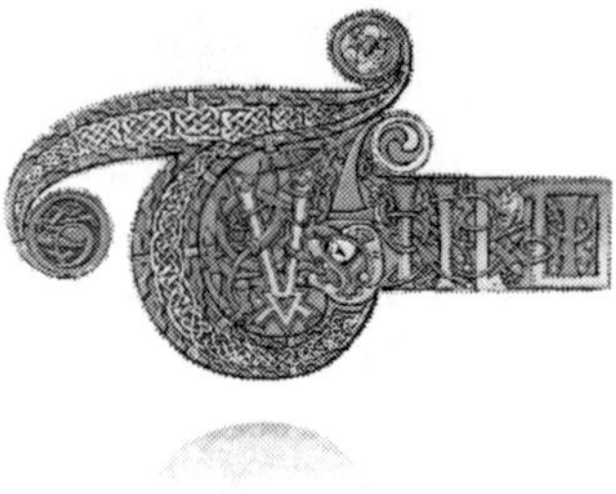

Gonzalo
I have great comfort from this fellow.
Methinks he hath no drowning mark upon him - his
complexion is perfect gallows.

The Tempest 1.1.27-29

Gonzalo, councilor to the King of Naples, says this when, in a tempest at sea, the boat he is on begins sinking. Then the salty Boatswain orders the royal passengers to get out of the way and go to their cabins.

Gonzalo: *This man gives me great consolation. He shows no sign of being destined to drown. His disposition offers certain proof that he is fated to hang.*

Nature as Teacher

MARCH 21

Duke Senior
And this our life, exempt from public haunt,
Finds tongues in trees, books in the running brooks,
Sermons in stones, and good in everything.
As You Like It 2.1.15-17

Duke Senior says this to his lords in the Forest of Arden, the place where he retreated after his brother had usurped the dukedom. Free from the pressures of public life and the company of society, Duke Senior and his men live life as students of nature, observing and reflecting.

Duke Senior: *Thus, free from the company of society, our way of life uncovers language in trees, erudition in the flowing springs, sermons in the rocks, and goodness in all things.*

Surfaces as Misleading

MARCH 22

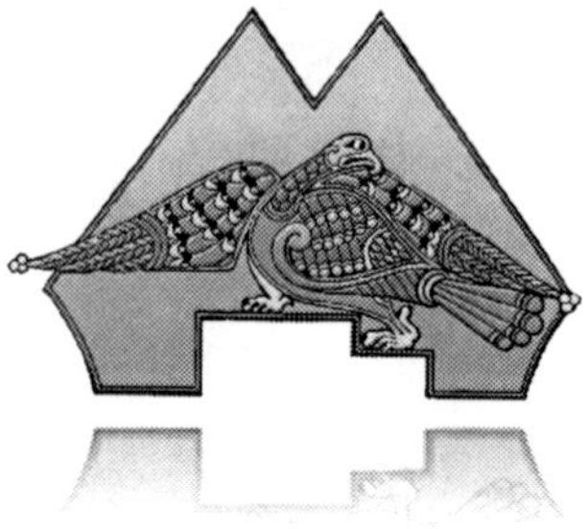

Bassanio

Look on beauty,
And you shall see 'tis purchas'd by the weight,
Which therein works a miracle in nature,
Making them lightest that wear most of it. . . .

The Merchant of Venice 3.2.88-91

Required to engage in a contest of sorts to win his beloved Portia, Bassanio must choose from among three caskets (gold, silver, and lead) the one that contains Portia's portrait. Anyone who fails can never afterwards marry. Looking at the gold casket, Bassanio surmises that it contains a trap.

Bassanio: *Observe a beautiful person or thing, and you'll find that artificial beauty is acquired by bulk. This fact produces a natural wonder, making those people sleaziest who possess the greatest amount of it.*

Marvelous Discovery

MARCH 23

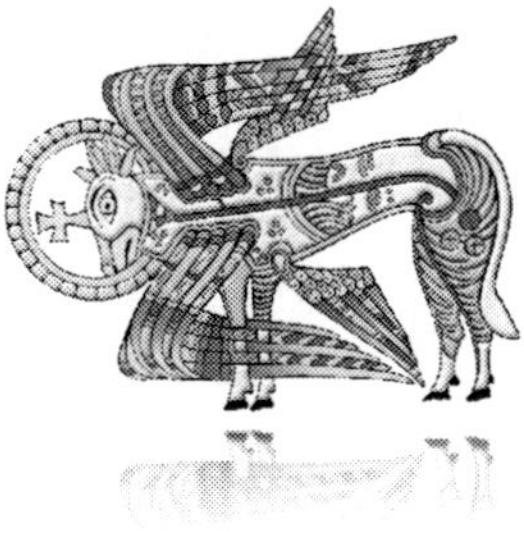

Miranda

How beauteous mankind is! O brave new world
That has such people in't.

The Tempest 5.1.183-84

Playing chess with her beloved Ferdinand, Miranda says this after her father Prospero breaks a spell he has cast on a group of shipwrecked people. These dignitaries from Milan, including Ferdinand's father, are the first crowd of human beings Miranda has ever seen. When she had encountered the shipwrecked Ferdinand three hours earlier, he was only the third man she had ever laid eyes on.

Miranda: *How beautiful the human species is! Oh, what a splendid, strange world it is that contains these kinds of people!*

Destiny

MARCH 24

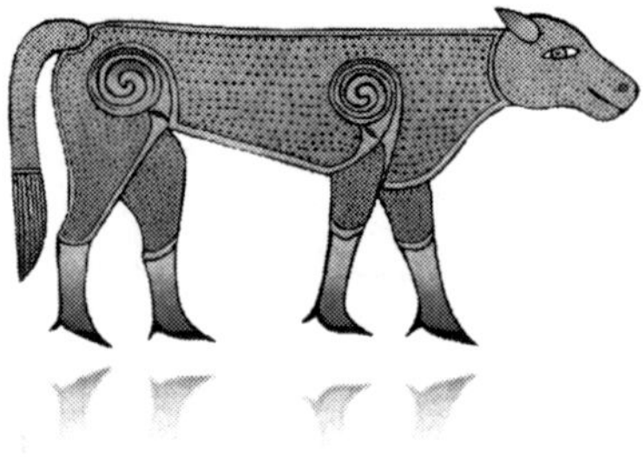

Hamlet

There is special providence in the fall of a sparrow. If it be now, 'tis not to come; if it be not to come, it will be now; if it be not now, yet it will come. The readiness is all.

Hamlet 5.2.218-22

Prince Hamlet says this to his friend Horatio as Horatio pleads with Hamlet not to engage in a duel with Laertes if Hamlet has any misgivings about it.

Hamlet: *There is direct divine intervention in the death of a sparrow. If death happens now, it won't in the future. If it be not in the future, it will happen in the present. If it doesn't happen now, it will nonetheless occur. Attentiveness is everything.*

Ease of Spreading Rumors

MARCH 25

Rumour

Rumour is a pipe
Blown by surmises, jealousies, conjectures,
And of so easy and so plain a stop
That the blunt monster with uncounted heads,
The still-discordant wav'ring multitude,
Can play upon it.

King Henry IV, Part 2 1.Induction.15-20

The character of Rumor, who opens the play, addresses himself to the audience. Rumor reveals that he is about to spread the news throughout the kingdom that Prince Hal has been slain by Hotspur in the battle at Shrewsbury. The truth, however, is just the opposite.

Rumor: *Rumor is a wind instrument played by the multitude, using the breath of speculation, envy, and supposition. The instrument is so simple that even the monster mob with innumerable heads, the ever-fighting, fickle mob, can play it.*

Mystery of Evil

MARCH 26

Lear

Is there any cause in nature that make
these hard hearts?

King Lear 3.6.75-76

King Lear, overcome by madness as a result of his daughters' cruelty, imagines that he is a judge conducting a trial of Regan, Goneril, and others. He proposes dissecting Regan to find out what is breeding about her heart. Then he asks this question.

King Lear: *Is there any motivating force in the physical universe or in human nature that produces the cruel dispositions of these daughters?*

Distraction

MARCH 27

Sonnet 113

Since I left you, mine eye is in my mind,
And that which governs me to go about
Doth part his function, and is partly blind,
Seems seeing, but effectually is out. . . .

Lines 1-4

Sonnet 113: *Since I parted from you, my sight has been overtaken by the images in my mind. My ability to see and maneuver in the world is divided: from an external perspective I appear to see and function, but my sight is really blinded by my thoughts of you.*

Temptation

MARCH 28

King
Most subject is the fattest soil to weeds. . . .
King Henry IV, Part 2 4.4.54

King Henry IV says this about his oldest son Hal, Prince of Wales and heir to the throne, when the King learns that Hal is absent from court and is instead hanging around with his disreputable pals in London.

King Henry: *The richest soil is the most vulnerable to being overrun by weeds.*

Inevitability of Slander

MARCH 29

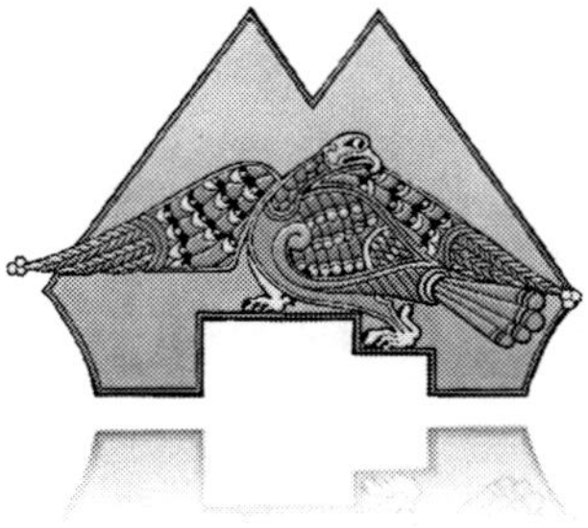

Duke
No might nor greatness in mortality
Can censure 'scape. Back-wounding calumny
The whitest virtue strikes. What king so strong
Can tie the gall up in the slanderous tongue?

***Measure for Measure* 3.2.178-81**

Dressed as a friar so as to secretly observe both his subjects and his chosen replacement, the disguised Duke of Vienna is speaking to himself. The Duke has just heard the fop Lucio shred the Duke's character with unwarranted accusations.

Duke: *Neither power nor greatness amongst human beings can avoid unfavorable judgment. Backbiting slander strikes the purest virtue. What king is there who is so strong that he can restrain the rancor of a slanderous tongue?*

Multiplying Sorrows

MARCH 30

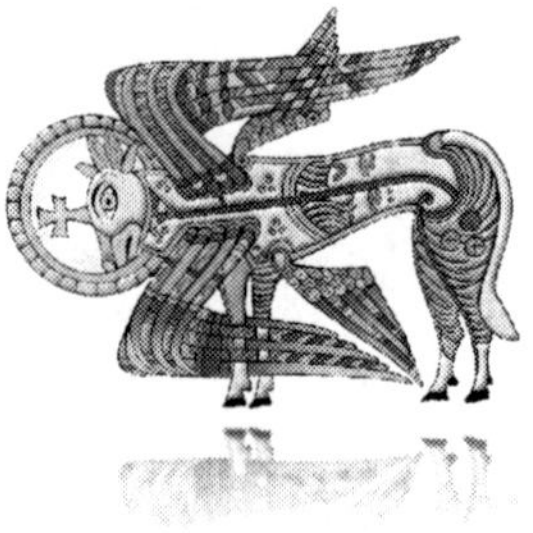

King
When sorrows come, they come not single spies,
But in battalions.

Hamlet 4.5.78-79

Just after the mad Ophelia leaves the room, King Claudius says this to his wife, Queen Gertrude, referring both to Ophelia's tragic circumstances and also to Claudius' and Gertrude's own situation. First, Ophelia's father is murdered by her beloved Prince Hamlet, then Hamlet is sent away from his native country. After these events Ophelia goes mad, and now her brother Laertes has secretly arrived from France. As Laertes arrives at the Danish court, a riotous rabble declares that Laertes will be king.

King Claudius: *When griefs come, they arrive not as single secret agents, but in entire military units.*

Heeding One's Own Advice

MARCH 31

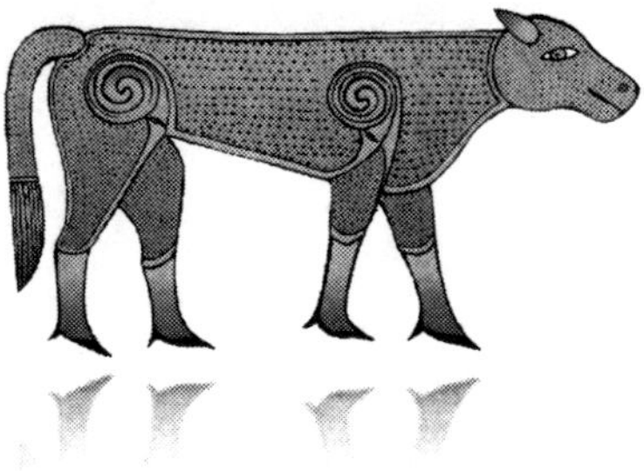

Ophelia

But good my brother,
Do not as some ungracious pastors do,
Show me the steep and thorny way to heaven,
Whilst like a puff 'd and reckless libertine
Himself the primrose path of dalliance treads,
And recks not his own reed.

Hamlet 1.3.46-51

Ophelia says this to her brother Laertes after he admonishes her to behave cautiously and chastely in her relationship with Hamlet, Prince of Denmark.

____

____

____

____

____

____

Ophelia: *But my dear brother, do not, as some wicked pastors do, point out to me the high and difficult road to heaven while, like a proud, rash, and loose man, you follow the licentious path of self-indulgence and ignore your own advice.*

Renewal

APRIL 1

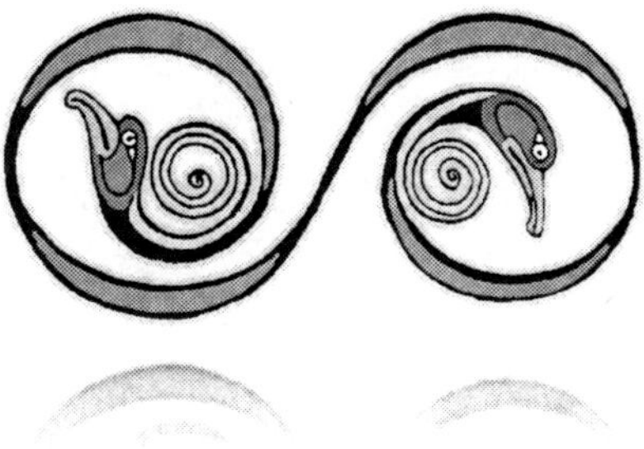

Sonnet 98

proud pied April, dressed in all his trim,
Hath put a spirit of youth in everything. . . .

Lines 2-3

Sonnet 98: *The bright, beautiful colors of April, draped in fine attire, breathe youthful vitality into all things.*

Not Being Understood

APRIL 2

Touchstone

When a man's verses cannot be
understood, nor a man's good wit seconded with the
forward child, understanding, it strikes a man more
dead than a great reckoning in a little room.

As You Like It 3.3.11-14

Touchstone, trying to woo the simple goatherd Audrey, tries to show off by making a reference to Ovid that goes right over Audrey's head. Unbeknownst to Touchstone, his reference is inaccurate.

Touchstone: *When a person's poetry isn't keenly grasped or apprehended by being understood, then it destroys a person more thoroughly than having a great reputation but being stuck in some insignificant place.*

Procrastination

APRIL 3

Hamlet

I do not know
Why yet I live to say this thing's to do,
Sith I have cause, and will, and strength, and means
To do't.

Hamlet 4.4.43-46

Hamlet, Prince of Denmark, here watches Fortinbras and his army pass by as they march across Denmark to do battle in Norway in order to avenge a slight against Fortinbras' own father. Hamlet pauses to berate himself for failing to act to avenge his own father's murder.

***Hamlet:** I don't understand why I am even alive to utter this phrase, "This act is still left for me to accomplish" since I have the justification, the motivation, and the physical ability to do it.*

Unintended Consequences

APRIL 4

Caliban
You taught me language, and my profit on't
Is I know how to curse.

The Tempest 1.2.364-65

Caliban says this to Miranda when she reminds Caliban that he was imprisoned by a spell in a rock until she released him and then taught him how to speak.

Caliban: *You have taught me to speak, and my advantage now is that I am skilled in profanity.*

Goodness in Evil

APRIL 5

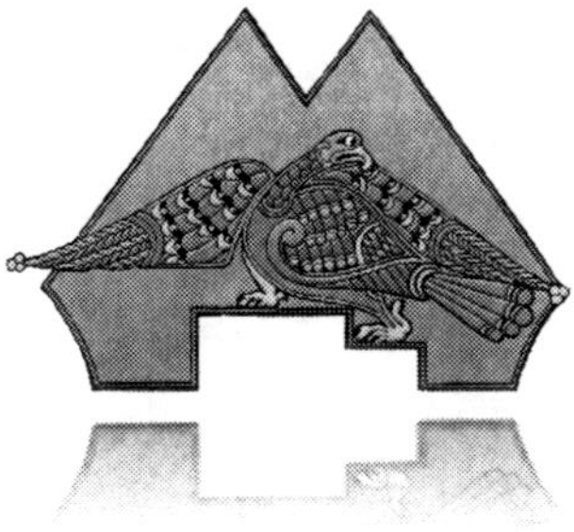

King Henry
There is some soul of goodness in things evil,
Would men observingly distil it out:
For our bad neighbour makes us early stirrers,
Which is both healthful and good husbandry.

King Henry V 4.1.4-7

Talking to the Duke of Gloucester and the Duke of Bedford, King Henry acknowledges that the English soldiers are facing great danger in their upcoming battle with the French who greatly outnumber them. By way of consolation, Henry makes this observation.

King Henry: *There is some essence of goodness in things that are evil if only people would extract it with great care. Our rowdy neighbor makes us early risers, something which is both good for our health and also good for the management of our household duties.*

Love as Impetuous

APRIL 6

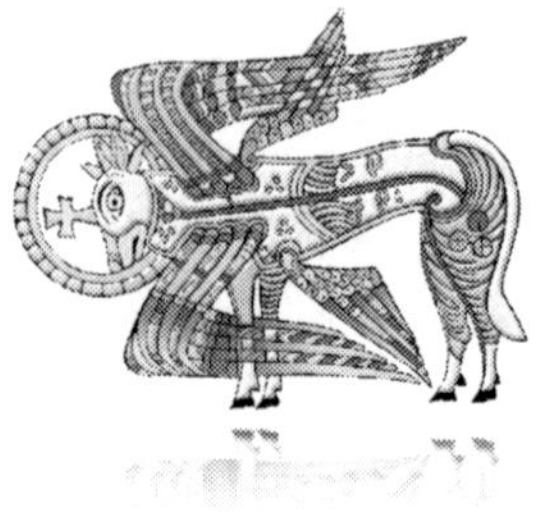

Helena
Love looks not with the eyes, but with the mind,
And therefore is wing'd Cupid painted blind;
Nor hath Love's mind of any judgement taste:
Wings, and no eyes, figure unheedy haste.
A Midsummer Night's Dream 1.1.234-37

Helena says this as she is spurned by Demetrius who loves Hermia who loves Lysander who has been forbidden to court Hermia.

***Helena:** Love does not see with the senses but rather with subjective desire. This is the reason winged Cupid is portrayed as blind. The judgment of the lover universally lacks discernment. Wings without sight symbolize impulsive speed.*

Healing Powers of Sleep

APRIL 7

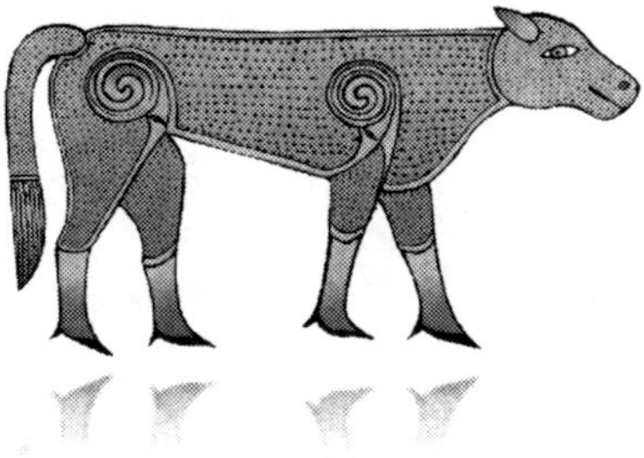

Gentleman
Our foster nurse of nature is repose. . . .

King Lear 4.4.12

The French officer says this to Cordelia, who has just reported to him that her father, King Lear, has been found in a nearby field, completely mad due to his horrific treatment at the hands of his other two cruel daughters.

Gentleman: *Rest is like a nursemaid to our bodies and minds.*

Love's Tinted Glasses

APRIL 8

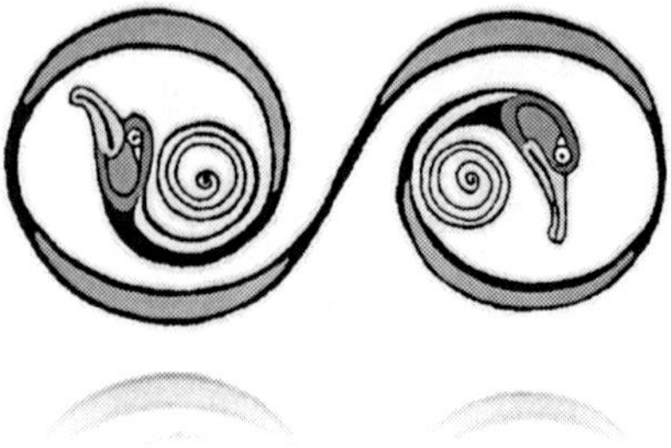

Sonnet 96

As on the finger of a throned queen
The basest jewel will be well esteemed,
So are those errors that in thee are seen
To truths translated, and for true things deemed.

Lines 5-8

Sonnet 96: *Just as the cheapest jewel on the finger of the queen is esteemed to be of great value, so are your transgressions changed into virtues and then perceived as genuinely good.*

Despair

APRIL 9

Hamlet

How weary, stale, flat, and unprofitable
Seem to me all the uses of this world!

Hamlet 1.2.133-34

In his grief over the death of his father and the all-too-hasty marriage of his mother, Hamlet, Prince of Denmark, is overwhelmed by melancholy.

Hamlet: *How tiresome, worn out, dull, and useless all the ways of this world seem to me!*

Goodness by Default

APRIL 10

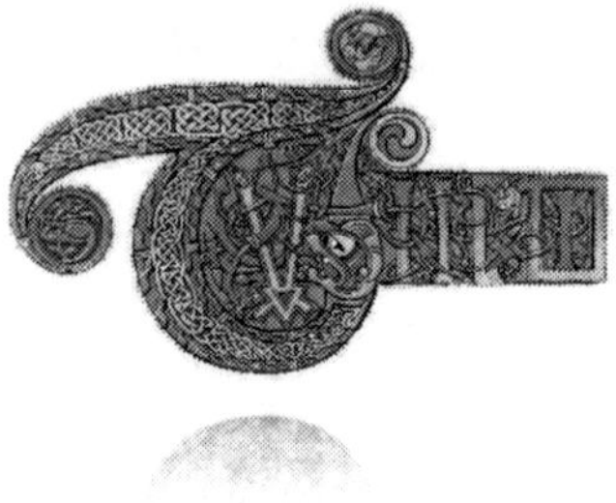

Antipholus S.

I see a man here needs not live by shifts
When in the streets he meets such golden gifts.

The Comedy of Errors 3.2.181-82

Angelo, the goldsmith, has just handed Antipholus of Syracuse a golden necklace, mistaking him for Antipholus of Ephesus, his long lost twin brother. Antipholus of Syracuse protests that he never ordered the chain and then offers to pay for it. Angelo refuses to take the money. After Angelo leaves, Antipholus of Syracuse makes this remark.

Antipholus S.: *I notice that here an individual doesn't have to thrive underhandedly since merely by wandering around town he encounters such rich presents.*

Tall Tales

April 11

Prince

I am not yet of Percy's mind,
the Hotspur of the north, he that kills me some six or
seven dozen of Scots at a breakfast, washes his hands,
and says to his wife, 'Fie upon this quiet life, I want
work'.

King Henry IV, Part 1 2.4.100-04

Frustrated with the inertia of the apprentice bartender Francis, Prince Hal thinks of a person the opposite of the slow Francis: Hal's rival Hotspur whose name reveals his fiery martial temperament. Hal imagines a typical Hotspur morning.

Prince: *I have not quite achieved the disposition of Percy, the Hotspur of northern England. This man decimates six or seven dozen Scots before breakfast, wipes off his hands, and then complains to his wife, "Damn this peaceful life, I want real work!"*

Virtue of Imperfections

APRIL 12

Mariana

They say best men are moulded out of faults,
And, for the most, become much more the better
For being a little bad.

***Measure for Measure* 5.1.436-38**

Mariana, Lord Angelo's discarded fiancée, pleads for Angelo's life when he is condemned to death for abusing his power as acting Duke of Vienna. Here Mariana pleads with Isabella, another woman Angelo has wronged, to beg for Angelo's life.

***Mariana:** The very best individuals are sculpted out of their imperfections. As a whole, such individuals are made even better because they have been slightly bad.*

Baiting a Fish

APRIL 13

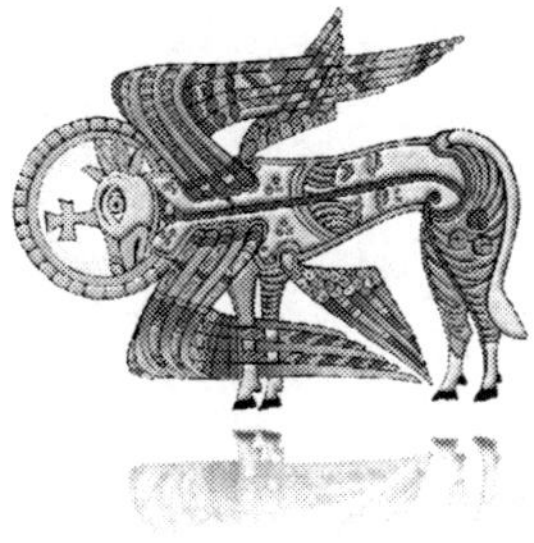

Ursula
The pleasant'st angling is to see the fish
Cut with her golden oars the silver stream,
And greedily devour the treacherous bait. . . .
Much Ado About Nothing 3.1.26-28

Ursula, Hero's waiting woman, says this to Hero as the two plan a scheme to trap Beatrice into loving Benedick. Ursula and Hero are planning to let Beatrice (who is hiding) overhear their conversation about how much Benedick loves Beatrice. They compare Beatrice to a fish and themselves to fishermen.

Ursula: *The most pleasurable fishing occurs when the fish is observed slicing the silver stream with her golden fins and hungrily swallowing the dangerous bait.*

Appropriate Time for Advice

APRIL 14

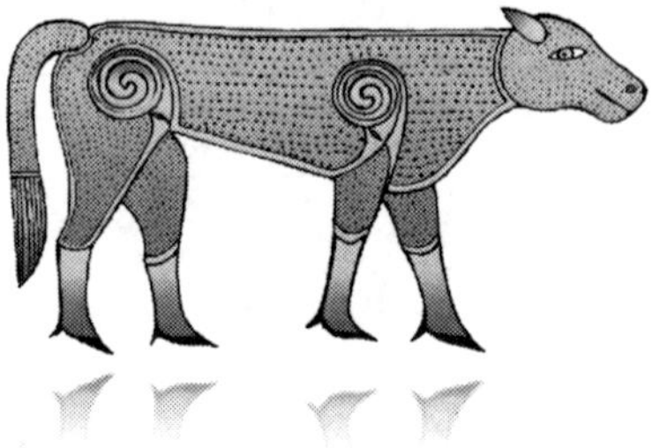

King

Chide him for his faults, and do it reverently,
When you perceive his blood inclin'd to mirth;
But being moody, give him time and scope,
Till that his passions, like a whale on ground,
Confound themselves with working.

King Henry IV, Part 2 4.4.37-41

Discovering that his son Hal, Prince of Wales, is once more absent from court and from official duties, King Henry IV criticizes Hal's younger brother, Thomas of Clarence, for not spending more time with Hal. Because Thomas is Hal's favorite brother, says Henry, he is in a special position to offer advice to Hal.

____

____

____

____

____

____

King Henry IV: *Call attention to his flaws respectfully when you notice he is in a good mood. When his mood is dark, leave him alone until his emotions wear themselves out like a struggling beached whale.*

Folly of Riches
APRIL 15

Duke

If thou art rich, thou'rt poor;
For, like an ass whose back with ingots bows,
Thou bear'st thy heavy riches but a journey,
And Death unloads thee.

Measure for Measure 3.1.25-28

The Duke of Vienna, disguised as a friar, counsels Claudio to face his execution the next day by reminding him of the folly of material success from a spiritual perspective.

Duke: *If you are wealthy, you are actually unfortunate. Like a pack mule weighted down with precious metals, you carry your burdensome wealth only a distance, and then Death takes it away from you.*

Necessity of Luxury

APRIL 16

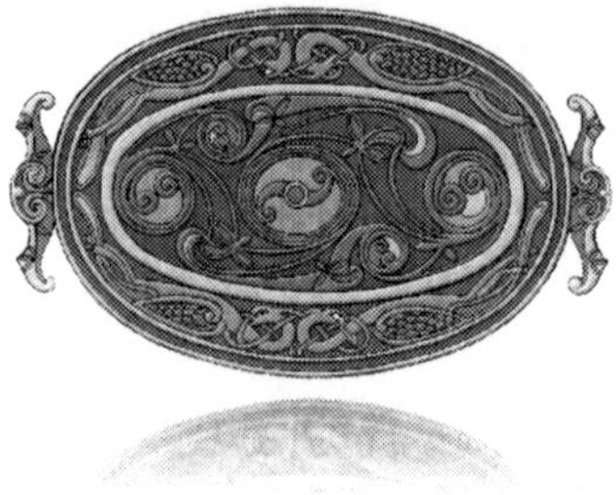

Lear

O, reason not the need! Our basest beggars
Are in the poorest things superfluous;
Allow not nature more than nature needs,
Man's life is cheap as beast's.

King Lear 2.2.456-59

King Lear says this when his greedy, manipulative daughters, Goneril and Regan, try to persuade him to reduce the size of his retinue. Regan asks him why he needs even one knight to accompany him.

Lear: *Don't question whether or not it is necessary. Our most wretched street people are extravagant with the most insignificant items. If you don't permit a creature of nature more than is necessary to survive, then human life is as worthless as an animal's.*

Our Own Worst Enemy

APRIL 17

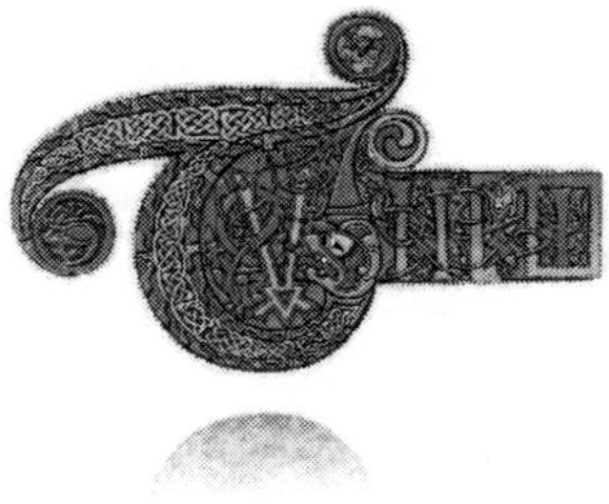

Falstaff

She's neither fish nor flesh, a man knows not where to have her.

Hostess

Thou art an unjust man in saying so, thou or any man knows where to have me, thou knave, thou.

King Henry IV, Part 1 3.3.128-33

Falstaff, mad at Mistress Quickly for demanding that he pay her the money he owes her, tries to insult her. Mistress Quickly unknowingly makes the insult even worse.

Falstaff: *She's neither amphibian nor human: a man can't figure out where to be intimate with her.*
Hostess: *You are utterly false in saying this! You--or any man--is familiar with exactly where to enjoy me, you villain, you!*

Paragon of Creation

APRIL 18

Hamlet

What piece of work is a man,
how noble in reason, how infinite in faculties, in form
and moving how express and admirable, in action how
like an angel, in apprehension how like a god: the
beauty of the world, the paragon of animals. . . .

Hamlet 2.2.305-09

Hamlet says this to his childhood acquaintances, Rosencrantz and Guildenstern, as Prince Hamlet is struggling with the recent death of his father, his mother's remarriage, and his father's ghost's revelation that he was murdered. Hamlet is being ironic.

Hamlet: *What an extraordinary work of art a human being is! How magnificent is the mind, how inexhaustible are the capabilities, how perfect and marvelous are the behavior and movement! How angelic is the demeanor and how godlike is the understanding. A human being is the ornament of the world and the supreme paradigm for all animals!*

Consolation of Hope

APRIL 19

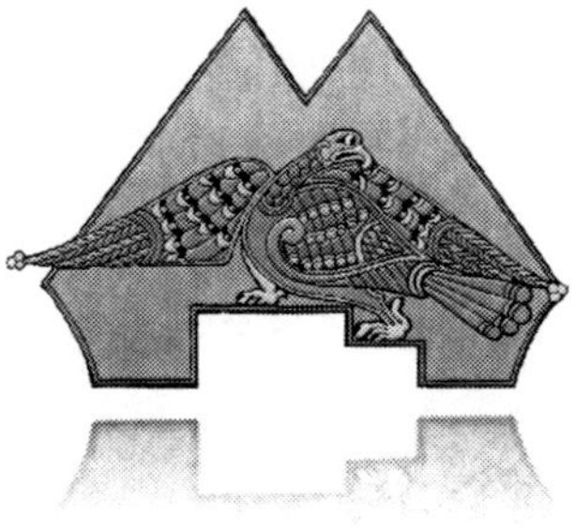

Pistol

Si fortuna me tormenta, spero me contenta.

King Henry IV, Part 2 5.5.97

Pistol says this as he, Falstaff, and their riotous crew are taken away to Fleet Prison, the debtor's jail. The Lord Chief Justice has ordered this action as the reformed King Henry V passes through London just after his coronation. Abandoned by his former drinking companion-turned-king, Pistol consoles himself with a garbled mix of Latin languages.

Pistol: *If fortune torments me, hope contents me.*

Love Beyond Time

APRIL 20

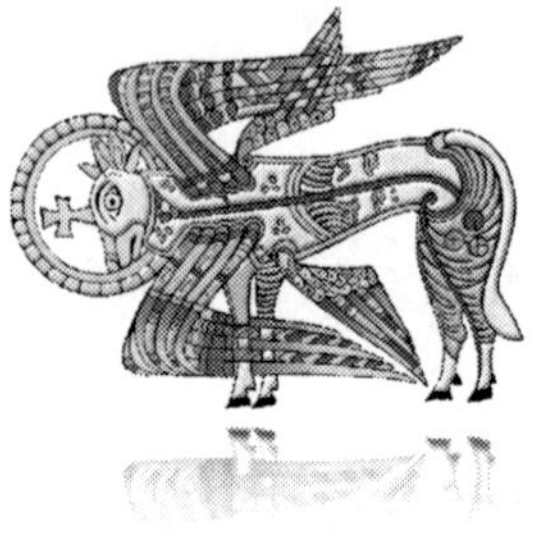

Sonnet 107

Not mine own fears, nor the prophetic soul
Of the wide world, dreaming on things to come,
Can yet the lease of my true love control,
Supposed as forfeit to a confined doom.

Lines 1-4

Sonnet 107: *Neither my anxieties nor the visionary spirit of the world looking into the future can limit the duration of my love for you, which is mistakenly thought to be subject to the limits of mortality.*

Framing Experience

APRIL 21

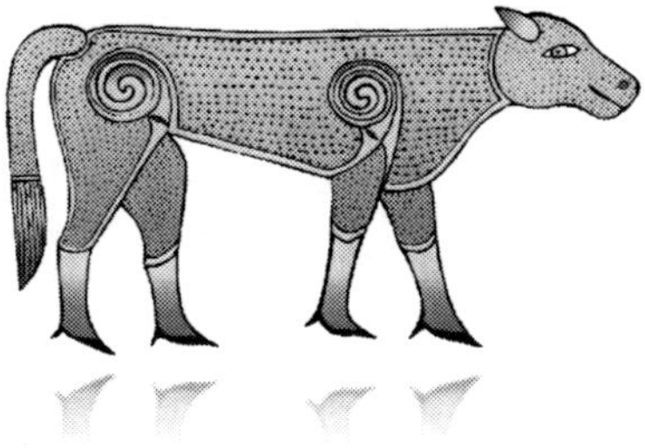

Hamlet

Meet it is I set it down
That one may smile, and smile, and be a villain. . . .

Hamlet 1.5.107-08

Hamlet says this to himself just after his father's ghost has appeared. The ghost has revealed that he did not die a natural death, as Prince Hamlet was led to believe, but rather has been murdered by the ghost's brother, Hamlet's uncle Claudius.

Hamlet: *Here is my notebook! How fitting it is for me to write down that a person may smile and smile and still be a crook.*

Sting of Ingratitude

APRIL 22

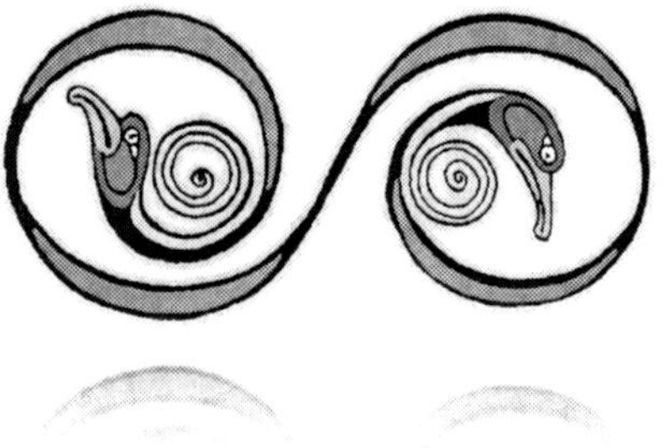

Lear

Ingratitude, thou marble-hearted fiend,
More hideous when thou show'st thee in a child
Than the sea-monster.

King Lear 1.4.251-53

King Lear says this after his daughter Goneril reverses roles and treats Lear like a child, insisting that he reduce his retinue in half. Having banished one of his daughters and divided his kingdom among the other two, Lear expects honor and gratitude, not callous disrespect.

Lear: *Ungratefulness, you devil with a heart like marble! You are more grotesque when you appear in one of my own flesh and blood than if you had appeared in a vicious ocean creature.*

The Poet's Triumph Over Time

APRIL 23

Sonnet 107
Now with the drops of this most balmy time
My love looks fresh, and death to me subscribes,
Since 'spite of him I'll live in this poor rhyme,
While he insults o'er dull and speechless tribes. . . .
Lines 9-12

Sonnet 107: *Because of propitious events at the present time, my love appears brand new. Death answers to me. While he struts around, scorning those who neither write nor speak well, I will triumph over death in the lasting power of these humble rhymes.*

Controlling Destiny

APRIL 24

Cassius
Men at some time are masters of their fates.
The fault, dear Brutus, is not in our stars
But in ourselves, that we are underlings.
***Julius Caesar* 1.2.138-40**

Cassius says this to Brutus who has just remarked on the fickle crowds of Roman citizens applauding new honors accorded to Caesar.

Cassius: *At one point or another, human beings are able to control their destinies. The blame for being subject to another's power lies not in the heavens, but in ourselves.*

Responding to Injustice

APRIL 25

Queen
The lion dying thrusteth forth his paw
And wounds the earth, if nothing else, with rage
To be o'erpow'r'd. . . .

King Richard II 5.1.29-31

Queen Isabel says this to her husband King Richard II when the two meet in London as Richard is on his way to the Tower. Richard says he is resigned to his fate and that she must do likewise.

Queen: *The dying lion fiercely throws out his paw and in his fury, if nothing else, at least strikes the earth in his helplessness.*

Intuiting Disaster

APRIL 26

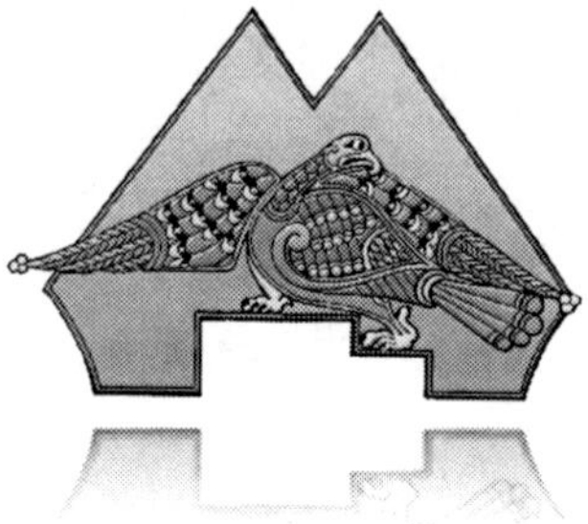

Northumberland

See what a ready tongue suspicion hath!
He that but fears the thing he would not know
Hath by instinct knowledge from others' eyes
That what he fear'd is chanced.

King Henry IV, Part 2 1.1.84-87

The Earl of Northumberland is speaking to Morton who has just run from the Battle of Shrewsbury to convey the dark news to Northumberland that his son Hotspur is dead. Even though Northumberland has been misled by false rumors indicating Hotspur is alive, as soon as Morton mentions Hotspur, Northumberland knows his son is dead.

Northumberland: *How quickly suspicion transforms into the spoken truth! A person who fears something he would deny can instinctively detect in the eyes of others that what was dreaded has actually taken place.*

Children Mirroring Our Youth

APRIL 27

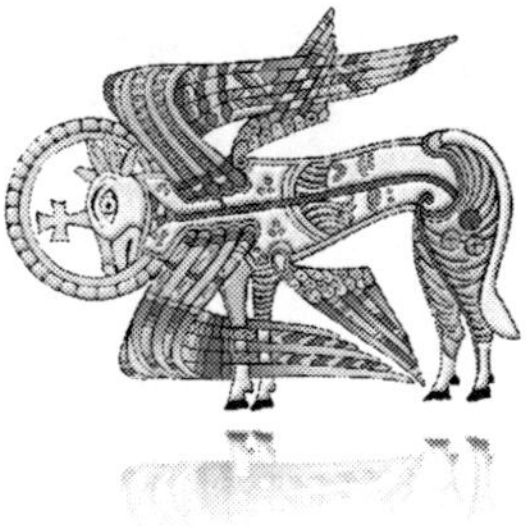

Sonnet 3

Thou art thy mother's glass, and she in thee
Calls back the lovely April of her prime:
So thou through windows of thine age shalt see,
Despite of wrinkles, this thy golden time.

Lines 9-12

____

____

____

____

____

____

Sonnet 3: *You are your mother's mirror. In you she recalls the beautiful springtime of the fullness of her youth. Likewise, from the perspective of age you will see in your own child your own flourishing youthful beauty.*

False Gravitas

APRIL 28

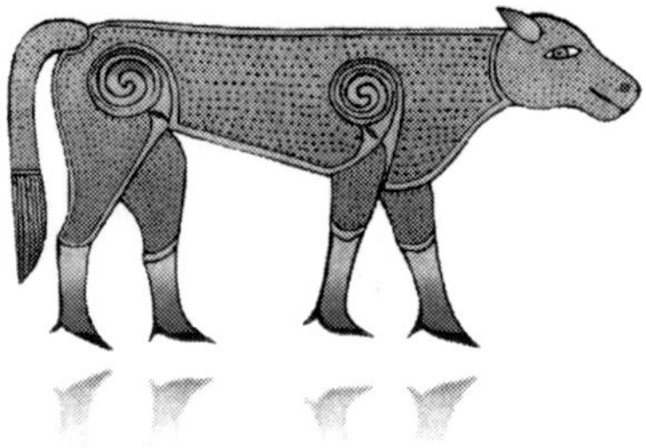

Gratiano

There are a sort of men whose visages
Do cream and mantle like a standing pond,
And do a wilful stillness entertain,
With purpose to be dress'd in an opinion
Of wisdom, gravity, profound conceit,
As who should say, 'I am Sir Oracle,
And when I ope my lips, let no dog bark.'

The Merchant of Venice 1.1.88-94

Trying to cheer up his friend Antonio who is sad for an unknown reason, Gratiano playfully caricatures the pretense of wisdom.

______

______

______

______

______

______

Gratiano: *There is a type of man whose face glasses over like a stagnant pool covered with scum. Such a person maintains an affected silence in order to be thought wise, grave, and deeply understanding. This person appears to be saying, "I am Sir Mouthpiece of the Deity, and whenever I start to speak, do not permit even a barking dog to interrupt."*

Turning the Tables

APRIL 29

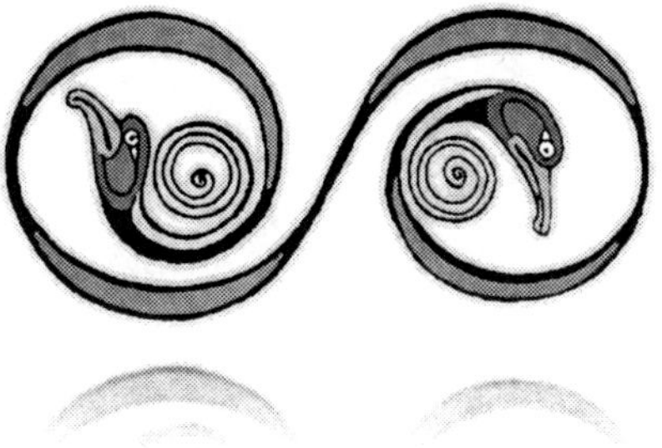

Hamlet
For 'tis the sport to have the enginer
Hoist with his own petard. . . .

Hamlet 3.4.208-09

King Claudius, correctly fearing that Hamlet suspects the King of murdering Hamlet's father, sends Prince Hamlet away from Denmark with sealed letters intending him harm. Rightfully suspecting Claudius' treachery, Hamlet tells his mother that he plans to turn the tables on his enemy.

Hamlet: *It is the common pastime to have the inventor blown up, using his/her own explosive device.*

License to Act Differently

APRIL 30

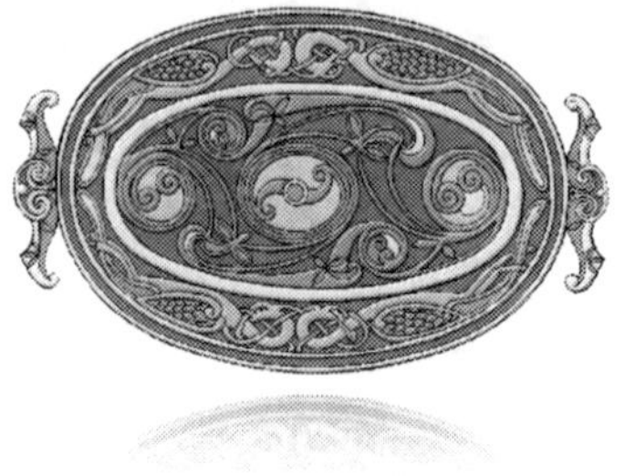

King

'tis ever common
That men are merriest when they are from home.

***King Henry V* 1.2.272-73**

Henry says this to Exeter after the King has received a mocking present from the French Dauphin of a metal casket full of tennis balls. Henry comments that the gift is a clear indication that the Dauphin is trying to embarrass King Henry by reminding him of his wilder days when he was away from court, not valuing his role as heir to the throne.

King Henry V: *It is usually the case that people are the most flippant when they are away from home.*

The Self-sufficient Laborer

MAY 1

Corin
Sir, I am a true labourer: I earn that I eat, get
that I wear; owe no man hate, envy no man's
happiness; glad of other men's good, content with my
harm; and the greatest of my pride is to see my ewes
graze and my lambs suck.

As You Like It 3.2.70-74

The shepherd Corin says this to the court fool Touchstone after Touchstone accuses the shepherd of lacking courtly manners and wit because he was never exposed to life at court.

***Corin:** I am an honest laborer: I earn what I eat, I work for what I wear, I bear no one hate, and I envy no one's happiness. I am happy for others' economic success, and I endure my own troubles. My greatest pride is to see my female sheep grazing and their young feeding.*

Desire as Relentless

MAY 2

Duke

This forenamed maid hath yet in her the
continuance of her first affection. His unjust
unkindness, that in all reason should have quenched
her love, hath, like an impediment in the current,
made it more violent and unruly.

Measure for Measure 3.1.238-42

The Duke of Vienna is discussing Mariana, a woman once betrothed to Angelo. Although he was engaged to her, Angelo spurned Mariana after her dowry--along with her brother--was lost in a shipwreck.

Duke: *The woman I mentioned, who has remained single, continues to desire her first love. His cruelty, which should have put out the fire of her affections, instead has affected her like an obstacle in a river's current that dams the river up, making the current stronger and more uncontrollable.*

Sanctioning Corruption

MAY 3

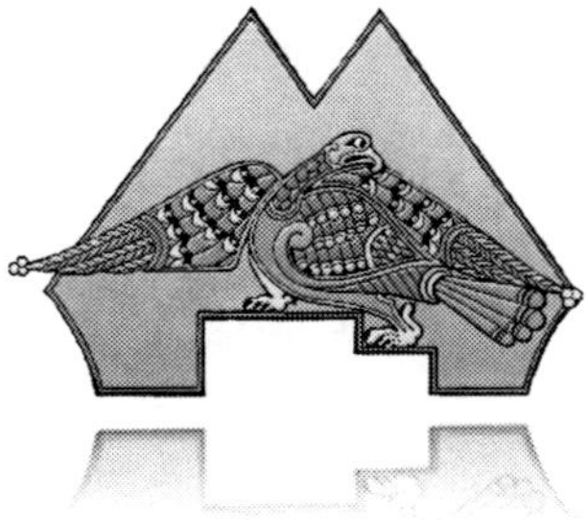

Angelo
Thieves for their robbery have authority,
When judges steal themselves.

***Measure for Measure* 2.2.176-77**

Angelo here is reflecting on his own lust for the pure Isabella because Angelo has condemned Isabella's brother Claudio to death for sleeping with his fiancée.

Angelo: *Robbers have official approval for their crimes when judges themselves are thieves.*

Despising One's Origins

MAY 4

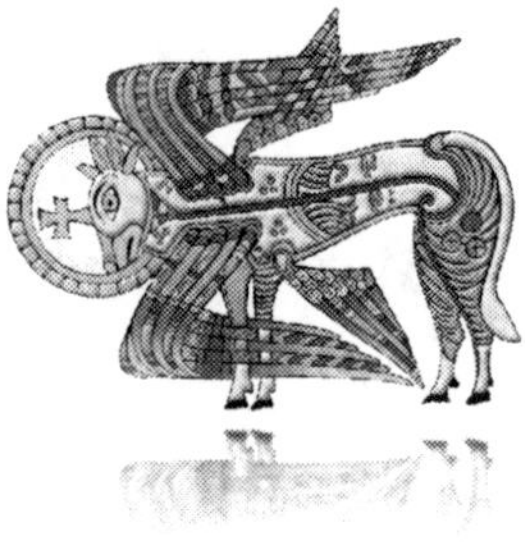

Brutus

But, 'tis a common proof
That lowliness is young ambition's ladder
Whereto the climber upward turns his face;
But when he once attains the upmost round
He then unto the ladder turns his back,
Looks in the clouds, scorning the base degrees
By which he did ascend.

Julius Caesar 2.1.21-27

Brutus says this to his servant Lucius after Brutus has awakened Lucius from sleep. Brutus muses mostly to himself about the reasons why Caesar should be assassinated.

Brutus: *It is a universal experience that humble origins are simply the means by which the ambitious person climbs higher. Once such a person reaches the top of the ladder, he ignores his origins, gazing only on the clouds and despising the lowly steps by which he rose.*

Humility in Victory

MAY 5

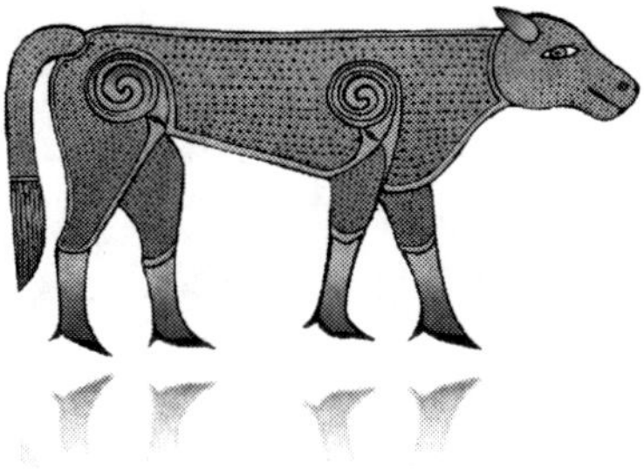

Montjoy

The day is yours.

King

Praised be God, and not our strength, for it!

King Henry V 4.7.85-86

Outnumbered by the French five to one and overwhelmed by the turmoil of battle, King Henry V does not know, when the French herald Montjoy approaches him, which side has won the Battle of Agincourt. Henry asks him, and Montjoy responds.

Montjoy: *The victory is yours.* **King:** *May God be praised for this victory rather than our army or our mortal power.*

Politicians

MAY 6

Hamlet

This
might be the pate of a politician which this ass now
o'er-offices, one that would circumvent God, might
it not?

***Hamlet* 5.1.77-80**

Prince Hamlet says this to Horatio as the gravedigger uncovers another skull in the new grave that he is digging.

Hamlet: *The skull which this jerk now treats with such disdain might once have been the head of a politician, might it not, one whose arguments would run circles around God?*

Stating the Obvious

MAY 7

Hamlet
There's never a villain dwelling in all Denmark
But he's an errant knave.
Horatio
There needs no ghost, my lord, come from the grave
To tell us this.

Hamlet 1.5.129-32

Prince Hamlet says this to his friend Horatio after Hamlet has just talked with his father's ghost and discovered that the former King Hamlet was murdered by his brother Claudius. When he makes this comment, Hamlet has in mind his uncle Claudius, who is now King.

Hamlet: *Every scoundrel living in Denmark is nothing but a shiftless lowlife.*
Horatio: *We don't need a ghost, my lord, appearing from the grave to teach us this.*

Emptiness of Honor

MAY 8

Falstaff

Can honour set to a leg?
No. Or an arm? No. Or take away the grief of a wound?
No. Honour hath no skill in surgery then? No. What is
honour? A word. What is that word honour? What
is that honour? Air. A trim reckoning! Who hath it?
He that died a-Wednesday.

King Henry IV, Part 1 5.1.131-36

Falstaff says this to himself after Prince Hal has just told Falstaff that he owes God a death. As Falstaff heads off to the Battle of Shrewsbury with a ragtag bunch of conscripts, he refuses to see honor within a patriotic military framework. Instead he looks upon it as a threat to his own skin.

Falstaff: *Can honor repair a broken leg? No. Or an arm? No. Or take away the pain of a wound? No. Honor has no talent as a surgeon, then? No. What is honor? A word. What is in this word "honor"? What constitutes honor? Air. A fine way of thinking about it! Who has it? The person who died on Wednesday.*

Discontent as Dangerous

MAY 9

Caesar
Let me have men about me that are fat,
Sleek-headed men, and such as sleep a-nights.
Yond Cassius has a lean and hungry look:
He thinks too much: such men are dangerous.
Julius Caesar 1.2.191-94

Caesar says this to Antony although Cassius is nearby. Cassius will be one of the conspirators to assassinate Caesar.

Caesar: *Let me have individuals around me who are plump and healthy and those who rest comfortably at night. Cassius over there looks underfed and ambitious. He broods too much: these types of men are treacherous.*

Power to Change One's Mind

MAY 10

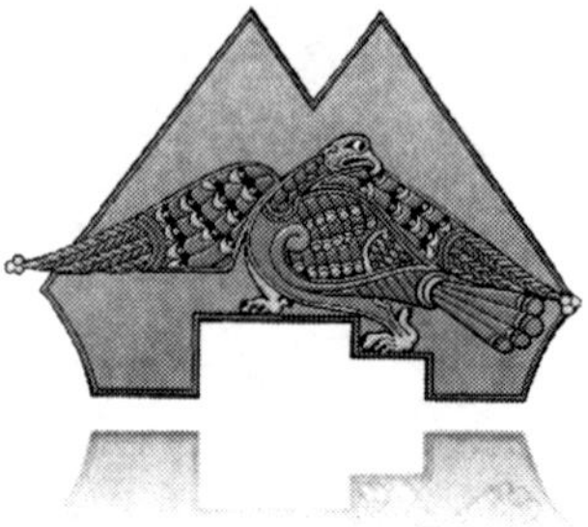

Angelo

He's sentenc'd, 'tis too late. . . .

Isabella

Too late? Why, no. I that do speak a word
May call it again.

Measure for Measure 2.2.55; 57-58

Lord Angelo, temporarily replacing the absent Duke of Vienna, reiterates his decision to execute Claudio, Isabella's brother, who has impregnated his fiancée Juliet.

Angelo: *He is already sentenced. It is too late.* ***Isabella:*** *Too late? But, no! I that called a word into action may command it back again.*

Genuine Affection

MAY 11

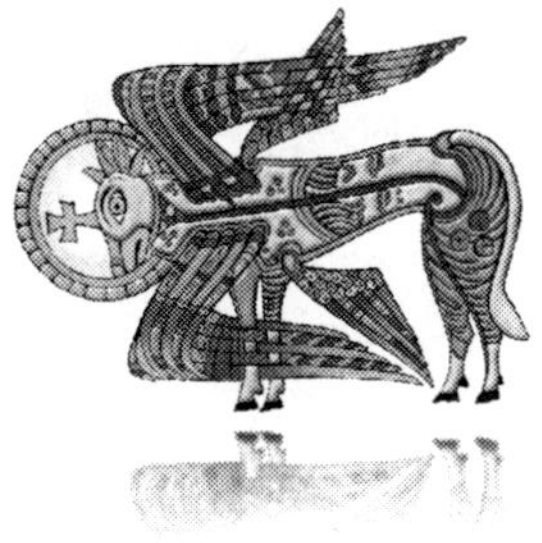

Doll
By my troth, I kiss thee with a most constant heart.

King Henry IV, Part 2 2.4.269-70

Falstaff's mistress, Doll Tearsheet, says this to Falstaff after he accuses her of giving him only flattering kisses.

Doll: *Truly, I kiss you with a very faithful heart.*

Not Being Ourselves

MAY 12

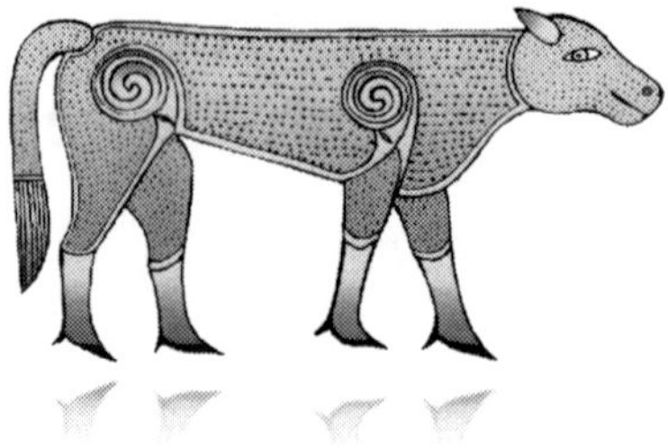

Lear

We are not ourselves
When nature, being oppressed, commands the mind
To suffer with the body.

King Lear 2.2.299-301

King Lear says this when his daughter Regan and son-in-law Cornwall refuse the King's command to see them. Lear tries to explain away this insult from his family members.

Lear: *We are not our true selves when, burdened by illness, our minds as well as our bodies suffer.*

Love's Power to Bind Us to Life

MAY 13

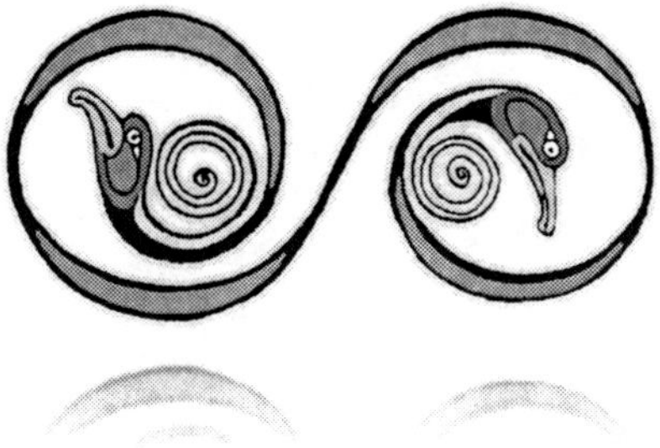

Solanio
I think he only loves the world for him. . . .
The Merchant of Venice 2.8.50

Solanio says this to his companion Salerio. Solanio is referring to the merchant Antonio's deep affection for Bassanio.

Solanio: *I believe he holds life dear only because of Bassanio.*

Warrior's Transformation

MAY 14

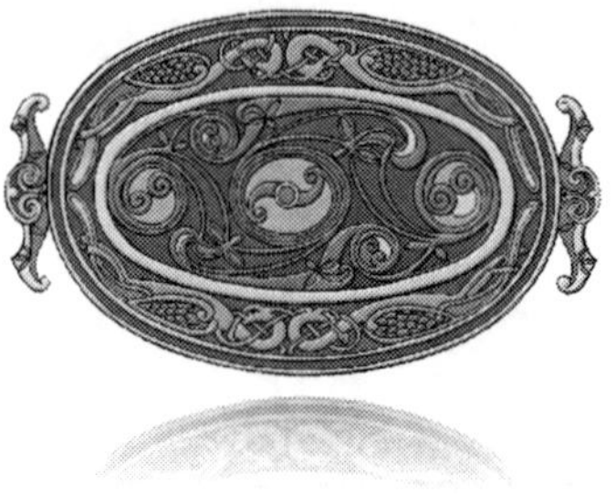

Vernon

All furnish'd, all in arms;
All plum'd like estridges, that with the wind
Bated, like eagles having lately bath'd,
Glittering in golden coats like images,
As full of spirit as the month of May,
And gorgeous as the sun at midsummer;
Wanton as youthful goats, wild as young bulls.

King Henry IV, Part 1 4.1.97-103

Sir Richard Vernon, fighting under Hotspur's rebel forces, says this to Hotspur who has condescendingly asked where the madcap Prince Hal and his men are. Vernon responds with an epic description of warriors armed to the teeth and ready for battle.

***Vernon:** They were fully outfitted, fully armed, feathered like ostriches with plumes like eagles that, having just bathed, flapped their wings against the wind. They sparkled in their brilliant armor like gilded statues. They were lively as the month of May, dazzling like the midsummer sun, playful as young goats, and fierce as young bulls.*

Moral Limits
MAY 15

Macbeth
I dare do all that may become a man;
Who dares do more, is none.

Macbeth 1.7.46-47

Macbeth says this in response to Lady Macbeth's claim that Macbeth will live only to consider himself a coward if he does not kill King Duncan.

Macbeth: *I have the courage to do everything that is fitting for a human being to do. Whoever goes beyond this essential nature is no longer human.*

Joy of Anticipation

MAY 16

Gratiano

That ever holds: who riseth from a feast
With the keen appetite that he sits down?
Where is the horse that doth untread again
His tedious measures with the unbated fire
That he did pace them first? - all things that are,
Are with more spirit chased than enjoy'd.

The Merchant of Venice 2.6.8-13

Gratiano says this to Salerio as the two wait to meet their friend Lorenzo and his beloved Jessica who has just fled her father's house. Lorenzo and Jessica are late, and Gratiano remarks that impatient lovers usually run ahead of time not behind it.

Gratiano: *It is always the case. Whoever gets up from a banquet with the same sharp desire that he/she arrived with? Where is there a horse that retraces its laborious steps with the same zest with which it started out? All things in existence are pursued with more passion than they are appreciated once possessed.*

Hidden Nature

MAY 17

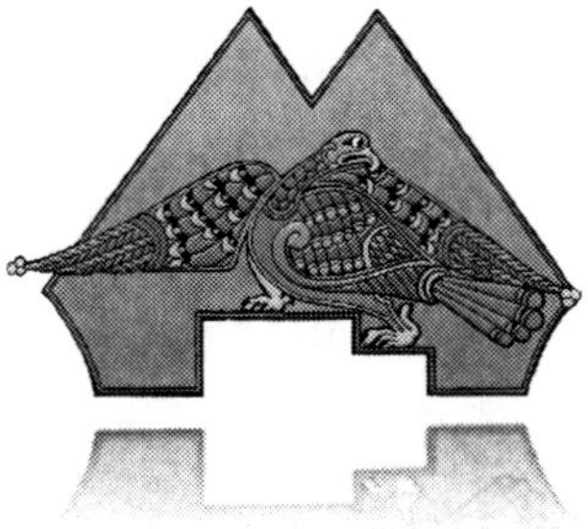

Duncan

There's no art
To find the mind's construction in the face. . . .

Macbeth 1.4.11-12

Duncan, King of Scotland, says this to his son Malcolm after Malcolm has described the Thane of Cawdor's expression of indifference as Cawdor was being executed as a traitor.

Duncan: *There is no field of knowledge that can perceive the mind's purpose simply by examining a person's face.*

Changing Tastes

MAY 18

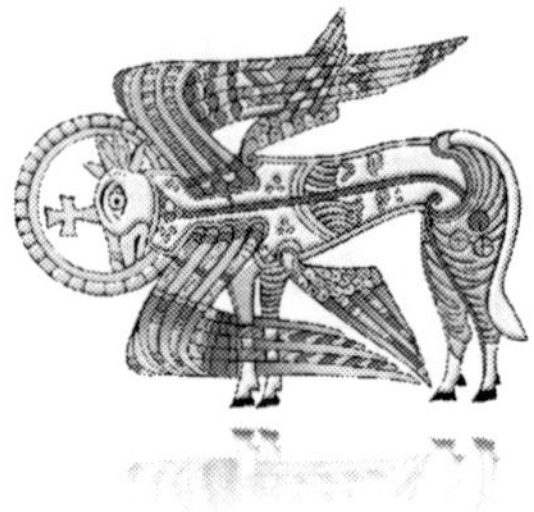

Benedick

A man loves the meat in his youth
that he cannot endure in his age.

Much Ado About Nothing 2.3.229-30

Benedick has been tricked into believing that Beatrice has spoken of her passionate love for Benedick. As a result, he decides that he must now endure the teasing that will come his way after he abandons his long-lived ranting about marriage and pursues a relationship with Beatrice.

Benedick: *A man when he is young craves the food that he is not able to stand when he is old.*

Love as a Disease

MAY 19

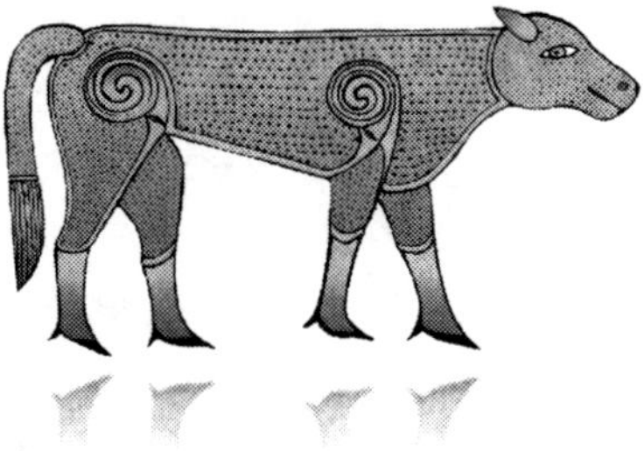

Sonnet 147

My love is as a fever, longing still
For that which longer nurseth the disease,
Feeding on that which doth preserve the ill,
Th'uncertain sickly appetite to please. . . .

Lines 1-4

Sonnet 147: *My love is like a disease that feeds on and craves that which simply prolongs the illness, satiating an unstable, unhealthy desire.*

Mistaking Obedience for Virtue

MAY 20

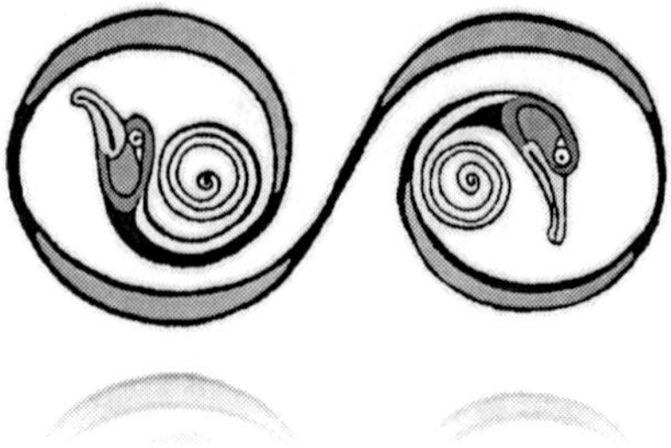

Falstaff

You call honourable boldness impudent
sauciness; if a man will make curtsy and say nothing,
he is virtuous.

***King Henry IV, Part 2* 2.1.123-25**

Falstaff says this to the Chief Justice who has ordered Falstaff to pay the debt he rightfully owes to Mistress Quickly. Always quick to defend his indefensible actions, Falstaff responds.

Falstaff: *You label honest confidence as insolence, but if a person is silent and obedient, then that individual is considered good and proper.*

War as Abscess

MAY 21

Hamlet

Two thousand souls and twenty thousand ducats
Will not debate the question of this straw!
This is th' impostume of much wealth and peace,
That inward breaks, and shows no cause without
Why the man dies.

***Hamlet* 4.4.25-29**

Prince Hamlet says this to the captain of Fortinbras' army as the soldiers from Norway pass through Denmark to fight over a small, useless patch of ground in Poland.

Hamlet: *Two thousand soldiers and twenty thousand ducats will not resolve the issue concerning this trifling piece of land. This battle is the abscess of too much money and too much peace that festers within the body politic and reveals no outward justification for the death of a soldier.*

Love's Difficult Questions

MAY 22

Celia

It is as easy to count atomies as to resolve the propositions of a lover.

As You Like It 3.2.229-30

Celia says this to Rosalind after Celia has just told her cousin that her beloved Orlando is in the Forest of Arden. Hearing this news, Rosalind fires off a dozen questions at her. Celia responds.

Celia: *Tallying the number of atoms in the universe is easier than trying to answer the questions of someone in love.*

Abuse of Religious Power

MAY 23

Morton

But now the Bishop
Turns insurrection to religion. . . .

King Henry IV, Part 2 1.1.200-01

The rebel messenger Morton observes that Hotspur struggled as a rebel to win his soldier's minds and hearts in addition to their arms. Now, after Hotspur's death, the Archbishop of York has no trouble attracting followers in his climb to power by calling upon the blood of King Richard II who was earlier vilified and now is presented as a saint.

Morton: *Now the Archbishop turns unlawful political action into religiously justified virtue.*

Virtue As Seductive

MAY 24

Angelo

Can it be
That modesty may more betray our sense
Than woman's lightness? Having waste ground enough,
Shall we desire to raze the sanctuary
And pitch our evils there?

Measure for Measure 2.2.168-72

Angelo, temporary ruler of Vienna in the Duke's absence, says this to himself after the novice Isabella has just left his chamber. The virtuous Isabella has been pleading with Angelo to reverse the execution order he placed on the head of Isabella's brother Claudio.

Angelo: *Is it possible that humble virtue may inflame our lust more than a promiscuous woman would? Having plenty of devastated land, why would we want to burn down a sacred site and erect evil in its place?*

Facing the Unknown

MAY 25

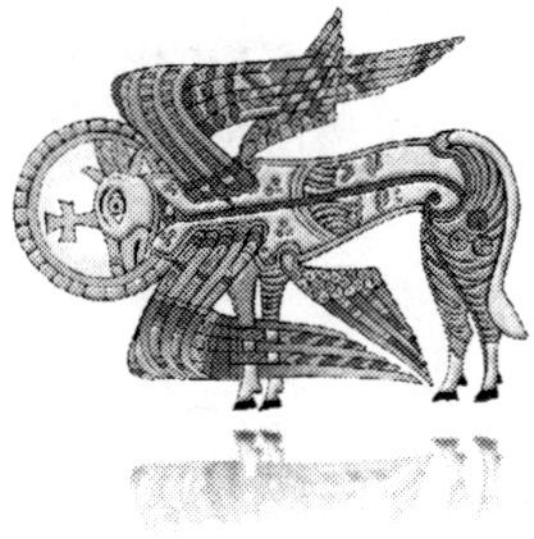

Marcellus

Thou art a scholar, speak to it, Horatio.

Hamlet 1.1.45

Marcellus, a member of the King's guard, has invited Horatio to stand watch with him after Marcellus and others have seen the ghost of King Hamlet for two successive nights. When the ghost appears again, Marcellus implores Horatio to do something about it.

Marcellus: *You're educated. You talk to it, Horatio.*

Rising Sun

MAY 26

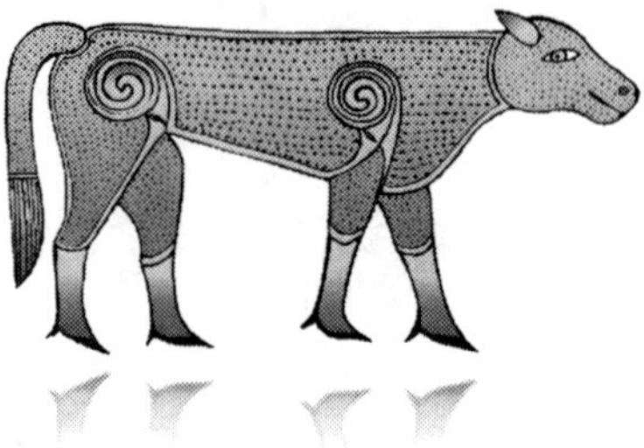

Montague

the all-cheering sun
. . . in the farthest east begin[s] to draw
The shady curtains from Aurora's bed. . . .

***Romeo and Juliet* 1.1.134-40**

Montague, Romeo's father, is describing his son's early morning retreats to a sycamore grove on the edge of the city. Distraught by Rosaline's rejection of his love, Romeo steals away to the grove in the very early morning hours and then returns home at dawn.

Montague: *The sun, that brings cheerfulness to everyone in the distant eastern horizon, starts to withdraw the shadowy curtains away from the bed of the goddess of dawn.*

Irrelevance of Time

MAY 27

Prince

What a devil hast thou to do with the time of the day? Unless hours were cups of sack, and minutes capons, and clocks the tongues of bawds, and dials the signs of leaping-houses, and the blessed sun himself a fair hot wench in flame-coloured taffeta, I see no reason why thou shouldst be so superfluous to demand the time of the day.

King Henry IV, Part 1 1.2.6-12

When Falstaff asks Prince Hal what time it is, Hal reminds Falstaff what a useless question this is coming from the king of debauched living.

Prince: *What the h--- do you care what time of day it is? Unless hours were glasses of wine and minutes roasted chicken, clocks and dials the voices of whores and ads for whorehouses, the very sun himself a shining silk-coated prostitute, then I see absolutely no reason why you should do something so unnecessary as to request the time of day.*

Doubts as Traitors

MAY 28

Lucio

Our doubts are traitors,
And makes us lose the good we oft might win
By fearing to attempt.

Measure for Measure 1.4.77-79

Hearing that her brother Claudio has been sentenced to die, the virtuous novice Isabella despairs of being able to help her brother. The fop Lucio challenges her conclusion.

Lucio: *Our doubts are traitors to us because they deprive us of the benefit we might have achieved if we weren't afraid to try.*

Ultimate Questions

MAY 29

Hamlet
To be, or not to be, that is the question. . . .

Hamlet 3.1.56

Walking by himself in the battlements of the castle, Hamlet, Prince of Denmark, is preoccupied with the question of how to respond to the ghost's news that he, King Hamlet, had been murdered by his brother Claudius, Prince Hamlet's uncle and the present King.

Hamlet: *To exist, or not to exist: that's the quandary.*

Brotherhood in Arms

MAY 30

King

This story shall the goodman teach his son,
And Crispin Crispian shall ne'er go by
From this day to the ending of the world
But we in it shall be remembered,
We few, we happy few, we band of brothers.
For he today that sheds his blood with me
Shall be my brother. . . .

***King Henry V* 4.3.56-62**

King Henry says this to his soldiers, trying to inspire courage in his troops as they face the French army which outnumbers the English five to one. This battle, fought at Agincourt, occurs on a special saints' day called the Feast of Crispian.

King: *This tale will the farmer teach his son. From now until the end of the world, the Feast of Crispian will not pass unnoticed without those of us in battle today being commemorated. We small but fortunate handful of soldiers are bonded as flesh-and-blood since anyone who dies or is wounded with me today will become my brother.*

An Enduring Profession

MAY 31

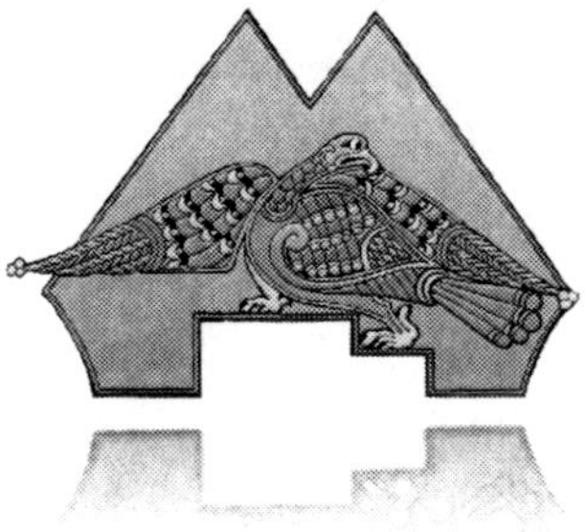

Gravedigger
What is he that builds stronger than
either the mason, the shipwright, or the carpenter?
Other Gravedigger
The gallows-maker, for that frame out lives a
thousand tenants.

Hamlet 5.1.41-44

The two gravediggers, digging Ophelia's grave, try to best one another with witty jokes, puzzles, and paradoxes.

Gravedigger: *Who can construct an edifice stronger than that which the stone mason, the ship builder, or the carpenter can build?* ***Other Gravedigger:*** *The one who constructs the gallows--that structure lasts longer than a thousand of its inhabitants.*

Delight in Country Air

JUNE 1

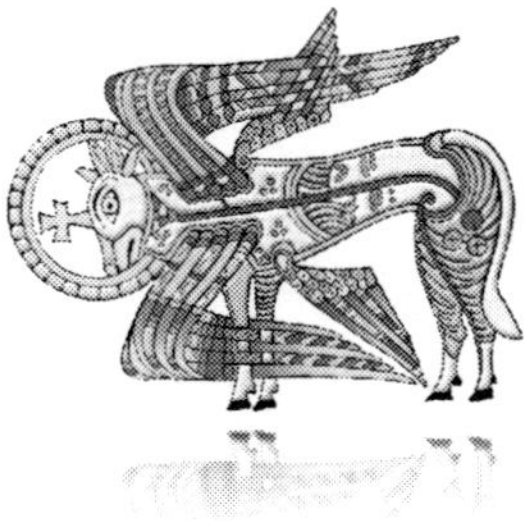

Duncan
This castle hath a pleasant seat; the air
Nimbly and sweetly recommends itself
Unto our gentle senses.

Macbeth 1.6.1-3

Duncan, King of Scotland, says this to Banquo as they approach the Inverness castle of Macbeth and his wife. Duncan praises the beauty of the immediate area.

Duncan: *This castle sits in delightful terrain. The brisk, sweet air gently offers itself to our senses.*

Inner and Outer Growth

JUNE 2

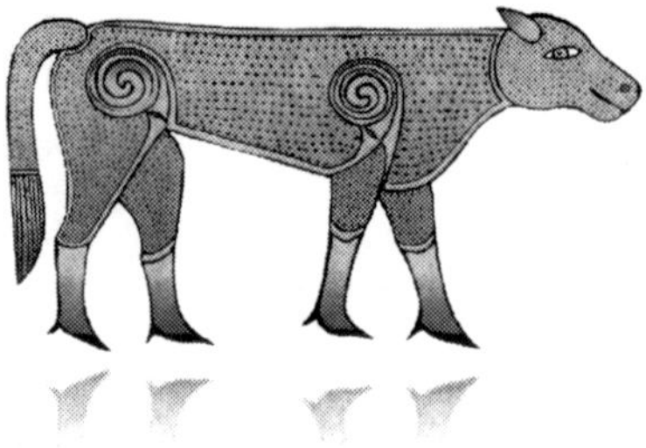

Laertes

nature crescent does not grow alone
In thews and bulk, but as this temple waxes,
The inward service of the mind and soul
Grows wide withal.

Hamlet 1.3.11-14

Laertes says this to his sister Ophelia as he cautions her not to take Hamlet's attention to her seriously because as heir to the throne Prince Hamlet's will is not his own.

Laertes: *A person growing does not increase in physical strength and mass only. Rather as the body grows, so an inner duty to one's conscience and self grows with it.*

Salvation as Undeserved

JUNE 3

Portia

in the course of justice, none of us
Should see salvation. . . .

The Merchant of Venice 4.1.197-98

Portia, disguised as the lawyer Balthazar, says this to Shylock, who has demanded strict justice from the court in giving him a pound of Antonio's flesh. This is the penalty Shylock specified for a forfeited bond when he loaned Antonio money. Portia is trying to argue Shylock out of his position.

Portia: *If each of us were judged according to the strict proceedings of the law, none of us would merit heaven.*

Rivalry

JUNE 4

Prince
Two stars keep not their motion in one sphere. . . .
***King Henry IV, Part 1* 5.4.64**

During the Battle of Shrewsbury, the newly transformed Prince Hal says this to his arch rival, the passionate rebel Hotspur, when the two finally meet.

Prince Hal: *Two such brilliant lights as we are cannot remain in the same orbit.*

Call for Reformation

JUNE 5

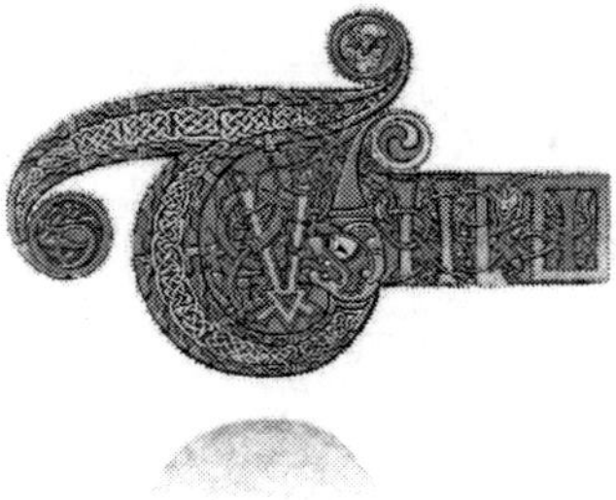

Doll

Thou whoreson little tidy Bartholomew boar-pig,
when wilt thou leave fighting a-days, and foining a-nights,
and begin to patch up thine old body for heaven?

***King Henry IV, Part 2* 2.4.230-33**

Falstaff's mistress Doll Tearsheet says this to Falstaff after he and a drunken Pistol have engaged in a sword fight that is broken up by Bardolf just in the nick of time.

Doll: *You detestable, plump little Bartholomew summer festival pig! When will you give up fighting by day and thrusting by night and start mending your torn up old body to meet your Maker?*

Embracing Battle

JUNE 6

Mowbray
Never did captive with a freer heart
Cast off his chains of bondage, and embrace
His golden uncontroll'd enfranchisement,
More than my dancing soul doth celebrate
This feast of battle with mine adversary.

King Richard II 1.3.88-92

Mowbray, Duke of Norfolk, says this to Bolingbroke, Duke of Hereford, as the two prepare to engage in a trial by combat that will decide the merits of their respective charges of treason against one another. Both contestants assert their innocence.

Mowbray: *Never did a captive more willingly discard his chains and clasp his precious freedom in his arms more than my ecstatic spirit rejoices in this desired combat with my opponent.*

Love as Reflected

JUNE 7

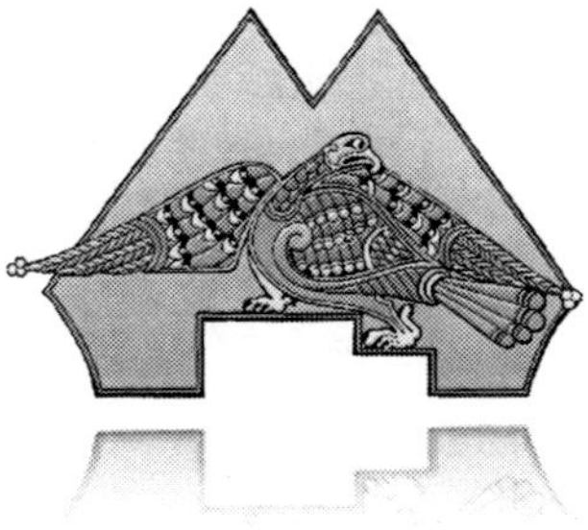

Sonnet 22

all that beauty that doth cover thee
Is but the seemly raiment of my heart,
Which in thy breast doth live, as thine in me. . . .

Lines 5-7

Sonnet 22: *All the beauty that adorns you is only the pleasing garment of my heart which dwells in your breast as your heart lives in mine.*

Restoring Peace

JUNE 8

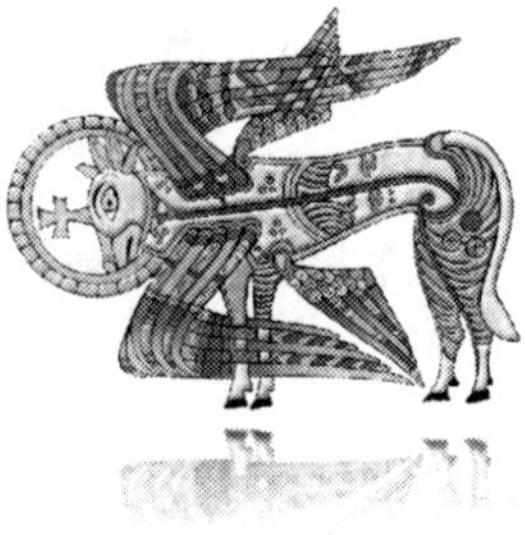

King
The edge of war, like an ill-sheathed knife,
No more shall cut his master.

King Henry IV, Part 1 1.1.17-18

Announcing a respite in the civil war that has ravaged England since Henry IV deposed Richard II, King Henry comments on the destructiveness of war.

King Henry IV: *The blade of war, that has been like an improperly encased knife, will no longer wound its owner.*

True Love

JUNE 9

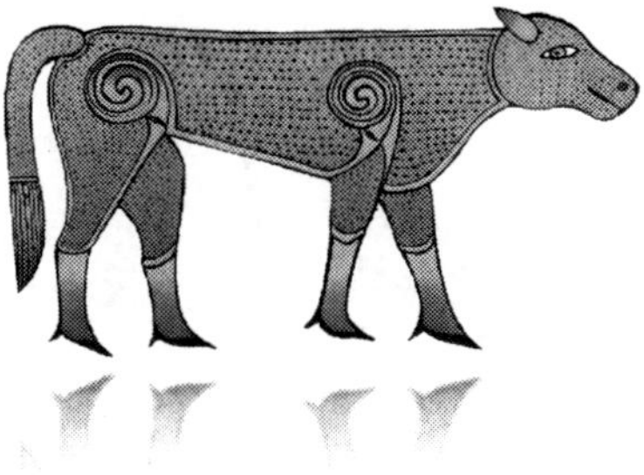

Sonnet 116

Let me not to the marriage of true minds
Admit impediments; love is not love
Which alters when it alteration finds,
Or bends with the remover to remove.
O no, it is an ever-fixed mark,
That looks on tempests and is never shaken. . . .

Lines 1-6

____

____

____

____

____

____

Sonnet 116: *May I never acknowledge any obstacles to the perfect union of two true lovers. Love which changes when it meets change is not love. Neither does love, like the stationary arm of a compass, bend when it traces a path. Instead, love is like the North Star that gazes down on chaotic storms but is never itself moved.*

Tiresome Company

JUNE 10

Hotspur

O, he is as tedious
As a tired horse, a railing wife,
Worse than a smoky house. I had rather live
With cheese and garlic in a windmill, far,
Than feed on cates and have him talk to me
In any summer house in Christendom.

King Henry IV, Part 1 3.1.153-58

Hotspur complains to his cousin Mortimer that Mortimer's father-in-law, the verbose Welshman Glendower, irritates him beyond endurance.

Hotspur: *He is as irritating as a worn-out mount or a nagging wife and worse than a smoke-filled house. I would rather live on skimpy snacks in a distant windmill than inhabit a luxurious summer home in Christendom, replete with choice foods, if I had to listen to Glendower all the time.*

License for Tyranny

JUNE 11

Cassius
And why should Caesar be a tyrant then?
Poor man, I know he would not be a wolf
But that he sees the Romans are but sheep.
He were no lion, were not Romans hinds.

***Julius Caesar* 1.3.103-06**

Caska, one of the conspirators, has just stated that all slaves possess in their own hands the ability to be free from subjection. Another of the conspirators, Cassius, challenges him.

Cassius: *Why would Caesar be a tyrant? Unfortunate man, I know he would not be a preying wolf except that the Roman people act like sheep. He would not be the formidable lion if the Romans did not behave like tame female deer.*

Empty Courtesy

JUNE 12

Brutus

When love begins to sicken and decay
It useth an enforced ceremony.
There are no tricks in plain and simple faith. . . .

***Julius Caesar* 4.2.20-22**

Brutus, friend and conspirator against Caesar, says this to the soldier Lucilius who has just come from Cassius' camp. When Brutus asks Lucilius how Cassius, another of the conspirators, received him, Lucilius admits that Cassius was courteous but not very friendly.

Brutus: *Love that is declining reverts to polite ritual as its form of communication. Honest, trusting love does not need any charades or deceit.*

Avoiding Attack

JUNE 13

Malcolm

This murtherous shaft that's shot
Hath not yet lighted, and our safest way
Is to avoid the aim. . . .

Macbeth 2.3.141-43

Suspecting that their father's murder was more than the act of drunken grooms, Malcolm and Donalbain, the sons of the dead King Duncan, decide to flee to England and Ireland, respectively, to save their lives.

Malcolm: *This deadly arrow that has already been discharged from the bow has not yet landed. Our safety lies in removing ourselves from the target.*

Value of a Faithful Heart

JUNE 14

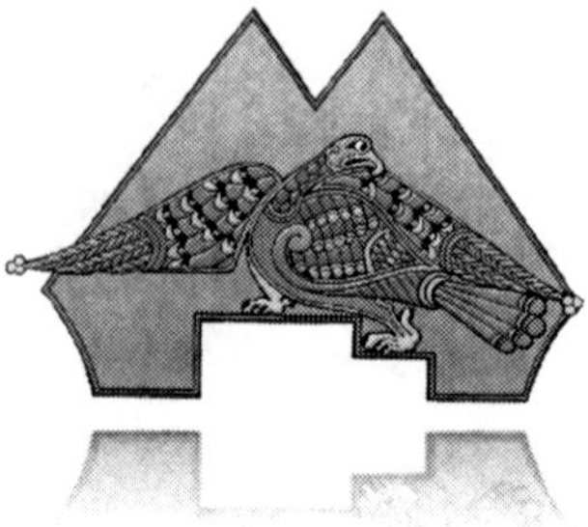

King

A good leg will fall, a straight back will stoop, a black beard will turn white, a curled pate will grow bald, a fair face will wither, a full eye will wax hollow; but a good heart, Kate, is the sun and the moon. . . .

King Henry V 5.2.158-62

Trying to woo Katherine of France, who speaks broken English, Henry, who only speaks broken French, tries to persuade Kate that because he is plain and blunt he is a good marriage prospect. Those who have no other adornments, King Henry argues, are forced to be good, loving husbands.

King Henry V: *A curtsey can collapse, an erect back can curve, a dark beard can turn gray, a curly head can grow bald, a beautiful face can wrinkle, and perfectly healthy sight can become blind. However, a faithful heart is everything under the heavens.*

Bewitchment

JUNE 15

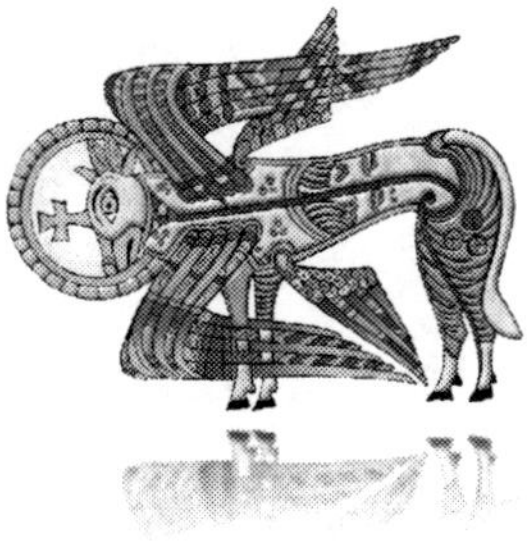

Miranda

I might call him
A thing divine, for nothing natural
I ever saw so noble.

The Tempest 1.2.418-20

Miranda, the daughter of Prospero who is the ousted Duke of Milan, says this after seeing Ferdinand, the first red-blooded male she has ever seen in her life, aside from her father and the primitive Caliban.

____

____

____

____

____

____

Miranda: *I would have to identify him as a heavenly creature, for I have never before seen any mortal creature so magnificent.*

War as Distraction

JUNE 16

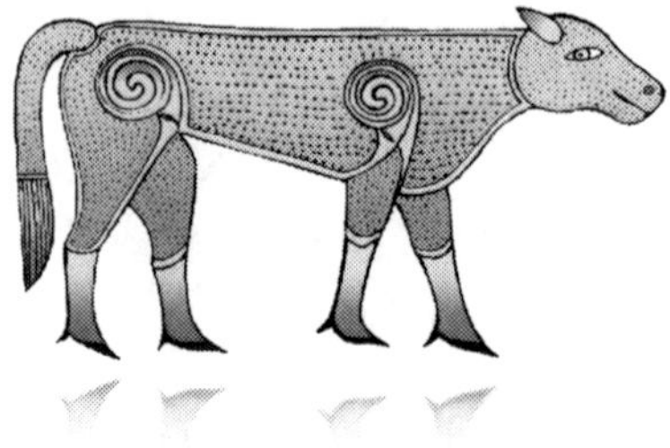

King

Therefore, my Harry,
Be it thy course to busy giddy minds
With foreign quarrels, that action hence borne out
May waste the memory of the former days.

King Henry IV, Part 2 4.5.212-15

The dying King Henry gives this advice to his son Prince Hal, heir to the throne. Recounting the troubles he has had with various rebellions during his illegitimate reign, King Henry offers his son tips on political strategy.

King Henry IV: *Therefore, my Harry, make it your plan of action to preoccupy the flighty minds of your subjects with foreign wars in order to obliterate their memory of the past.*

Playing the Odds

JUNE 17

Horatio
You will lose, my lord.
Hamlet
I do not think so. . . .
I shall win at the odds.

Hamlet 5.2.208-10

Prince Hamlet and his dear friend Horatio discuss Hamlet's upcoming duel with Laertes. Unbeknownst to both Hamlet and Horatio, Laertes has agreed to King Claudius' scheme to ensure Hamlet's death by poisoning Laertes' sword tip.

Horatio: *You are going to lose, my lord.*
Hamlet: *I don't believe so. . . . The favorable odds will give me victory.*

Choosing Self-denial

JUNE 18

Macbeth
To know my deed, 'twere best not know myself.

Macbeth 2.2.72

Having just bloodied the daggers of the drunken grooms to give the impression that they--not Macbeth--killed King Duncan, Lady Macbeth chides her husband for being lost in thought concerning his murder of Duncan.

Macbeth: *To acknowledge what I have done would require splitting myself off from the person that I have been.*

Consciousness Prompting Cowardice

JUNE 19

Hamlet

Thus conscience does make cowards of us all,
And thus the native hue of resolution
Is sicklied o'er with the pale cast of thought,
And enterprises of great pitch and moment
With this regard their currents turn awry
And lose the name of action.

Hamlet 3.1.83-88

Suspended in doubt and inaction, Prince Hamlet disparages his own failure to avenge his father's (King Hamlet's) death at the hands of his uncle Claudius.

Prince Hamlet: *And so, consciousness and thought make us fear action. As a result, the natural color of conviction is made to fade by the pallid shading of reflection. And arduous undertakings of great magnitude and cause, as a result of this deliberation, divert their course and are deprived of their very designation as endeavors.*

Self-recrimination

JUNE 20

Sonnet 88
When thou shalt be disposed to set me light
And place my merit in the eye of scorn,
Upon thy side, against myself I'll fight,
And prove thee virtuous, though thou art forsworn:
With mine own weakness being best acquainted,
Upon thy part I can set down a story
Of faults concealed, wherein I am attainted,
That thou, in losing me, shall win much glory. . . .

Lines 1-8

Sonnet 88: *When you are in a mood to disparage me and to scorn my worth, I will take your side and argue your truthfulness even though you are breaking your promise to me. Because I best know my own faults, I can create a convincing tale of my hidden flaws and so thoroughly convict myself that in separating from me you will be praised by everyone.*

Sunrise Revelry

JUNE 21

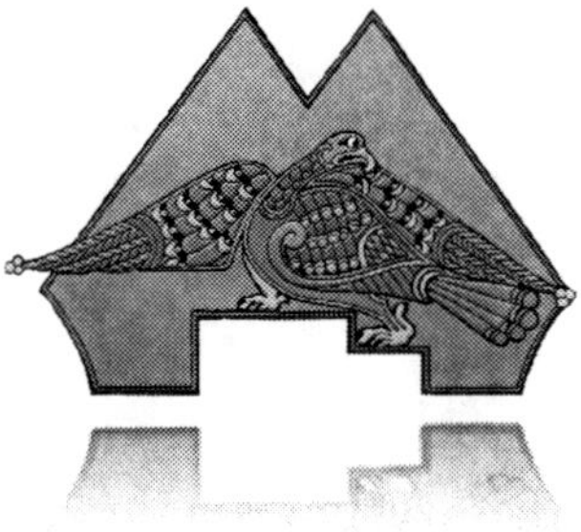

Oberon
I with the Morning's love have oft made sport;
And like a forester the groves may tread
Even till the eastern gate, all fiery-red,
Opening on Neptune with fair blessed beams,
Turns into yellow gold his salt green streams.
A Midsummer Night's Dream 3.2.389-93

In contrast to the damned spirits, the ghosts who roam the night and fear the day, Oberon, King of Fairies, revels in the beauty of sunrise.

Oberon: *I have often taken my pleasure with the goddess of the dawn. Like a royal forest keeper, I have often traversed the fields even as the beams of the rising sun in the eastern sky shone on the ocean. The beautiful, divine rays turned the sharp green water into bright gold.*

Principle Versus Practice

JUNE 22

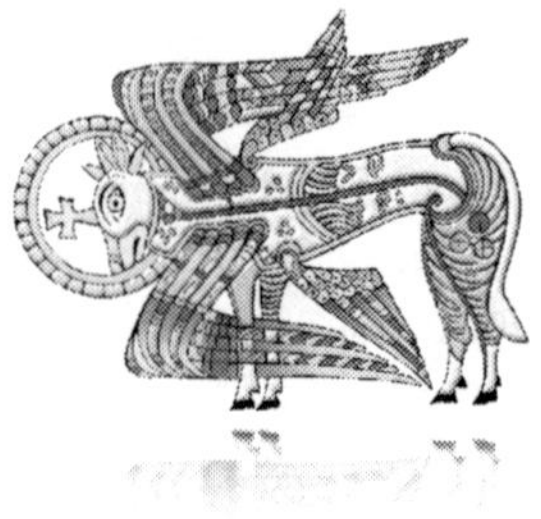

Gaunt
Things sweet to taste prove in digestion sour.
King Richard II 1.3.236

Old Gaunt, King Richard's uncle and advisor, says this to King Richard after the two have jointly decided a quarrel between two subjects charging each other with treason. The penalty for both subjects is banishment from England. Unfortunately, one of those two is Gaunt's own son, Bolingbroke. When Richard asks Gaunt why he agreed to the verdict earlier, only to lament it now, Gaunt responds.

Gaunt: *Those things which are delectable to eat turn out to be bitter once they are digested.*

Fear and Guilt

JUNE 23

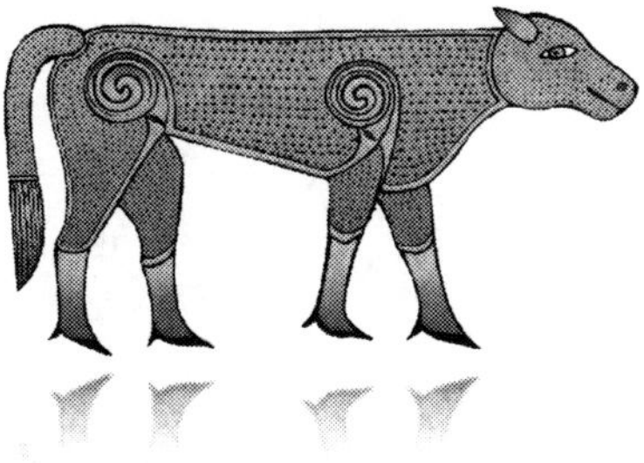

Queen

To my sick soul, as sin's true nature is,
Each toy seems prologue to some great amiss.
So full of artless jealousy is guilt,
It spills itself in fearing to be spilt.

Hamlet 4.5.17-20

Hearing that Ophelia has gone mad after her father's violent death and that she insists on seeing the Queen, Gertrude reluctantly grants Ophelia's request. Gertrude hesitates to see Ophelia because it is Hamlet, Gertrude's own son, who has mistakenly killed Ophelia's father. Now Gertrude is married to her former husband's brother, Claudius, and Hamlet has just told his mother that it was Claudius who murdered the former King Hamlet.

____

____

____

____

____

____

Gertrude: *To my sick conscience, illness being the true nature of sin, each trifling event seems to herald some great catastrophe. Since fear permeates guilt, the guilty one exposes herself in fearing exposure.*

Injury and Stereotyping

JUNE 24

Hamlet

Frailty, thy name is woman. . . .

Hamlet 1.2.146-47

Prince Hamlet says this in soliloquy in reference to his mother's, the Queen's, too hasty marriage to Claudius, the brother of her former husband, after the death of King Hamlet.

Prince Hamlet: *Moral weakness, you are indistinguishable from feminine nature.*

Irresolute Nature

JUNE 25

Cassius
Well, Brutus, thou art noble: yet I see
Thy honourable mettle may be wrought
From that it is disposed.

***Julius Caesar* 1.2.307-09**

Cassius, one of the conspirators, mutters this to himself after he and Brutus have been listening to Caska reporting that Caesar publicly refused the crown three times. After Brutus leaves, Cassius reveals that he believes he can win Brutus over to his (Cassius') plot to assassinate Caesar.

Cassius: *So, Brutus, you do possess great character, but I notice that your admirable disposition may be molded in a different direction from that which it naturally tends.*

Hypocrisy

JUNE 26

Hotspur
Why, what a candy deal of courtesy
This fawning greyhound then did proffer me!
King Henry IV, Part 1 1.3.247-48

Hotspur says this concerning King Henry IV who was helped to his throne by Hotspur's father, Northumberland. Feeling dishonored and neglected by King Henry, Hotspur re-evaluates Henry's former courtesy.

Hotspur: *What a sugary slice of good manners did this flattering predator then offer me!*

Inner Strength

JUNE 27

Hamlet

and blest are those
Whose blood and judgment are so well commeddled
That they are not a pipe for Fortune's finger
To sound what stop she please.

Hamlet 3.2.69-72

Prince Hamlet says this to his beloved friend Horatio, praising him for his uniquely balanced heart and mind.

Prince Hamlet: *Those people are supremely happy whose passions and ability to reflect are so well mixed that they do not make themselves instruments upon which Fortune plays any pitch she desires.*

Serendipity

JUNE 28

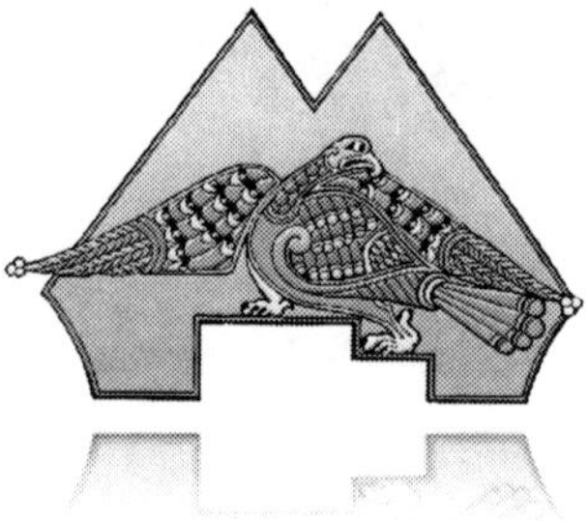

Antony

He comes upon a wish. Fortune is merry
And in this mood will give us anything.

Julius Caesar 3.2.256-57

Antony says this to a servant who comes to announce that Octavius, once Caesar's enemy and the man who will be one of the three triumvirs to rule the new Rome after Caesar's assassination, has already arrived in Rome. Earlier, Antony had dispatched a servant to tell Octavius to remain with his army outside the city until further notice. Now, however, after finishing his brilliant address to the Roman people, Antony is glad to see Octavius.

Antony: *Octavius has arrived just at the time I want him to be here. Fortune is agreeable and in this frame of mind will give us anything we desire.*

Sweet Summer Air

JUNE 29

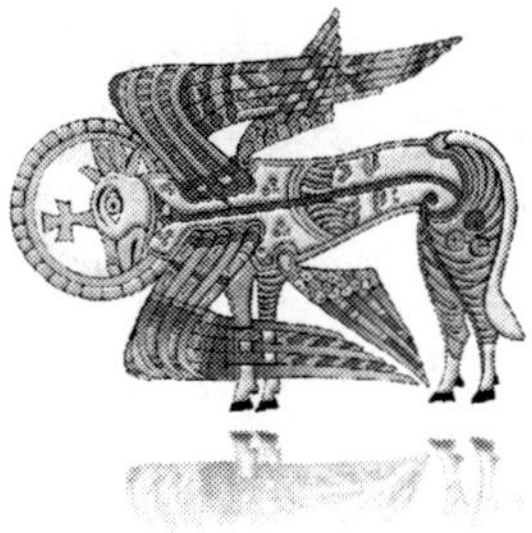

Banquo

This guest of summer,
The temple-haunting martlet, does approve
By his loved mansionry, that the heaven's breath
Smells wooingly here. . . .

Macbeth 1.6.3-6

Accompanying Duncan, King of Scotland, to Macbeth's castle, Banquo says this after Duncan calls attention to the fresh air surrounding the castle they are entering.

Banquo: *A summer visitor, the castle-invading martlet, demonstrates by his well-loved nest on the castle wall that the mountain air smells pleasant.*

Providence

JUNE 30

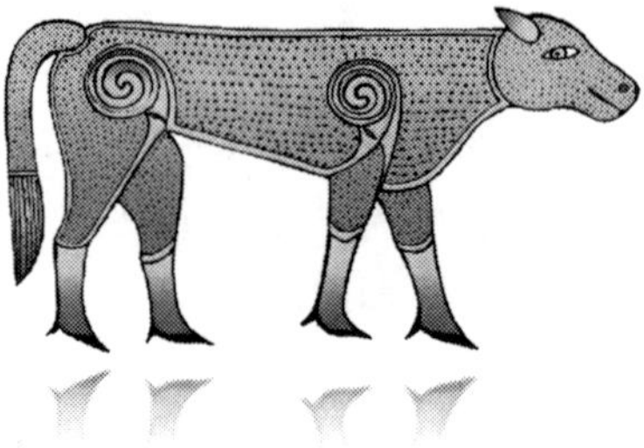

Hamlet
Our indiscretion sometime serves us well
When our deep plots do pall; and that should learn us
There's a divinity that shapes our ends,
Rough-hew them how we will. . . .

Hamlet 5.2.8-11

Impulsively opening the sealed royal commission sent from Claudius to the King of England, Prince Hamlet discovers orders for his own death. Recounting this event later to his friend Horatio, Hamlet remarks on the good fortune that drove him to uncover this document, to unlawfully open it, and to defend himself against it.

___

___

___

___

___

___

Prince Hamlet: *Our lack of judgment at times works in our favor when our artful schemes fail. This fact should teach us that there is a divine being that fashions our ultimate destinies, however crudely we may carve them.*

Pleasures of Conversation

JULY 1

Northumberland
These high wild hills and rough uneven ways
Draws out our miles and makes them wearisome,
And yet your fair discourse hath been as sugar,
Making the hard way sweet and delectable.
King Richard II 2.3.4-7

Arriving from exile, Bolingbroke is met by Northumberland. As the two travel to Berkeley Castle to meet the Duke of York, Northumberland expresses his pleasure with Bolingbroke's company.

Northumberland: *The steep, desolate terrain and the difficult rugged paths lengthen our journey and tire us out. However, your pleasing conversation has been like sugar, making the harsh journey delightful.*

The Miraculous

JULY 2

1 Gentleman

there was speech in their dumbness, language in
their very gesture; they looked as they had heard of a
world ransomed, or one destroyed: a notable passion
of wonder appeared in them. . . .

***The Winter's Tale* 5.2.14-17**

The Shepherd, whose daughter Perdita is not his actual child, reveals the true identity of the babe he found abandoned on the shore sixteen years earlier. The Shepherd unknowingly discloses this news to Polixenes and to his trusted old friend Camillo. Both of these men are overcome with wonder when they realize that this young woman is the abandoned daughter, believed to be dead, of their estranged friend Leontes.

1 Gentleman: *There was expression in their silence, language in each gesture. They looked as if they had just heard news of an entire world released from captivity or else of one utterly demolished. A noticeable feeling of the miraculous arose in them.*

Revenge

JULY 3

Hamlet

Haste me to know't, that I with wings as swift
As meditation or the thoughts of love
May sweep to my revenge.

Hamlet 1.5.29-31

Hamlet, Prince of Denmark, says this to the ghost of his father just after the apparition has revealed that he was murdered by his own brother Claudius.

Hamlet: *Tell me quickly so that with wings as fast as the speed of thought or of the lover's imagination, I may swiftly and forcefully carry out my revenge.*

War and Peace

JULY 4

King Henry

In peace there's nothing so becomes a man
As modest stillness and humility;
But when the blast of war blows in our ears,
Then imitate the action of the tiger:
Stiffen the sinews, conjure up the blood,
Disguise fair nature with hard-favoured rage.

King Henry V 3.1.3-8

As the English troops begin their siege of Harfleur, King Henry urges on his troops, asking that they forgo peacetime civility and don the mask of the warrior.

King Henry: *In peacetime nothing is more befitting an individual than modesty and calmness in moderation. But when war's cacophony assaults our ears, then model ourselves after the tiger: clench the muscles, summon the spirit, and cover over our purer natures with the fierce face of fury.*

Proverbial Wisdom

JULY 5

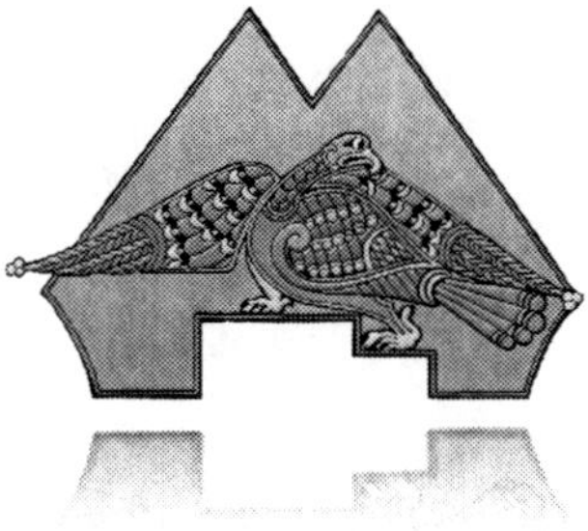

Nerissa
The ancient saying is no heresy,
Hanging and wiving goes by destiny.

The Merchant of Venice 2.9.83-84

The waiting woman Nerissa says this to her mistress Portia as suitors seek the hand of Portia in marriage. Following a ritual set up by Portia's dead father, each suitor must choose either a lead, silver, or gold casket. Failure to pick the right casket means the suitor must leave immediately and agree never to marry.

Nerissa: *The old proverb is true: swinging from the gallows and choosing a partner are both matters determined only by fate.*

Hope in Misery

JULY 6

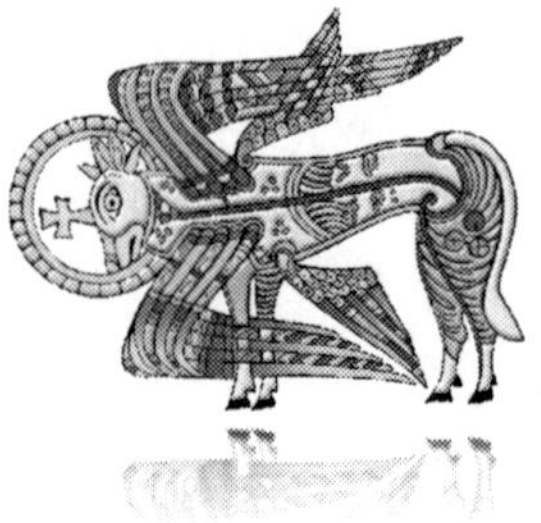

Kent

Nothing almost sees miracles

But misery.

King Lear 2.2.166-67

Trying to defend King Lear's honor against the insolence of Goneril's servant Oswald, the Earl of Kent gets into an argument with Oswald and is punished by being put in the stocks. Grateful that the moon beams are bright enough to allow him to read a letter from virtuous Cordelia, Lear's banished daughter, Kent makes this observation.

Kent: *Almost no experience imagines miracles as suffering does.*

Inflated Self-image

JULY 7

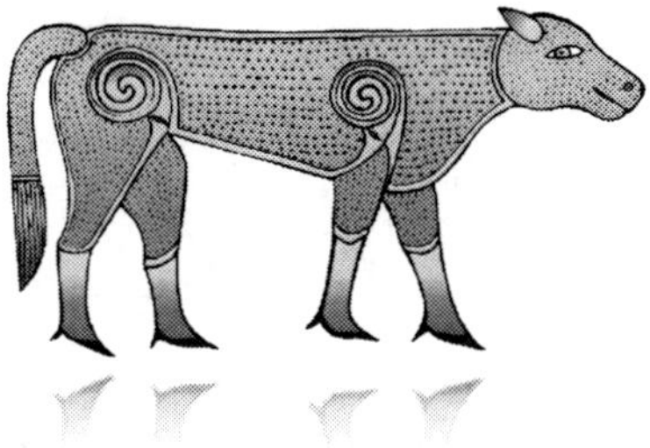

Rosalind
'Tis not her glass but you that flatters her,
And out of you she sees herself more proper
Than any of her lineaments can show her.
As You Like It 3.5.54-56

Rosalind, the daughter of Duke Senior who is disguised as the boy Ganymede, says this to the earnest shepherd Silvius, who is in love with the foul-tongued shepherdess Phebe.

Rosalind: *It is not looking in her mirror but listening to you that pampers her. Because of you she views herself as better looking than any of her facial features can reveal to her.*

Virtues As Enemies

JULY 8

Adam
Know you not master, to some kind of men,
Their graces serve them but as enemies?
No more do yours. Your virtues, gentle master,
Are sanctified and holy traitors to you.

As You Like It 2.3.10-13

The faithful old family servant Adam says this to his master Orlando who has just won a wrestling match against a formidable champion. After the victory, Orlando is identified as the son of an enemy of the Duke Frederick, and he is banished.

Adam: *Do you not know, my master, that with certain types of enviable people, their pleasing qualities work against them? Yours are no better. Your virtues, albeit blessed and divine, still betray you to the enmity of others.*

Slave to Fashion

JULY 9

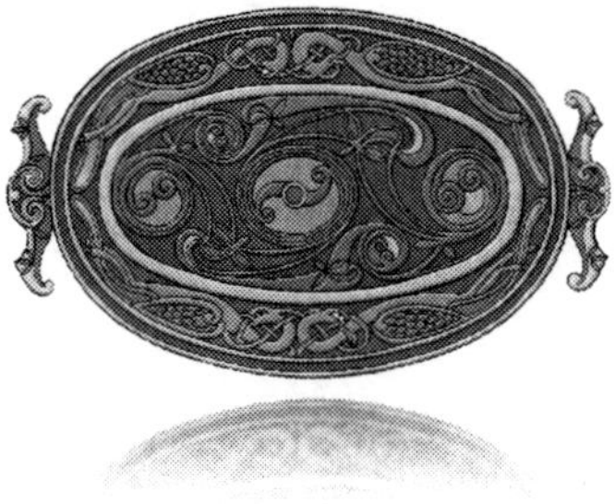

Hamlet

Thus has he - and many more of the same bevy that I know the drossy age dotes on - only got the tune of the time and, out of an habit of encounter, a kind of yeasty collection, which carries them through and through the most fanned and winnowed opinions; and do but blow them to the trial, the bubbles are out.

***Hamlet* 5.2.189-95**

Horatio says this about the fawning courtier Osric. Prince Hamlet mocks Osric and others like him for their slavery to fashion and to trendy ideas.

Hamlet: *Thus has he--and many of the same crowd of people that the frivolous age is infatuated with--only grasped the lingo of the day along with an ostentatious form of courtesy, a superficial assortment of ideas, which sustains them through discussion of the most carefully considered judgments. However, if you put these ideas to the test, the bubbles pop.*

Exposing Weakness

JULY 10

Mowbray
Well, by my will we shall admit no parley.
Westmoreland
That argues but the shame of your offence:
A rotten case abides no handling.

King Henry IV, Part 2 4.1.159-61

The Earl of Westmoreland has been sent by Prince John of Gaunt to try to negotiate with the rebels, led by Mowbray, Hastings, and the Archbishop. Justifiably fearing a trap, Mowbray initially refuses to meet with Prince John.

Mowbray: *We will not with my consent agree to discuss a truce.* ***Westmoreland:*** *This position exposes the guilt of your harmful actions. A flimsy case cannot survive the scrutiny of the legal process.*

Inability to Be Objective

JULY 11

Cassius
Tell me, good Brutus, can you see your face?
Brutus
No, Cassius; for the eye sees not itself
But by reflection, by some other things.

Julius Caesar 1.2.51-53

Cassius, preparing to enlist Brutus in the conspiracy to assassinate Caesar, asks Brutus whether or not he can perceive the way he appears to others.

***Cassius:** Tell me, dear Brutus, can you see your own face?*
***Brutus:** No, Cassius, the eye cannot see itself except when it is mirrored back by other objects.*

Advice for Writers

JULY 12

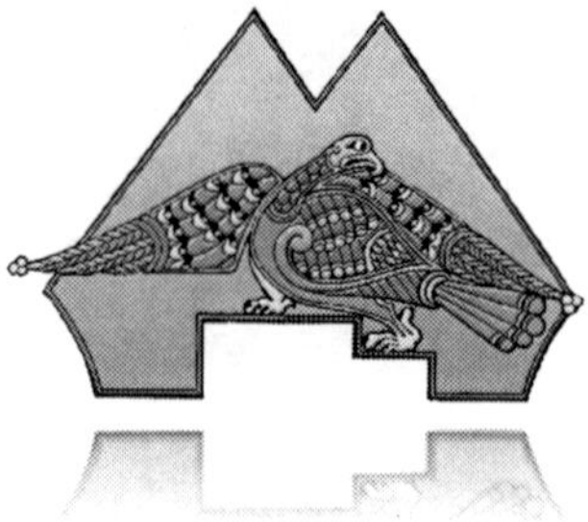

Sonnet 77

Look what thy memory cannot contain,
Commit to these waste blanks, and thou shalt find
Those children nursed, delivered from thy brain,
To take a new acquaintance of thy mind.
    These offices, so oft as thou wilt look,
    Shall profit thee, and much enrich thy book.

Lines 9-14

***Sonnet** 77: Write down on paper what your memory can't hold. Once freed from the mind's grasp, your written ideas will grow and appear fresh to you as do children sent away to be nursed. These practices will benefit you and will bring greater richness to your writing.*

Inspiration and Its Loss

JULY 13

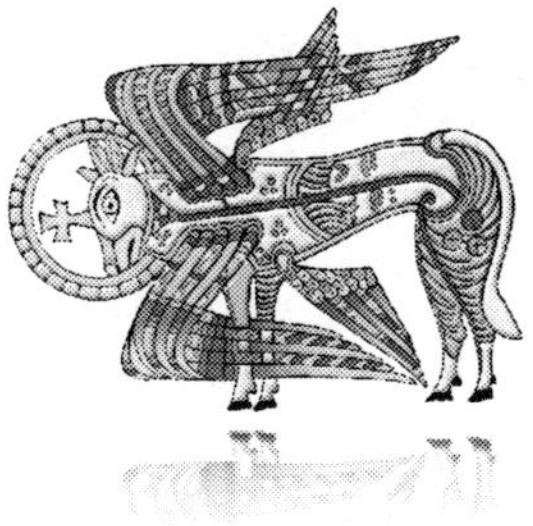

Morton
In few, his death, whose spirit lent a fire
Even to the dullest peasant in his camp,
Being bruited once, took fire and heat away
From the best-temper'd courage in his troops. . . .

King Henry IV, Part 2 1.1.112-15

Morton, a messenger, describes to Northumberland the effects on the rebel troops of his son Hotspur's death.

Morton: *Briefly, Hotspur's spirit fired up even the most lethargic fellow in his camp. The moment his death was reported, it stole inspiration and passion away from even the most finely wrought courage of his soldiers.*

Imitating Bad Behavior

JULY 14

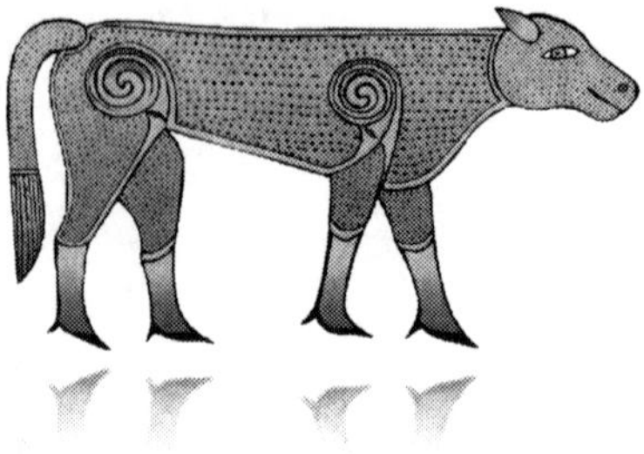

Fluellen
If the enemy is an ass and a fool and a
prating coxcomb, is it meet, think you, that we should
also, look you, be an ass and a fool and a prating
coxcomb . . . ?

King Henry V 4.1.77-80

When the Welsh captain Fluellen bawls out his fellow officer Gower for speaking too loudly so close to the enemy line, Gower tries to defend himself by saying that the French have been talking noisily all night long. Fluellen continues trying to mend Gower's ill behavior.

Fluellen: *If our opponent is an imbecile and a jerk and a blubbering idiot, does it make sense that we should likewise be an imbecile, a jerk, and a blubbering idiot?*

Readiness

JULY 15

King
All things are ready, if our minds be so.

King Henry V 4.3.71

King Henry says this just before the Battle of Agincourt when Salisbury comes to tell him that the French have already assumed their battle position and, therefore, the battle is about to begin.

King Henry: *If we are mentally prepared, then everything else around us is ripe for action.*

Natural Course of Love

JULY 16

Lysander
The course of true love never did run smooth. . . .
A Midsummer Night's Dream 1.1.134

Lysander says this to his beloved Hermia after Hermia has just been ordered to marry Demetrius, the man her father has chosen for her, or else die or become a nun.

Lysander: *The current of faithful love has never flowed without obstructions.*

Danger of Leniency

JULY 17

Escalus

Mercy is not itself, that oft looks so;
Pardon is still the nurse of second woe.

Measure for Measure 2.1.278-79

The wise old Lord Escalus says this while discussing Claudio's case with a local magistrate. When the magistrate comments that Lord Angelo is too exacting in condemning Claudio to death for getting his fiancée pregnant, Escalus responds.

Escalus: *When mercy too frequently shows itself, it becomes something other than what it is. Too frequent forgiveness fosters misfortune.*

Danger of Interfering

JULY 18

Hamlet

'Tis dangerous when the baser nature comes
Between the pass and fell incensed points
Of mighty opposites.

***Hamlet* 5.2.60-62**

Confiding to his friend Horatio, Prince Hamlet reveals that he has switched a death order that Claudius issued on Hamlet's head. In its place Hamlet has substituted a death order for the messengers carrying the order, Rosencrantz and Guildenstern, who have become Claudius' pawns. Since Claudius has murdered Hamlet's father, it is Claudius that Hamlet refers to as his powerful opponent.

Hamlet: *It is hazardous for an inferior nature to place itself in the space between the tip of angered swords and the thrust of those swords in a duel of two powerful enemies.*

Love's Teachings
JULY 19

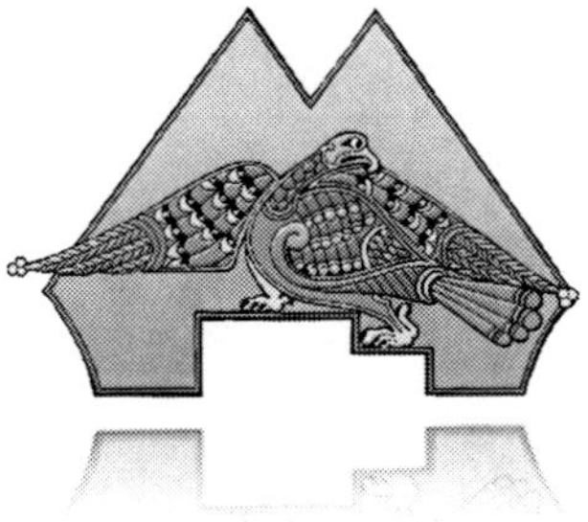

Sonnet 14

from thine eyes my knowledge I derive,
And, constant stars, in them I read such art
As truth and beauty shall together thrive. . . .

Lines 9-11

Sonnet 14: *Whatever I know I obtain from your eyes. I learn such wisdom in your eyes, faithful stars to me, as the knowledge that virtue and beauty will prosper only in the company of one another.*

Lies

JULY 20

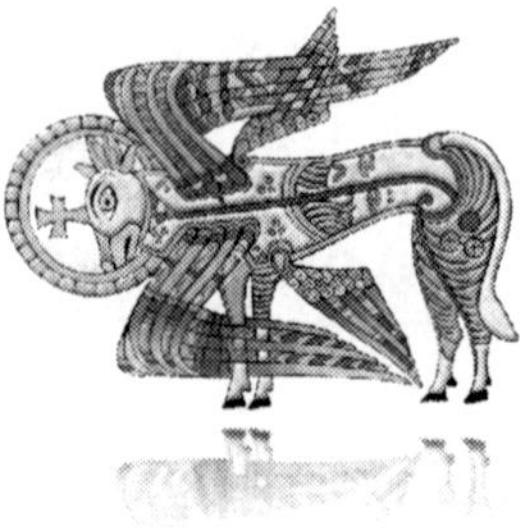

Prince
These lies are like their father that begets them,
gross as a mountain, open, palpable.
King Henry IV, Part 1 2.4.221-22

Prince Hal says this to Sir John Falstaff who has just constructed an enormous fabrication about his foiled robbery attempt earlier that day. Since Hal and Poins had disguised themselves and participated in this adventure, Hal knows beyond any shadow of a doubt that Falstaff is lying through his teeth.

Prince Hal: *These lies are the spitting image of the father that created them: huge as a mountain, unmistakable, and obvious.*

Sleeplessness

JULY 21

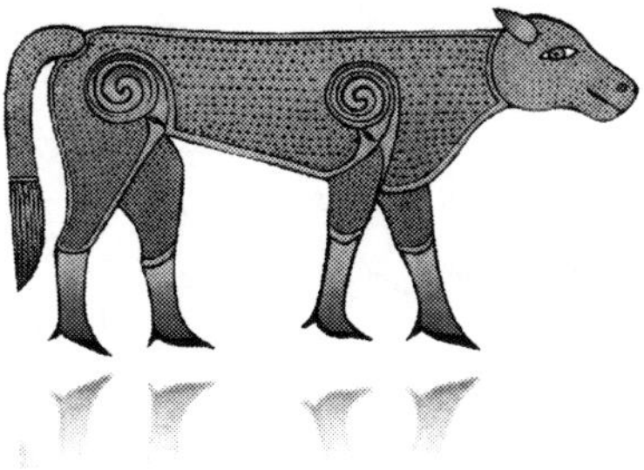

King

O sleep, O gentle sleep,
Nature's soft nurse, how have I frighted thee,
That thou no more wilt weigh my eyelids down,
And steep my senses in forgetfulness?

King Henry IV, Part 2 3.1.5-8

King Henry IV says this to himself as he walks about late at night at court in his nightgown, ill yet still at work. He has just ordered his page to summon the Earls of Surrey and Warwick to a meeting to discuss Northumberland's planned rebellion against King Henry. Northumberland was once Henry's closest ally.

____

____

____

____

____

____

***King Henry IV:** Sleep, wonderful sleep, nature's gentler caretaker, how did I scare you away so that you no longer close my eyes in slumber nor bathe my senses in unconsciousness?*

Flattery

JULY 22

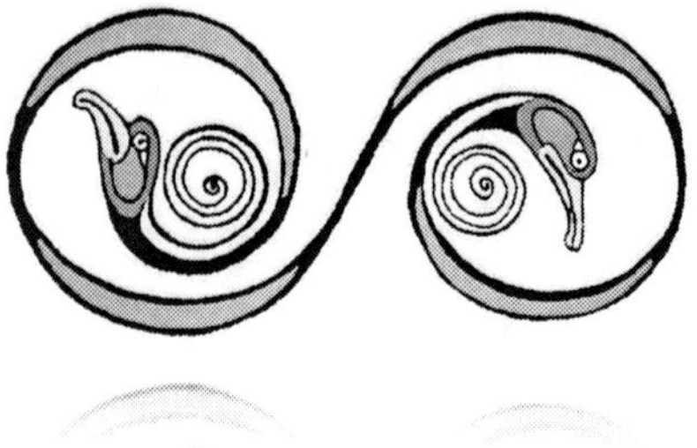

Decius

when I tell him he hates flatterers,
He says he does, being then most flattered.

Julius Caesar 2.1.206-07

Decius says this to Brutus, Cassius, Cinna, and other conspirators when Decius learns that Caesar plans to stay home from the Capitol on the day planned for his assassination. Decius says that he can persuade Caesar to leave by using flattery.

Decius: *When I tell Caesar that he despises insincere praise, he agrees with me. At that very moment he is a victim of flattery.*

Deliberation as Insurrection

JULY 23

Brutus

Between the acting of a dreadful thing
And the first motion, all the interim is
Like a phantasma or a hideous dream:
The genius and the mortal instruments
Are then in council, and the state of man,
Like to a little kingdom, suffers then
The nature of an insurrection.

Julius Caesar 2.1.63-69

Brutus says this to himself as he ponders whether or not he should join Cassius in rising up against Caesar.

Brutus: *Between the first inclination towards a momentous action and the act itself, everything in between has the character of an illusion or nightmare. The rational soul and the body's appetites and passions debate as if they were advisors of state. Then when action does take place, the kingdom of the individual experiences an armed rebellion within itself.*

Transformation

JULY 24

King

The tide of blood in me
Hath proudly flow'd in vanity till now.
Now doth it turn, and ebb back to the sea,
Where it shall mingle with the state of floods,
And flow henceforth in formal majesty.

King Henry IV, Part 2 5.2.129-33

The newly designated King Henry V says this to the Chief Justice who reminds Henry of his wilder days as Prince when the Chief Justice arrested him.

***King Henry V:** The current of my passion has forcefully flowed in foolish arrogance until now. Presently, it shifts and flows back to the sea where it will mix with the tide and move in dignified sovereignty.*

Love's Injury

JULY 25

Sonnet 40

love knows it is a greater grief
To bear love's wrong, than hate's known injury.

Lines 11-12

Sonnet 40: *Those who love someone know it's much harder to suffer a beloved's or friend's hurtful act than to endure an enemy's obvious injury.*

Licentiousness

JULY 26

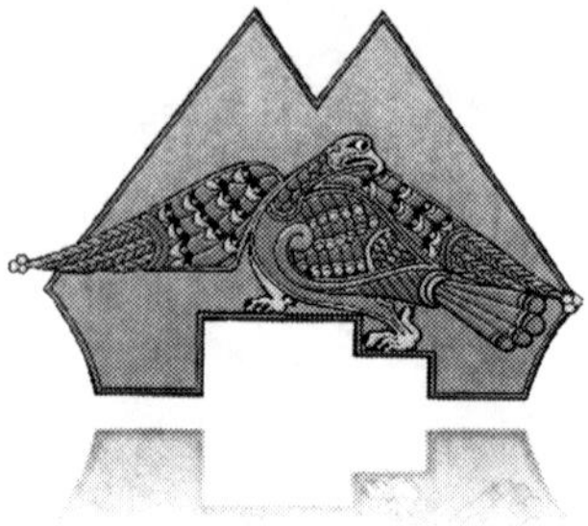

Claudio

too much liberty, my Lucio. Liberty,
As surfeit, is the father of much fast;
So every scope by the immoderate use
Turns to restraint. Our natures do pursue,
Like rats that ravin down their proper bane,
A thirsty evil; and when we drink, we die.

Measure for Measure 1.2.124-30

Claudio has just been arrested for getting Juliet, his betrothed, pregnant. As Claudio passes, guarded by three officers of the law, Lucio, a fop, asks him what has caused his arrest.

______

______

______

______

______

______

Claudio: *Too much liberty, my Lucio, excess liberty. Every instance of freedom, stretched to excess, must end in restriction. Like rats swallowing a delectable poison that fires their thirst for more, when we ingest the poison of license, we die.*

Danger of Envy

JULY 27

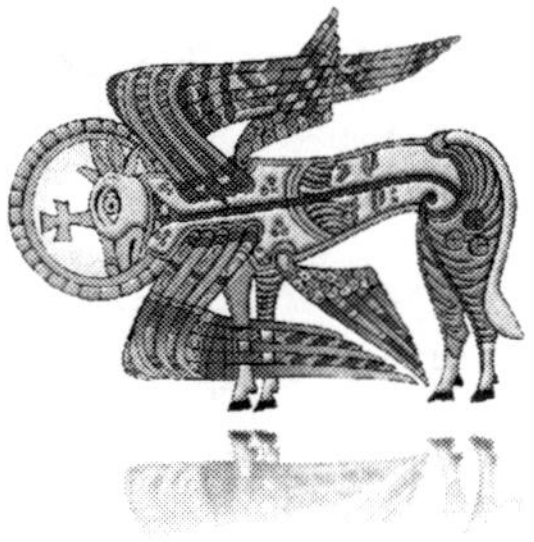

Caesar

He loves no plays
As thou dost, Antony; he hears no music.
Seldom he smiles, and smiles in such a sort
As if he mocked himself and scorned his spirit
That could be moved to smile at anything.
Such men as he be never at heart's ease
Whiles they behold a greater than themselves,
And therefore are they very dangerous.

Julius Caesar 1.2.202-09

Having just returned from the Lupercalia games, Caesar says this to Antony. Caesar states that if he were capable of fear, there is no one he would fear more than Cassius.

____

____

____

____

____

____

Caesar: *He does not enjoy plays as you do, Antony. He is sullen and even treacherous, untouched by music. He does not often smile, and when he does, it is only to mock himself for smiling. Such a person as he is will never rest content as long as he is aware of someone superior to him. Therefore, such a person is extremely menacing.*

Discomfort of New Roles

JULY 28

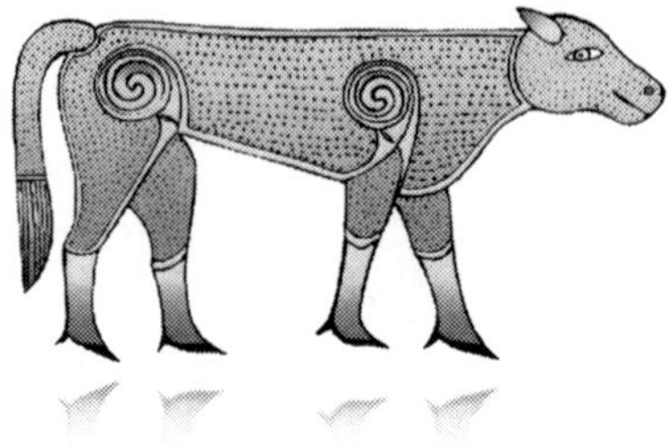

Banquo

New honours come upon him,
Like our strange garments, cleave not to their mould,
But with the aid of use.

Macbeth 1.3.145-47

Banquo says this about Macbeth who has just been named Thane of Cawdor. Macbeth is distracted because he is debating whether or not to murder Duncan in order to fulfill the second prophecy of the witches. Banquo, however, believes Macbeth is behaving oddly because he is not used to his new, unexpected title.

Banquo: *The title that has recently been bestowed upon him, like brand new clothes, does not fit his form and will do so only with repeated wear.*

Value As Relative

JULY 29

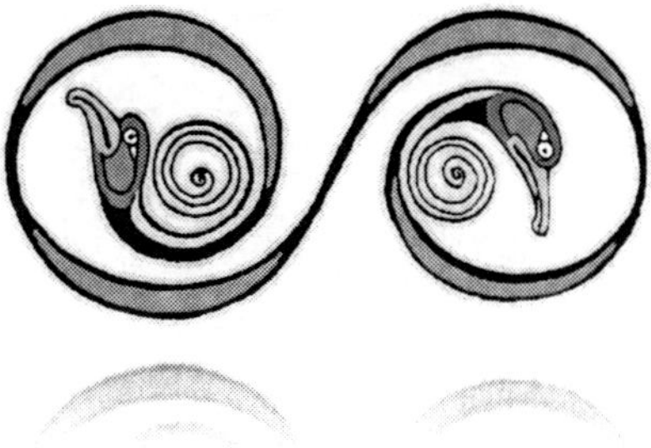

Portia
Nothing is good (I see) without respect. . . .
The crow doth sing as sweetly as the lark
When neither is attended. . . .
The Merchant of Venice 5.1.99, 102-03

Returning to Belmont after her sojourn to Venice disguised as a lawyer, Portia remarks to her waiting woman Nerissa that the music coming from Portia's house sounds better at night when they are returning home than it usually does by day.

Portia: *Nothing is valued outside of a particular context. When both birds are by themselves and no one is listening, the crow sings as melodiously as the lark.*

Bad Acting

JULY 30

Hamlet

O, it offends me to the soul to hear a robustious periwig-pated fellow tear a passion to tatters, to very rags, to split the ears of the groundlings. . . . I would have such a fellow whipped. . . .

Hamlet 3.2.8-11; 13

Having just given some of the actors visiting Elsinore a speech to perform, Prince Hamlet then bemoans the bad acting styles currently seen on stage.

Hamlet: *It offends my very being to hear a loud-mouthed actor with a wig, ripping a feeling to shreds--to mere scraps--shattering the ears of the audience in the inexpensive seats. I would order such a person to be flogged.*

Blessing

JULY 31

Old Man
God's benison go with you; and with those
That would make good of bad, and friends of foes!

Macbeth 2.4.40-41

As both Macduff and Rosse, noblemen in troubled Scotland, decide not to go to the coronation of Macbeth in Scone but to go their separate ways, the Old Man offers a blessing to Rosse.

Old Man: *May God's blessings go with you and also with whomever desires to fashion good out of evil and friends from enemies.*

The Beloved

AUGUST 1

Sonnet 18
Shall I compare thee to a summer's day?
Thou art more lovely and more temperate. . . .

Lines 1-2

Sonnet 18: *How can I speak of you as comparable to a pleasant summery day? You are more beautiful and more gentle.*

Loyalty

AUGUST 2

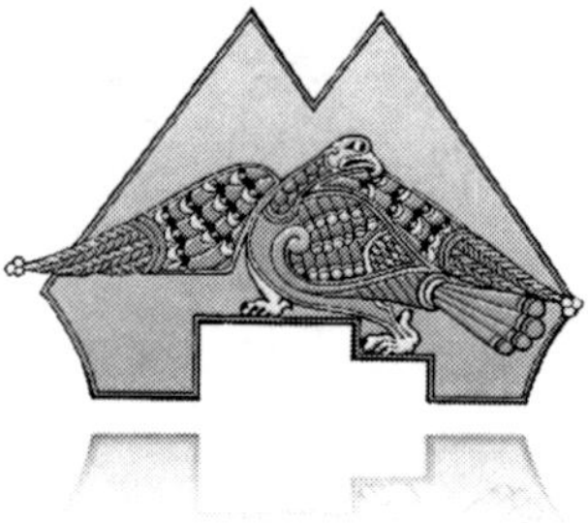

Orlando
O good old man, how well in thee appears
The constant service of the antique world,
When service sweat for duty, not for meed.

***As You Like It* 2.3.56-58**

In contrast to his brother Oliver, who is consumed with greed, Orlando sees Adam's selfless devotion to the family as a reflection of a golden world long gone. Adam is Oliver's servant.

***Orlando:** O kind old man, how readily one sees in you the steady devotion of the ancient world when those who served labored out of a sense of respect, not for recompense.*

Navigating Reality

AUGUST 3

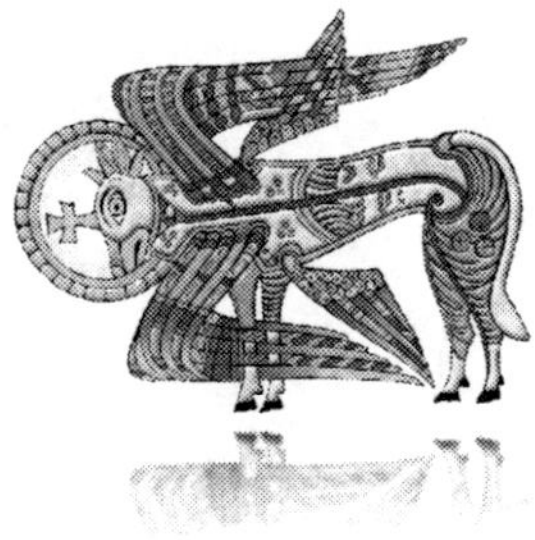

Hamlet

I am but mad north-north-west. When the
wind is southerly, I know a hawk from a handsaw.

Hamlet 2.2.379-80

Sent by the King and Queen to detect the source of Hamlet's madness, Guildenstern and Rosencrantz listen to Hamlet's defense. Prince Hamlet claims that his uncle Claudius and his mother Gertrude, who have recently married, are deceived: he is not completely out of his mind.

Hamlet: *I am only crazy intermittently. When the wind blows from the south, I can tell the difference between a bird of prey and a heron.*

Beauty

AUGUST 4

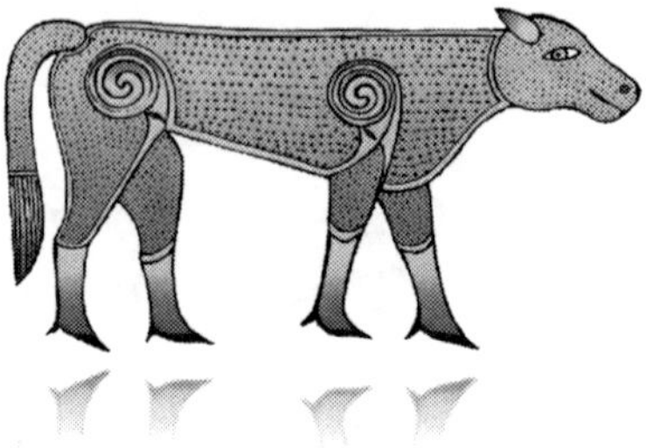

Sonnet 130

My mistress' eyes are nothing like the sun;
Coral is far more red than her lips' red;
If snow be white, why then her breasts are dun;
If hairs be wires, black wires grow on her head. . . .
I grant I never saw a goddess go;
My mistress when she walks treads on the ground.
    And yet, by heav'n, I think my love as rare
    As any she belied with false compare.

Lines 1-4, 11-14

Sonnet 130: *My lover's eyes' cannot be said to be like the sun. Neither can her lips be compared to coral, which is much redder. Snow might be white, but my lover's breasts are a dull brown. If hairs are likened to wires, then hers have to be described as black. I admit I never actually saw a goddess walk. My mistress--when she walks--traverses the earth. And yet I swear my beloved is as precious as any who might be set against her in a misleading comparison.*

Appearance as Deceiving

AUGUST 5

All Three Witches
Fair is foul, and foul is fair:
Hover through the fog and filthy air.

Macbeth 1.1.11-12

As the play opens, the three witches are the only characters on stage. Also known as the Weird Sisters, the witches chant these lines in unison at the end of the first short scene, thereby setting the tone of the play. They announce that they will meet again after a battle is both lost and won. It is not until the third scene of Act 1 that Macbeth and Banquo will happen upon the witches.

All Three Witches: *That which is virtuous is wicked, and that which is ugly is beautiful. Let us linger here in this murky atmosphere.*

Restraint

AUGUST 6

Sonnet 94

They that have the power to hurt, and will do none,
That do not do the thing they most do show,
Who, moving others, are themselves as stone,
Unmoved, cold, and to temptation slow:
They rightly do inherit heaven's graces. . . .

Lines 1-5

Sonnet 94: *Those who are in a position to hurt another and refrain from it act contrary to what their appearance might suggest. They sway and move others but are like rock: steady, cool, and difficult to provoke. Such people justly receive heavenly blessings.*

Underhanded Maneuvering

AUGUST 7

Polonius

See you now,
Your bait of falsehood takes this carp of truth;
And thus do we of wisdom and of reach,
With windlasses and with assays of bias,
By indirections find directions out.

***Hamlet* 2.1.62-66**

Meddling Polonius says this to his servant Reynaldo who is following Polonius' son Laertes into France. Polonius has asked Reynaldo to spy on Laertes in Paris by approaching members of Laertes' social circle, making slightly damaging comments about Laertes' character, and then seeing whether slime or cream rises to the surface.

Polonius: *See here, your baiting lie will hook the truth, and, therefore, we are able with our cleverness and ability to uncover the truth in a roundabout way, using backhanded methods.*

Limitations of Art

AUGUST 8

Chorus

Can this cockpit hold
The vasty fields of France? Or may we cram
Within this wooden O the very casques
That did affright the air at Agincourt?

King Henry V 1.Prologue.11-14

Apologizing for the inadequacy of the stage to depict the grand scale of human events and of history, the Chorus at the beginning of the play asks the audience these questions. The Chorus offers an apology for the audacity of the players to try to represent on stage one of the greatest English kings, Henry V, and one of the most infamous battles in English history, the English victory over the French at Agincourt in 1415.

Chorus: *Can this theatre, [a place where cockfights also take place], contain the immense lands of France? Or is it possible for us, the actors, to force into the confines of this stage the actual helmets that created an atmosphere of terror at the Battle of Agincourt?*

Dullness

AUGUST 9

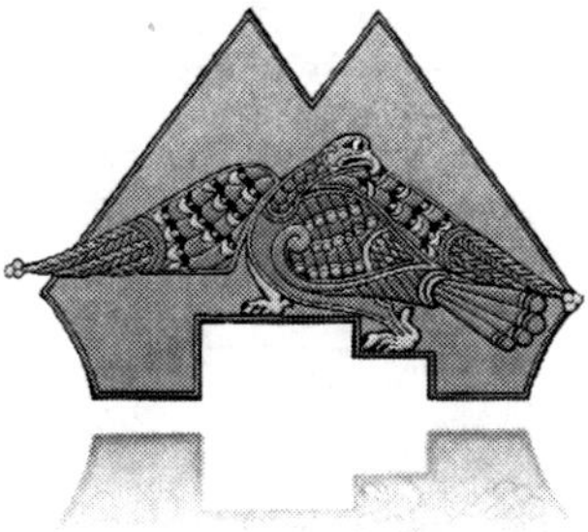

Gravedigger
Cudgel thy brains no more about it, for
your dull ass will not mend his pace with beating.

***Hamlet* 5.1.56-57**

The first gravedigger is mocking the second gravedigger for not being able to come up with an answer to a riddle. The riddle is a question: who builds stronger than a mason, a shipwright, or a carpenter?

Gravedigger: *Don't bludgeon your brain any longer thinking about the matter, for like a slow ass that refuses to budge, your dull mind will not improve its speed after the beating.*

Bombast

AUGUST 10

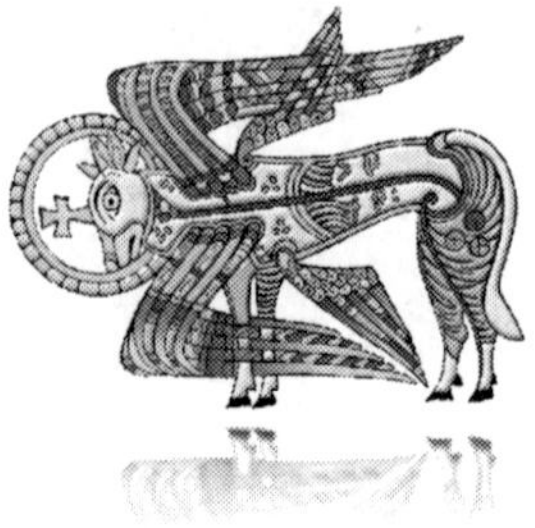

Benedick

his words are a very
fantastical banquet, just so many strange dishes.
Much Ado About Nothing 2.3.20-21

Benedick is very distressed to see his friend Claudio change so much after falling in love with Hero. Instead of contemplating battle armor, Claudio now worries about the fashion of his clothes. Instead of speaking directly and to the purpose, Claudio's speech is unrecognizable.

Benedick: *His words are an excessively fanciful feast--simply a multitude of unfamiliar foods.*

A Good Name
AUGUST 11

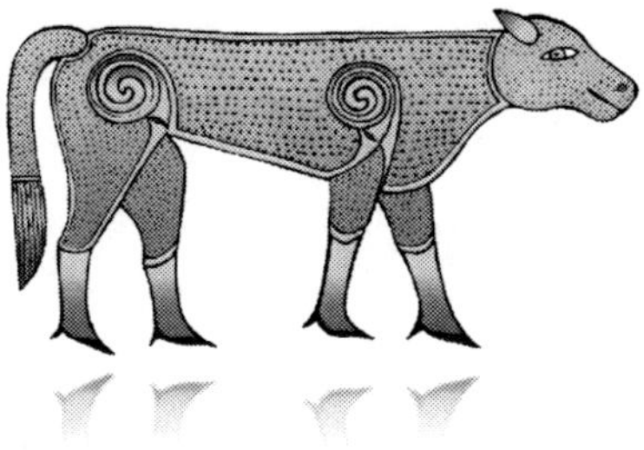

Mowbray
The purest treasure mortal times afford
Is spotless reputation - that away,
Men are but gilded loam, or painted clay.
King Richard II 1.1.177-79

Accused by Bolingbroke of treason and of taking money that was sent for his soldiers and using it for his own pleasure, Mowbray flatly rejects the accusations, challenging Bolingbroke to a duel. When King Richard II tries to stop the duel, Mowbray refuses, arguing that without a duel the shame of accusation will continue to stain his name.

***Mowbray:** The best reputation life can offer is one without any stain whatsoever. Without that, individuals are nothing more than decorated plaster or camouflaged clumps of earth.*

Balanced Justice

AUGUST 12

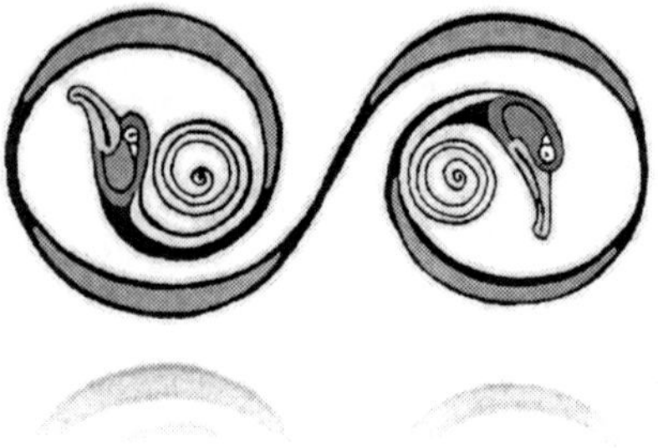

Angelo
We must not make a scarecrow of the law,
Setting it up to fear the birds of prey,
And let it keep one shape till custom make it
Their perch, and not their terror.
Escalus
Ay, but yet
Let us be keen, and rather cut a little,
Than fall, and bruise to death.

***Measure for Measure* 2.1.1-6**

Angelo, left in charge of the city when the Duke of Vienna announces his departure to Poland, argues with wise old Escalus about the proper means of enforcing the law.

Angelo: *We must not use the law simply as a scarecrow which, though intended to frighten birds of prey, becomes too familiar and, instead of scaring birds away, provides them a landing place.*
Escalus: *Yes, but let us be wise and chop carefully rather than let the sword fall heavily and crush to death whatever is beneath it.*

Prayer for Courage

AUGUST 13

King
O God of battles, steel my soldiers' hearts;
Possess them not with fear. Take from them now
The sense of reckoning, if th'opposed numbers
Pluck their hearts from them.

King Henry V 4.1.285-88

King Henry says this to himself, having wandered through his camp the night before battle, disguised as a common soldier. Facing a French army that is twenty times the size of the English army, Henry laments the heavy burden placed upon him and upon his soldiers.

King Henry V: *Oh Lord of war, make the heart of my troops as tough as steel. Make them incapable both of anticipating the future and of counting so that the vast quantity of enemy soldiers will not steal my men's courage.*

Necessity As a Virtue

AUGUST 14

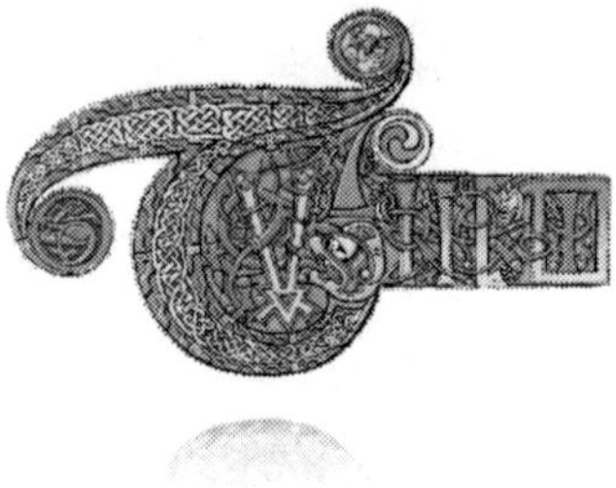

Gaunt
All places that the eye of heaven visits
Are to a wise man ports and happy havens.
Teach thy necessity to reason thus. . . . .
King Richard II 1.3.275-77

Having been banished from England, Bolingbroke bids goodbye to his father Gaunt. Bolingbroke says that his six years of exile will bring only grief. His father tries to persuade him to look at the situation more optimistically.

Gaunt: *To the wise person all places on earth under heaven are gateways and joyous, secure harbors. In the unavoidable constraints of your banishment, tell yourself that there is no better opportunity for developing virtue than there is in the force of circumstance.*

Companionship

AUGUST 15

Edgar

Who alone suffers, suffers most i'the mind,
Leaving free things and happy shows behind.
But then the mind much sufferance doth o'erskip,
When grief hath mates and bearing fellowship.

King Lear 3.6.102-05

Edgar says this as he watches Kent and the Fool leave bearing the mad King Lear. Lear has been woken from a desperately needed sleep in order to flee to Dover to avoid a death threat from his daughters Regan and Goneril.

***Edgar:** Those who suffer alone increase their mental anguish by banishing good people and pleasing sights. The suffering mind bypasses a lot of pain when sorrow is shared with friends and when anguish is relieved by companionship.*

Call to Celebrate

AUGUST 16

Iris

You sunburned sicklemen, of August weary,
Come hither from the furrow and be merry;
Make holiday!

The Tempest 4.1.134-36

The goddess Iris is a character in the masque celebrating the contract of love between Ferdinand, son of the King of Naples, and Miranda, daughter of the dispossessed Duke of Milan, Prospero. Iris says this to a group of farm laborers. This entire scene is an illusion that Prospero has conjured up.

Iris: *You weathered reapers, tired of the August harvest, break away from the cornfields and be happy. Celebrate!*

Effects of Misfortune

AUGUST 17

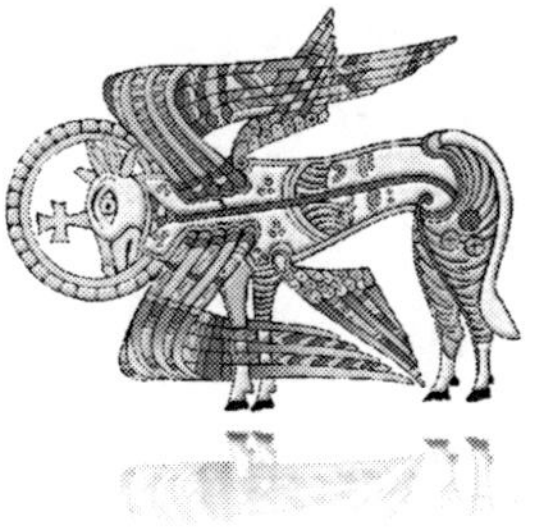

Trinculo

Misery acquaints a man with strange bedfellows!

***The Tempest* 2.2.39-40**

Shipwrecked on Prospero's island with the rest of the crew from Naples, Trinculo stumbles upon the creature Caliban, the offspring of the witch Sycorax, who is spread flat on the ground. Trinculo does not know if the silent Caliban is fish or fowl, human or vegetable. Nonetheless, Trinculo takes refuge under Caliban's ample garment in order to shelter himself from the storm that is brewing.

Trinculo: *Suffering introduces a person to unexpected intimacies with strangers.*

Self-Recrimination

AUGUST 18

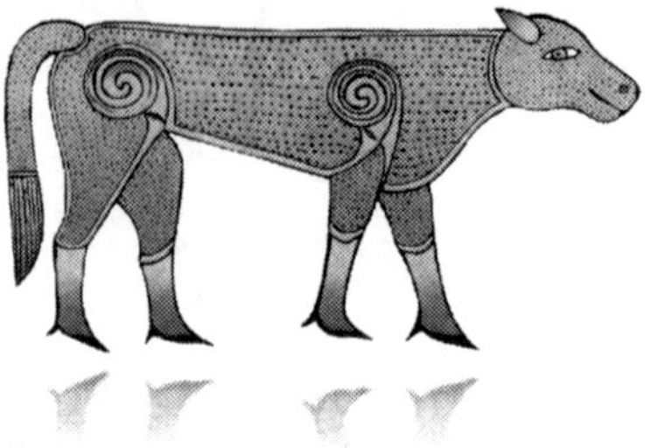

Hamlet

Bloody, bawdy villain!
Remorseless, treacherous, lecherous, kindless villain!
Why, what an ass am I!

Hamlet 2.2.582-84

Hamlet, Prince of Denmark, says this to himself after just having heard a seasoned visiting actor recite the tale of Pyrrhus' killing of old Priam as his frantic wife Hecuba watches. Spurred to feelings of revenge against the man who killed his father, Hamlet curses Claudius--and condemns his own inaction.

Hamlet: *Bloodthirsty, obscene wretch! Pitiless, treacherous, lecherous, unnatural bastard! What a fool I am!*

Mercy

AUGUST 19

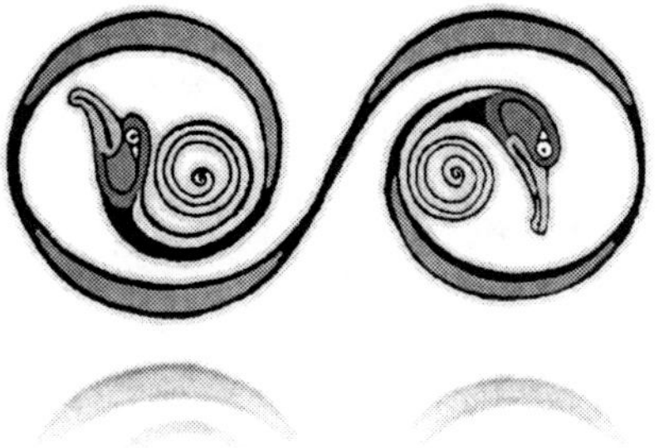

Portia
The quality of mercy is not strain'd,
It droppeth as the gentle rain from heaven
Upon the place beneath: it is twice blest,
It blesseth him that gives, and him that takes,
'Tis mightiest in the mightiest, it becomes
The throned monarch better than his crown.

The Merchant of Venice 4.1.182-87

In the Venetian court the merchant Antonio admits that he has contracted a financial bond with the moneylender Shylock. This bond requires a pound of Antonio's flesh if Antonio fails to pay his debt on time. Since the due date has passed and all of Antonio's ventures at sea have apparently failed, Shylock demands his pound of flesh. Disguised as a doctor of law from Rome, Portia expounds on the nature of mercy.

Portia: *Mercy's essence is not squeezed out by pressure. Instead, it falls from the heavens on the earth below. It is blessed in two ways: it blesses both the person who dispenses mercy and the one who receives it. It is the most powerful in the person who has the most power. It adorns a seated head of state better than a crown.*

Rewards of Nature

AUGUST 20

Caliban

I prithee, let me bring thee where crabs grow,
And I with my long nails will dig thee pignuts,
Show thee a jay's nest, and instruct thee how
To snare the nimble marmoset.

The Tempest 3.1.165-68

The unrestrained child of nature Caliban, who is the son of a witch, says this to Stephano, the drunken sailor, who has given Caliban alcohol for the first time ever in his life. Now drunk, Caliban believes Stephano is a god and offers to teach him the secrets of the natural treasures of the island.

Caliban: *Please let me show you the place where crabs breed. With my claws I will scoop out tasty roots for you. I will locate a blue jay's nest and teach you how to trap an agile monkey.*

Love's Folly

AUGUST 21

Touchstone

I remember when I was in love I broke my sword upon a stone, and bid him take that for comin-a-night to Jane Smile; and I remember the kissing of her batler, and the cow's dugs that her pretty chopt hands had milked; and I remember the wooing of a peascod instead of her. . . . We that are true lovers run into strange capers. . . .

As You Like It 2.4.44-49, 51-52

Watching the young shepherd Silvius suffering pangs of love for the disdainful Phebe, Touchstone recalls his own folly under the influence of love.

***Touchstone:** Once when I was in love, I struck a stone with my sword and told the stone my actions were revenge for daring to approach my love at night. I recall kissing the paddle my love had used to do the laundry and also kissing the udder of the cow that my love's lovely chapped hands had milked. I also wooed a pea pod in her absence. We that are truly in love do some strange things.*

Importance of Ceremony

AUGUST 22

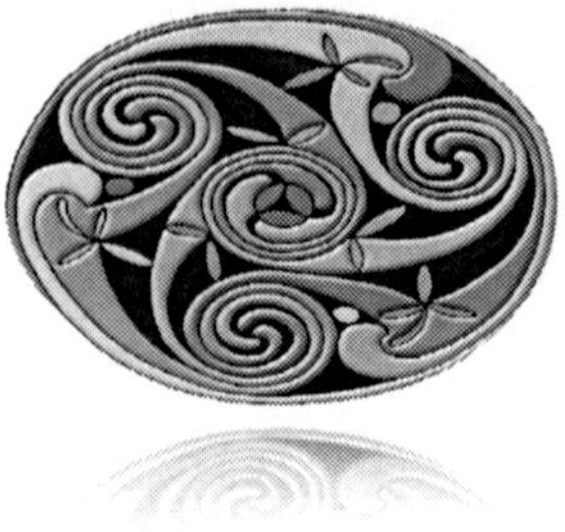

Lady Macbeth

the feast is sold,
That is not often vouch'd, while 'tis a-making,
'Tis given with welcome: to feed were best at home;
From thence, the sauce to meat is ceremony;
Meeting were bare without it.

Macbeth 3.4.32-36

Lady Macbeth chides her husband for abandoning his guests instead of presiding over the banquet. Macbeth had earlier left to meet with the two men paid to murder Banquo and his son. When Macbeth returns to the table, Lady Macbeth reprimands him.

Lady Macbeth: *That banquet is cheapened that is not repeatedly embellished while it is in progress. A successful feast needs heartfelt gratitude reiterated to the guests. Simply to eat is better done at home. Away from home the relish accompanying the main course is festive ritual. Without this, the occasion is stripped threadbare.*

Power of Innocence

AUGUST 23

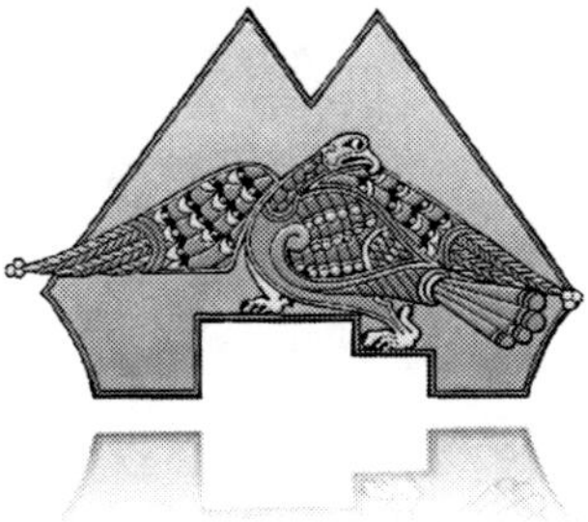

Paulina
The silence often of pure innocence
Persuades, when speaking fails.

The Winter's Tale 2.2.41-42

Paulina says this to the attendant of Queen Hermione who has just delivered a baby in prison, having been falsely accused of infidelity by her husband Leontes. Paulina offers to bring the babe before the enraged King to try to soften his heart and to persuade him to see the situation more in line with the truth.

Paulina: *The muteness of absolute innocence often successfully pleads its own case when speech itself falls flat.*

Pleasures of Friendship

AUGUST 24

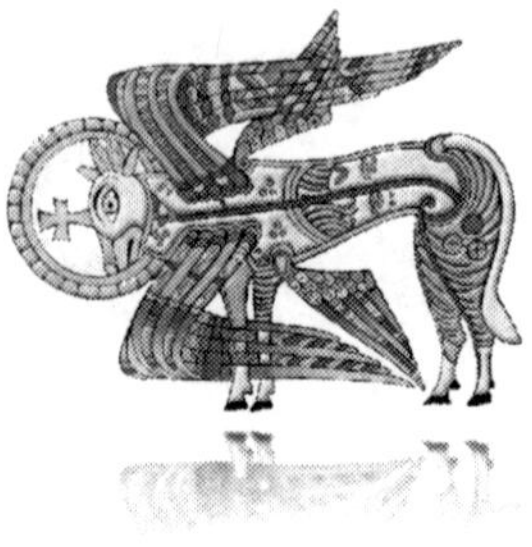

Bolingbroke
I count myself in nothing else so happy
As in a soul rememb'ring my good friends . . . .
King Richard II 2.3.46-47

Against the orders of King Richard II, Bolingbroke returns to England from exile and is met by his rebel supporters. When Hotspur offers his service to Bolingbroke, Bolingbroke thanks him.

Bolingbroke: *I consider myself in nothing so fortunate as in being able to call to mind my dear friends.*

Misrepresentation

AUGUST 25

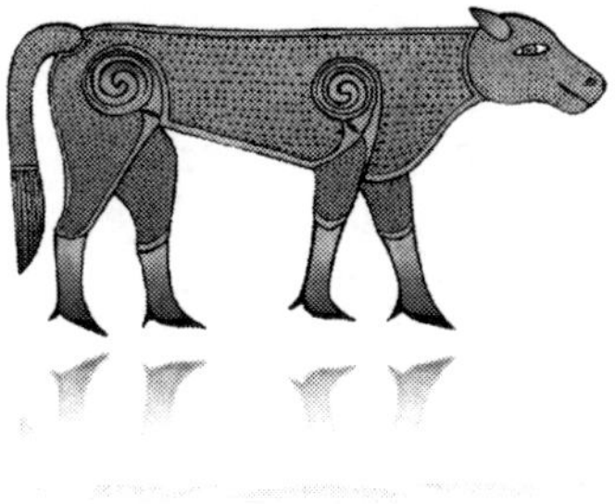

Antonio

The devil can cite Scripture for his purpose, -
An evil soul producing holy witness
Is like a villain with a smiling cheek,
A goodly apple rotten at the heart.

The Merchant of Venice 1.3.96-99

Antonio, who is borrowing money on Bassanio's behalf from the moneylender Shylock, says this to his friend Bassanio. Shylock has just told Antonio and Bassanio a story from the Old Testament to defend his (Shylock's) practice of charging interest. Antonio responds with disdain.

Antonio: *Even the devil, an enemy of God, can quote the divine word to suit his/her own ends. A corrupt soul offering sacred testimony is like a criminal with a beaming face: an apple that is pleasing on the outside but rotten at the core.*

Bearing Bad News

AUGUST 26

Messenger

Gracious madam,
I that do bring the news made not the match.

Antony and Cleopatra 2.5.66-67

The Messenger says this in response to the Egyptian Queen Cleopatra's hysteria when he tells her that her beloved Antony has married Octavia in Rome. Cleopatra beats the messenger and threatens his life.

Messenger: *Dear woman, I who am delivering this message did not set up the marriage.*

Burdens of Kingship

AUGUST 27

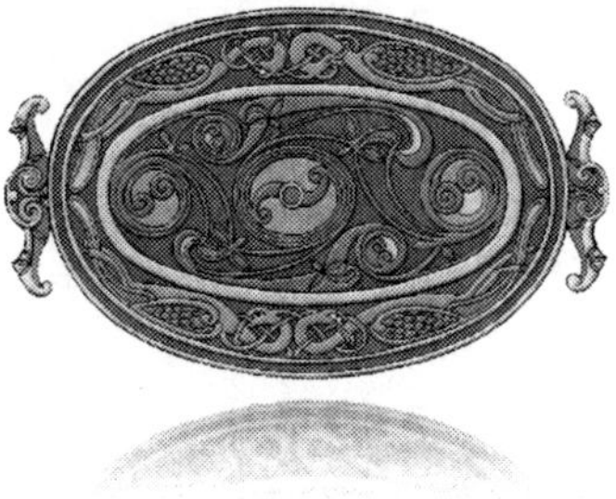

Prince

Why doth the crown lie there upon his pillow,
Being so troublesome a bedfellow?
O polish'd perturbation! golden care!
That keep'st the ports of slumber open wide
To many a watchful night!

King Henry IV, Part 2 4.5.20-24

Returning to court to find his father seriously ill, Prince Hal, heir to the throne, sits by his father's sickbed and addresses the crown that King Henry had requested be placed on the pillow next to him.

Prince Hal: *Why does the crown just sit there on his pillow when it is such a disturbing bedmate? Oh, shimmering trouble, golden burden! You keep the gates of sleep thrown wide for many a sleepless night.*

Love's Contradictions

AUGUST 28

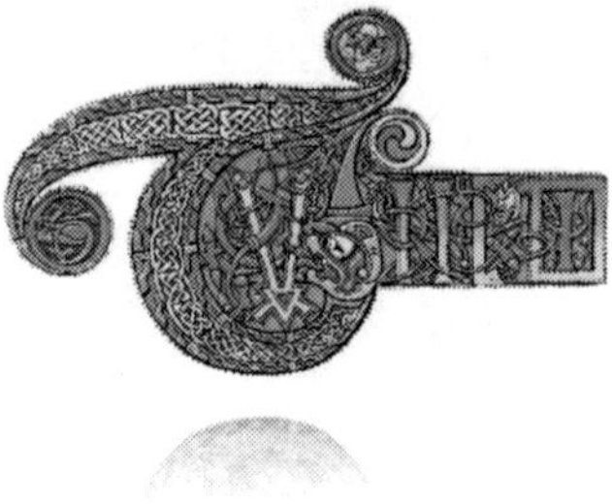

Romeo

O heavy lightness, serious vanity,
Misshapen chaos of well-seeming forms!
Feather of lead, bright smoke, cold fire, sick health,
Still-waking sleep that is not what it is!
This love feel I that feel no love in this.

Romeo and Juliet 1.1.178-82

Romeo begins this speech talking about the conflict between his family, the Montagues, and the Capulet family. However, he quickly digresses to a discussion of his own pre-Juliet obsession with fair Rosaline. Cast in the role of the Petrarchan lover whose love is unrequited, Romeo experiences only extremes in love.

Romeo: *Oh, burdensome joy, profound folly, confusion in apparently ordered structures! Feather of lead, radiant smoke, icy heat, sick vitality, sleep that keeps one awake! This passion I feel lacks even the remotest semblance of love.*

Repudiating Goodness
AUGUST 29

Albany
Wisdom and goodness to the vile seem vile;
Filths savour but themselves.

King Lear 4.2.39-40

Albany says this after his cruel, ambitious wife Goneril has just driven her own father, King Lear, out into a merciless storm without any cover or provisions. When Albany remarks upon the fact that he fears the disposition of a person who will treat her own father in such a manner, Goneril condemns her husband's compassion for Lear. Albany responds.

Albany: *Wisdom and goodness to the wicked seem wicked. Depraved creatures desire only those who are like themselves.*

Basking in Confinement

AUGUST 30

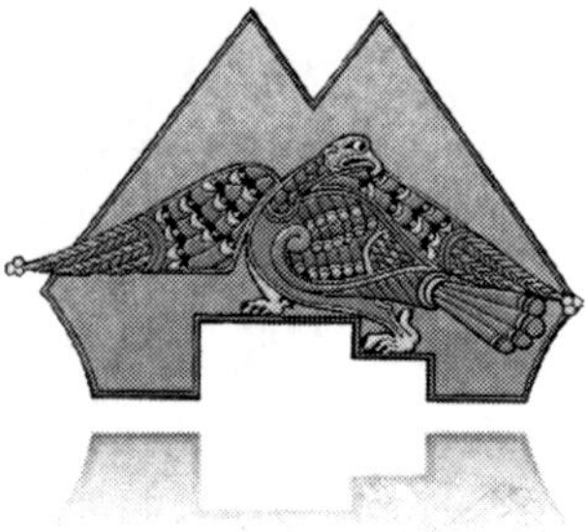

Ferdinand

All corners o'th' earth
Let liberty make use of; space enough
Have I in such a prison.

The Tempest 1.2.492-94

Ferdinand, son of the King of Naples, says this to Prospero, the deposed Duke of Milan, who has cast a spell on Ferdinand to make him fall in love with Miranda, Prospero's daughter, and also to confine him in one place.

Ferdinand: *Allow freedom to occupy the four corners of the earth. I have all the room I need here in my cramped state of confinement.*

Urgency

AUGUST 31

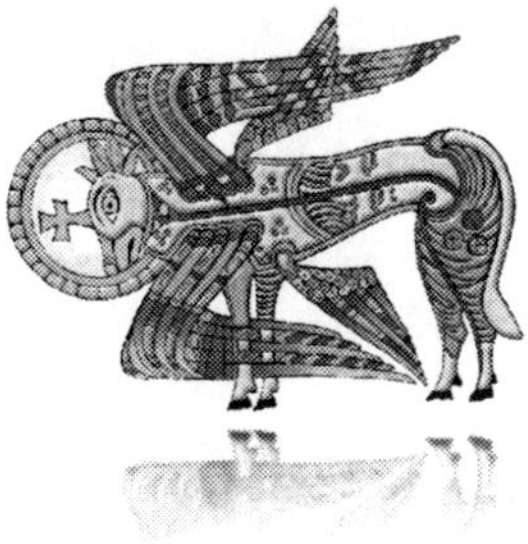

Hastings
We are time's subjects, and time bids be gone.
King Henry IV, Part 2 1.3.110

Regrouping the rebel forces after their defeat at Shrewsbury, Mowbray asks Hastings if it isn't time to face the King's armies. Hastings responds.

Hastings: *We are creatures of time, and time urges us to move on.*

Breaking Away From Idleness

SEPTEMBER 1

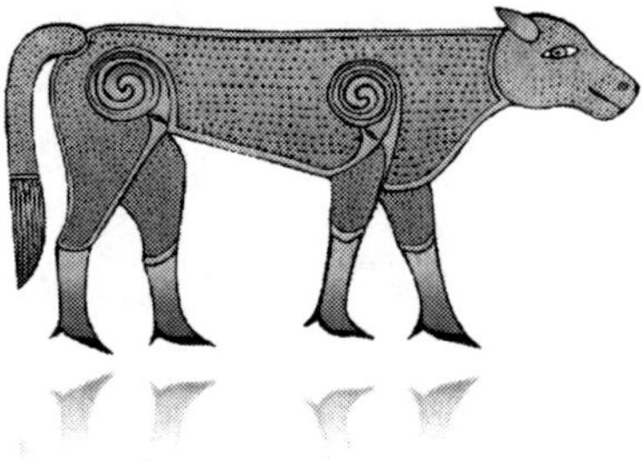

Antony

I must from this enchanting queen break off.
Ten thousand harms, more than the ills I know,
My idleness doth hatch.

Antony and Cleopatra 1.2.133-35

Antony says this after learning that while he has been luxuriating in Egypt with his lover Cleopatra, his wife Fulvia has died in Sicyon.

Antony: *I have to tear myself away from this bewitching queen. My dalliance here breeds a great multitude of troubles, more evils than I am even aware of.*

Love's Lunacy

SEPTEMBER 2

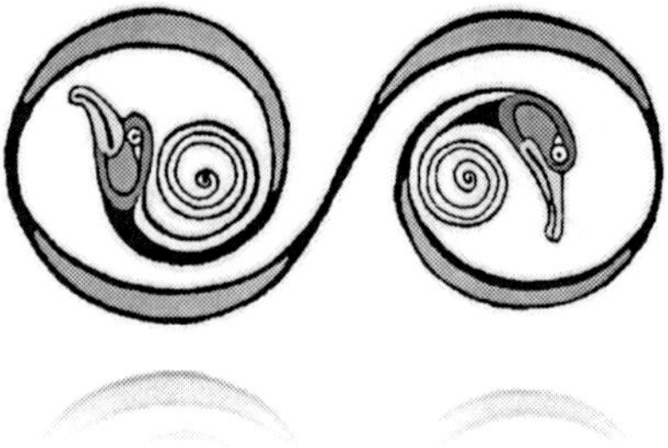

Rosalind

Love is merely a madness, and I tell you,
deserves as well a dark house and a whip as madmen
do; and the reason why they are not so punished and
cured is that the lunacy is so ordinary that the
whippers are in love too.

As You Like It 3.2.389-93

Rosalind, disguised as a man, tries to talk Orlando, the man she loves, out of being in love.

Rosalind: *Love is nothing but insanity, and, I say, merits confinement to a room and being thrashed just as much as lunatics are. But the reason lovers are not disciplined in this fashion is that the madness is so common that those who are handing out the punishment are themselves in love.*

The World as Prison

SEPTEMBER 3

Hamlet

O God, I could be bounded in a nutshell and
count myself a king of infinite space - were it not that
I have bad dreams.

***Hamlet* 2.2.255-57**

Sent by King Claudius and Gertrude to spy upon Hamlet and to ferret out the cause of his apparent madness, Hamlet's childhood friends Rosencrantz and Guildenstern banter with Prince Hamlet, prodding and poking him to get Hamlet to expose himself. Only partially jesting, Rosencrantz accuses Hamlet of ambition, and Hamlet responds by expressing his utter revulsion of the world.

Hamlet: *Oh God! I could be imprisoned inside a nutshell and still consider myself ruler of the cosmos--except for the fact that I have frightening suspicions of reality.*

Value of Bad Companions

SEPTEMBER 4

Warwick

My gracious lord, you look beyond him quite.
The Prince but studies his companions
Like a strange tongue, wherein, to gain the language,
'Tis needful that the most immodest word
Be look'd upon and learnt; which once attain'd,
Your Highness knows, comes to no further use
But to be known and hated.

***King Henry IV, Part 2* 4.4.67-73**

Despondent at his son's absence from court, King Henry predicts that when he dies, only riot and excess will govern Prince Hal's rule, producing danger and corruption. One of Henry's nobles, Warwick, challenges Henry's dire predictions.

Warwick: *My gracious lord, you misrepresent him. The Prince merely observes his companions in order to educate himself as someone would do while learning a foreign language. Once mastered, such words will not be used but only known and despised.*

Self-recrimination

SEPTEMBER 5

Hotspur
O, I could divide myself, and go to
buffets, for moving such a dish of skim milk with so
honourable an action!

King Henry IV, Part 1 2.3.31-33

Plotting an action to overthrow King Henry, Hotspur reads a letter from one of the rebels who is backing out of the scheme, arguing that it is too dangerous and too ill-supported. Angry that he has invited the man, Hotspur talks to himself.

***Hotspur:** Oh, I could split myself in two and fight it out between my two halves for inviting such a cowardly lightweight to do so noble a deed.*

Advice For Actors

SEPTEMBER 6

Hamlet

Suit the action to the word,
the word to the action, with this special observance,
that you o'erstep not the modesty of nature.

Hamlet 3.2.18-20

Hamlet, Prince of Denmark, says this to the members of the acting troupe visiting the royal court at Elsinore when he is instructing them how to deliver a speech that he has written.

Hamlet: *Make the gesture fit the words and the words correspond to the physical movement, paying particular attention to avoid extremes and instead to depict what is natural.*

Quick Thinking
SEPTEMBER 7

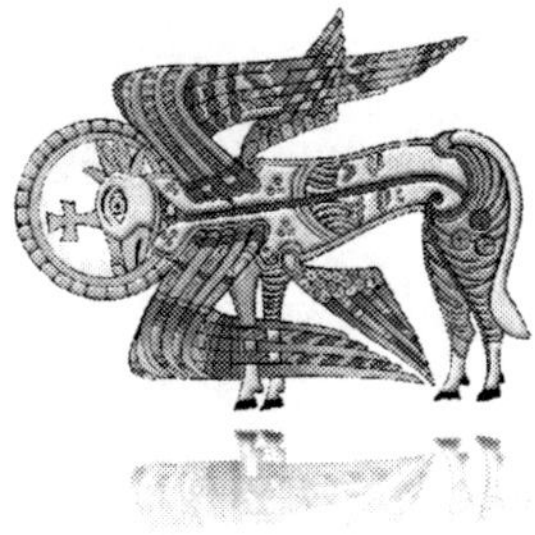

Falstaff

The better part of valour is discretion, in the which better part I have saved my life.

King Henry IV, Part 1 5.4.118-20

Having just killed his archrival, the rebel Hotspur, Prince Hal notices Falstaff's body on the ground and mistakenly believes Falstaff is dead. Giving an impromptu comic eulogy, Hal resolves to prepare Falstaff's body for burial after the Battle of Shrewsbury is over. As soon as Hal leaves, Falstaff pops up like an inflated roly-poly doll and then rationalizes his skin-saving pretense of being dead.

Falstaff: *The more important part of bravery is wise judgment. It is this portion that has saved my skin.*

Despair

SEPTEMBER 8

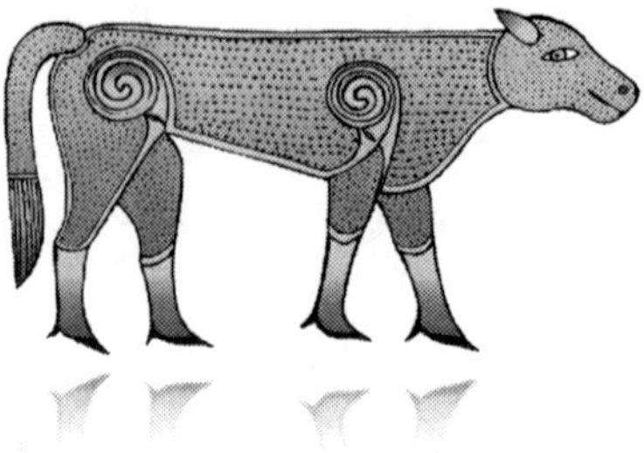

King

My words fly up, my thoughts remain below.
Words without thoughts never to heaven go.

Hamlet 3.3.97-98

In a posture of prayer, yet unwilling to give up the fruits of his sin (his wife and his crown), Claudius finds himself unable to pray.

____

____

____

____

____

____

King Claudius: *My words float up into the air, but my intentions stay behind on the earth. Prayers without conviction can never reach heaven.*

Keeping Faith

SEPTEMBER 9

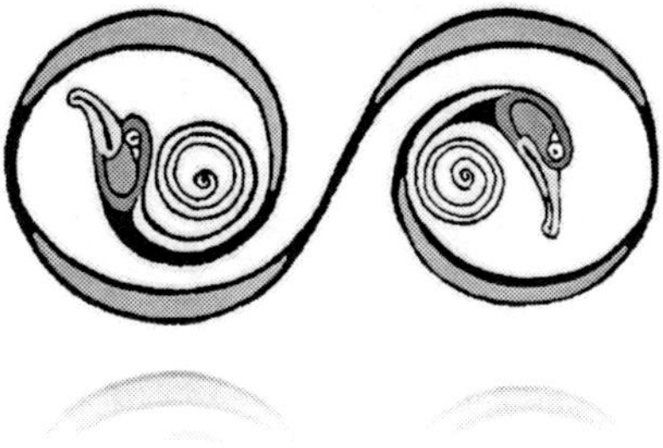

Orlando

Why how now Adam? No greater heart in
thee? Live a little, comfort a little, cheer thyself a little.

As You Like It 2.6.4-5

Orlando says this to kindly old Adam, the faithful family servant who has accompanied Orlando to the forest as he flees for his life. When Adam says he is simply too tired and too hungry to continue and then asks Orlando to measure out his grave, Orlando responds.

Orlando: *What's this, Adam? Have you lost your will to live? Stay alive a while longer, be consoled a bit, lift your spirits some.*

False Threats

SEPTEMBER 10

Duke

Now, as fond fathers,
Having bound up the threatening twigs of birch,
Only to stick it in their children's sight
For terror, not to use, in time the rod
Becomes more mock'd than fear'd. . . .

Measure for Measure 1.3.23-27

Duke Vincentio, the ruler of Venice, admits privately to the Friar that the firm laws on the books of Venice, which were necessary to constrain the appetites of the citizens, have not been enforced properly for the past fourteen years.

Duke: *When foolish fathers tie together a bunch of birch twigs and wave it at their children as a threat rather than a punishment, after a while the tool of discipline is more often mocked than feared.*

Speaking Authentically

SEPTEMBER 11

Edgar

The weight of this sad time we must obey,
Speak what we feel, not what we ought to say.

King Lear 5.3.322-23

Edgar says this to Kent and Albany when after the virtuous Cordelia and King Lear die, Albany offers the kingship to Kent and Edgar. Kent refuses; Edgar accepts.

Edgar: *The heaviness of this grave state of affairs we must submit to. We must speak from the heart and not from a sense of propriety.*

Hope As Healing

SEPTEMBER 12

Claudio

The miserable have no other medicine
But only hope. . . .

***Measure for Measure* 3.1.2-3**

Disguised as a friar, the Duke of Vienna counsels the condemned Claudio who is to be executed the next day for sleeping with his fiancée Juliet. The Duke then asks him if he has hope that he will be pardoned.

Claudio: *Those who are downtrodden have only hope as a remedy to treat their suffering.*

Home as a Castle
SEPTEMBER 13

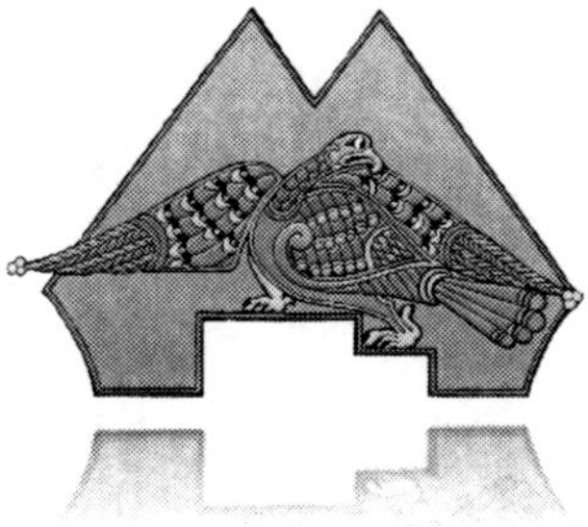

Prospero

Welcome, sir.
This cell's my court; here have I few attendants,
And subjects none abroad.

***The Tempest* 5.1.166-168**

Prospero, the deposed Duke of Milan, says this to Alonso, the King of Naples, who has given Prospero back his usurped kingdom. Prospero is referring to the humble life he has led in banishment on an island that has fed his needs and served as home for him and his daughter Miranda.

Prospero: *This confined space is my kingdom. I have very few servants here and no vassals outside of this island.*

Veil-Like Texture of Existence

SEPTEMBER 14

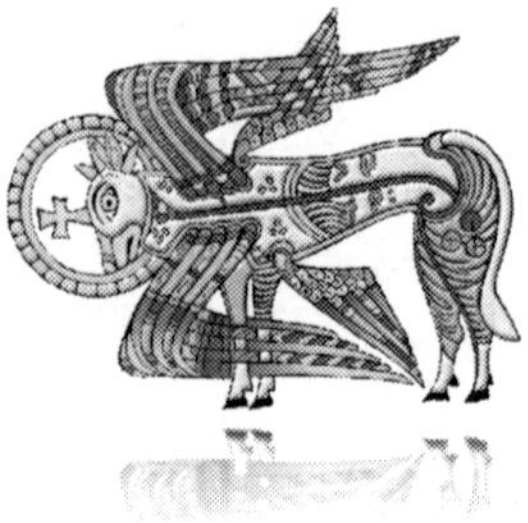

Prospero

We are such stuff
As dreams are made on, and our little life
Is rounded with a sleep.

The Tempest 4.1.156-58

The magician (and deposed Duke of Milan) Prospero says this to his daughter Miranda. He reflects here on the beautiful masque he has conjured to celebrate the betrothal of Miranda to Ferdinand, son of the King of Naples.

Prospero: *We are made of the very same substance from which dreams are created. Our brief life is brought to completeness by a lasting slumber.*

Emptiness of Ambition
SEPTEMBER 15

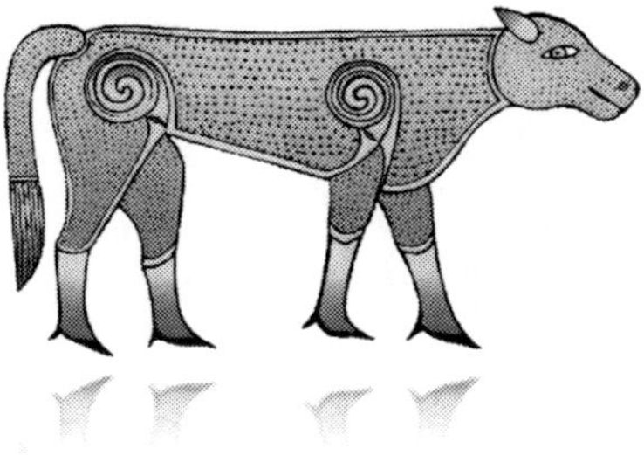

Prince
Ill-weav'd ambition, how much art thou shrunk!
When that this body did contain a spirit,
A kingdom for it was too small a bound;
But now two paces of the vilest earth
Is room enough.

King Henry IV, Part 1 5.4.87-91

Prince Hal says this over the cold body of the rebel Hotspur whom Hal has just killed in battle. Praising Hotspur's bravery, Hal nonetheless laments Hotspur's towering ambition.

____

____

____

____

____

____

Prince Hal: *Poorly fashioned ambition, how greatly diminished you are! When this body had a soul, the vast expanse of the English realm was too small a space for it. But now two steps' worth of the most despicable land is adequate lodging!*

Prayer

SEPTEMBER 16

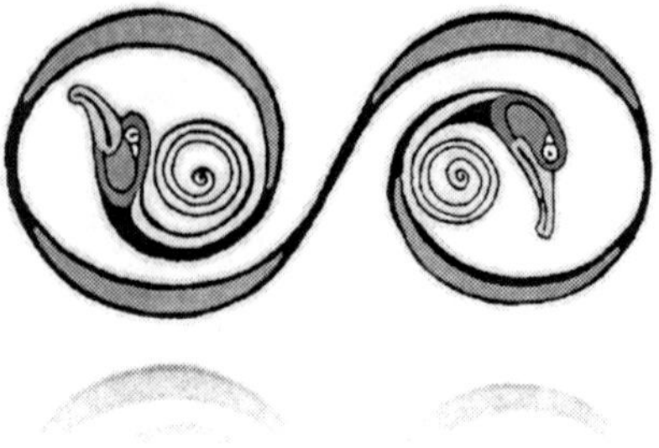

Bolingbroke
Strong as a tower in hope, I cry amen.

King Richard II 1.3.102

In his trial by combat with Mowbray, Bolingbroke says this to the Marshall who has just finished measuring Bolingbroke's and his opponent's lances to ensure that they are both of equal length. As the Marshall returns Bolingbroke's lance, he pronounces the wish that God may defend the right cause in this trial. Bolingbroke responds.

Bolingbroke: *Fortified like a stronghold with hope, I shout "so be it."*

Animals' Rights

SEPTEMBER 17

Duke Senior
Come, shall we go and kill us venison?
And yet it irks me the poor dappled fools,
Being native burghers of this desert city,
Should in their own confines with forked heads
Have their round haunches gor'd.

As You Like It 2.1.21-25

As he is about to shoot a deer, Duke Senior observes that the deer are more native to the land than the hunters who come after them.

Duke Senior: *Shall we go kill a deer? Still it bothers me that these pitiful spotted creatures, the natural rulers of this desolate city, should in their own territory, being armed with antlers on their heads, have their plump backs pierced.*

Hypocrisy

SEPTEMBER 18

Polonius
'Tis too much prov'd, that with devotion's visage
And pious action we do sugar o'er
The devil himself.

Hamlet 3.1.47-49

Polonius, Gertrude, and King Claudius devise a plan to test the cause of Hamlet's madness. They have asked the object of Hamlet's love, Ophelia, to pretend to read a book as she walks in the path of Hamlet's approach. Polonius and the others plan to hide and watch Hamlet's reaction to her.

Polonius: *It is too often demonstrated that with a saintly appearance and fake piety, we sugarcoat the devil himself.*

Wisdom of Inaction

SEPTEMBER 19

Macbeth

If Chance will have me King, why, Chance may crown
me,
Without my stir.

Macbeth 1.3.144-45

The news that Macbeth has received the title of Thane of Cawdor has thrown Macbeth into a frenzy. With this announcement the first of the witches' two prophecies for Macbeth has now come true, leaving only the title of King ahead. As he first imagines the murder of Duncan, Macbeth is overcome by fear and trembling. However, in a moment of short-lived lucidity (speaking to himself), he decides to leave the decision to the hands of fate.

Macbeth: *If fortune will make me king, then fortune will bring me the crown without my slightest effort to attain it.*

True Perception

SEPTEMBER 20

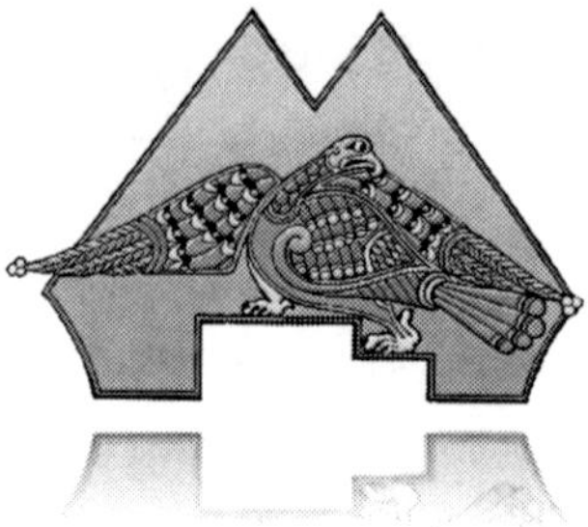

Lear

Your eyes are in a
heavy case, your purse in a light, yet you see how this
world goes.

Gloucester

I see it feelingly.

King Lear 4.6.142-45

The mad Lear says this to blind Gloucester who has been driven from his house upon pain of death for his kindness to Lear.

Lear: *Your eyes are in sad shape, your purse is lacking in weight, yet you perceive the way this world works.* ***Gloucester:*** *I see it with my heart.*

Impermanence of All Things

SEPTEMBER 21

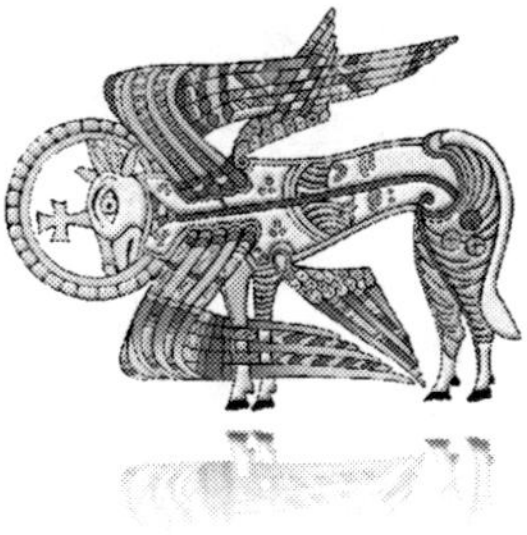

Sonnet 60

Time doth transfix the flourish set on youth,
And delves the parallels in beauty's brow;
Feeds on the rarities of nature's truth,
And nothing stands but for his scythe to mow.

Lines 9-12

Sonnet 60: *Time breaks through the shiny surface bestowed on the young and digs furrows into the forehead of beauty. Time nourishes itself on the striking specimens of natural life: nothing remains that isn't cut down by his blade.*

Love of Solitude

SEPTEMBER 22

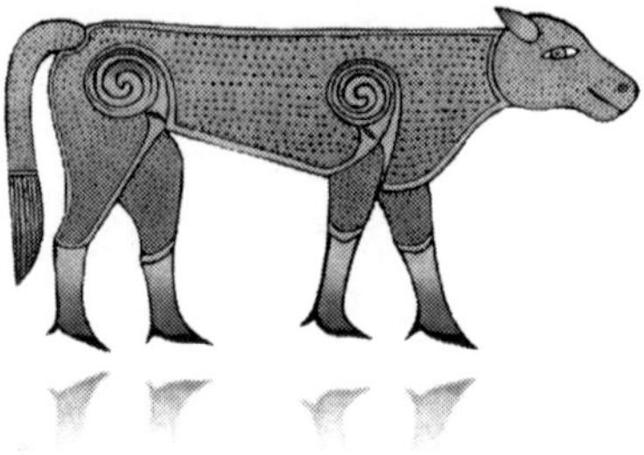

Duke
My holy sir, none better knows than you
How I have ever lov'd the life remov'd,
And held in idle price to haunt assemblies,
Where youth, and cost, witless bravery keeps.

Measure for Measure 1.3.7-10

The Duke has stepped down from his position as the head of the government in Vienna so that he might secretly observe his subjects as well as the deputy he has temporarily left in charge. Here the Duke asks Friar Thomas' help in supplying him with a religious habit in which to disguise himself as a friar.

Duke: *My reverend Friar, no one knows more than you do how I have always loved a secluded life and thought it frivolous to frequent those gatherings where youth and the latest fashion keep company with foolhardy bravado.*

Curse

SEPTEMBER 23

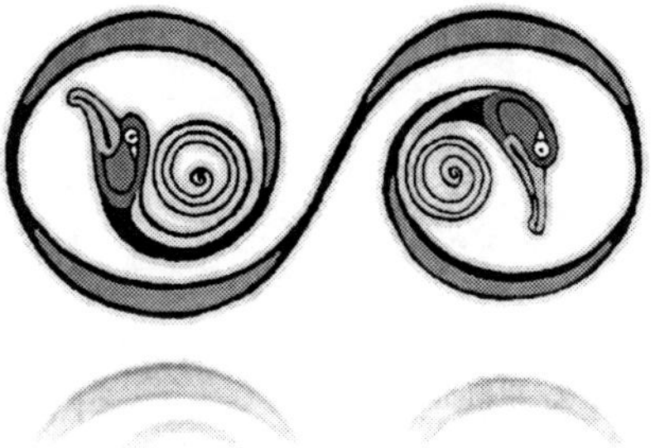

Prospero
Go, charge my goblins that they grind their joints
With dry convulsions, shorten up their sinews
With aged cramps, and more pinch-spotted make them
Than pard or cat o'mountain.

The Tempest 4.1.259-62

Prospero says this to the spirit Ariel after the two of them have thwarted the assassination of Prospero by Caliban, Stephano, and Trinculo. Prospero here tells Ariel to command the spirits to punish these three.

Prospero: *Hurry away, and order the spirits under my command to strike these men's joints with harsh spasms, tighten their muscles with the cramps of old people, and give these men more dark bruises than panthers or leopards have.*

Prerogatives of Birth

SEPTEMBER 24

Richard
We were not born to sue, but to command. . . .
King Richard II 1.1.196

King Richard and the venerable old Gaunt, Richard's uncle, cannot persuade Mowbray and Bolingbroke, Gaunt's son, to drop their respective charges of treason against one another. The King and Gaunt also fail to convince the two enemies to forego trial by combat. At this point, Richard interrupts to set a date for the combat.

King Richard: *As King, I was brought into this world not to beg but to rule.*

Secret of Longevity

SEPTEMBER 25

Adam
Though I look old, yet I am strong and lusty;
For in my youth I never did apply
Hot and rebellious liquors in my blood. . . .
Therefore my age is as a lusty winter,
Frosty, but kindly.

As You Like It 2.3.47-49; 52-53

When Orlando flees the court of the usurping duke, Duke Frederick, in order to save his own life, Orlando's old faithful servant Adam offers to accompany Orlando into the Forest of Arden. In support of his offer, Adam says this.

Adam: *Though I appear advanced in years, I am still physically powerful and vigorous. The reason is that when I was young, I didn't pour strong, unruly liquors into my body. As a result, my old age is like an exceptionally strong winter: extremely cold, but favorable.*

Regret

SEPTEMBER 26

Polixenes

better not to have had thee than
thus to want thee.

The Winter's Tale 4.2.12-13

Polixenes says this to Camillo who once saved Polixenes' life but who had to flee his native Sicily as a consequence. Absent from his home for fifteen years, the aging Camillo asks Polixenes' permission to return home to Sicily. Polixenes responds.

Polixenes: *It is better never to have had your companionship than to be deprived of you now.*

Childhood Innocence

SEPTEMBER 27

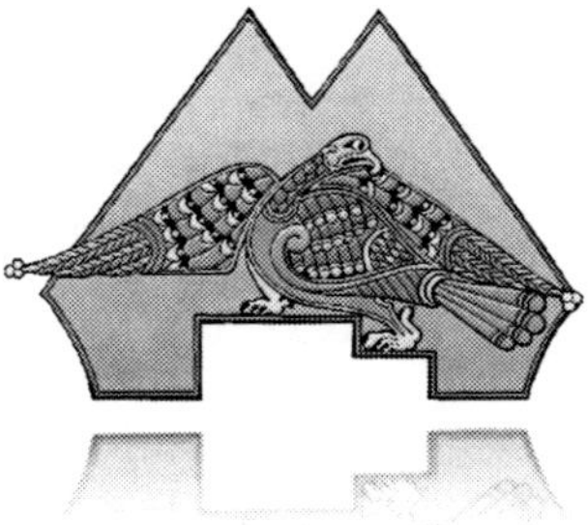

Polixenes

We were as twinn'd lambs that did frisk i'th' sun,
And bleat the one at th'other: what we chang'd
Was innocence for innocence: we knew not
The doctrine of ill-doing, nor dream'd
That any did.

The Winter's Tale 1.2.67-71

Polixenes, King of Bohemia, says this of his childhood friend Leontes, King of Sicilia, in response to Leontes' wife's question as to which of them was the more blatant rogue.

Polixenes: *We were like lambs born at the same time that played all day, calling back and forth to one another. We exchanged one form of purity for another. We had no knowledge of evil nor did we imagine anyone else did.*

Lasting Connections
SEPTEMBER 28

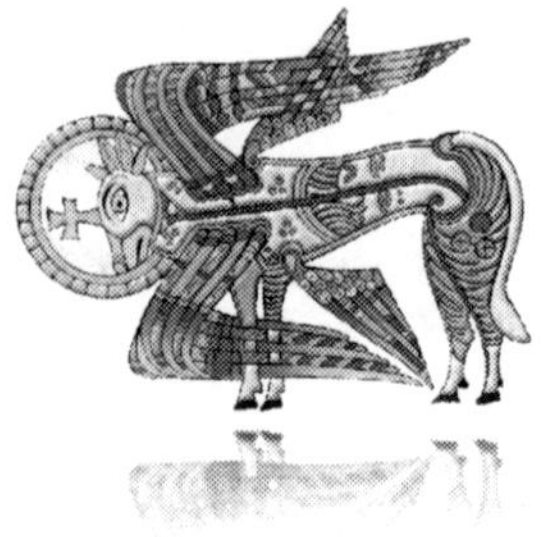

Sonnet 74
But be contented when that fell arrest
Without all bail shall carry me away;
My life hath in this line some interest,
Which for memorial still with thee shall stay.
When thou reviewest this, thou dost review
The very part was consecrate to thee;
The earth can have but earth, which is his due.
My spirit is thine, the better part of me. . . .

Lines 1-8

Sonnet 74: *Do not be troubled. When death takes me away, part of me will remain with you in these lines of poetry. As you reread this poetry, you will re-experience the part of my life devoted entirely to you. The earth can have my body, which belongs to the soil. But my spirit, my better part, is yours.*

Betrayal

SEPTEMBER 29

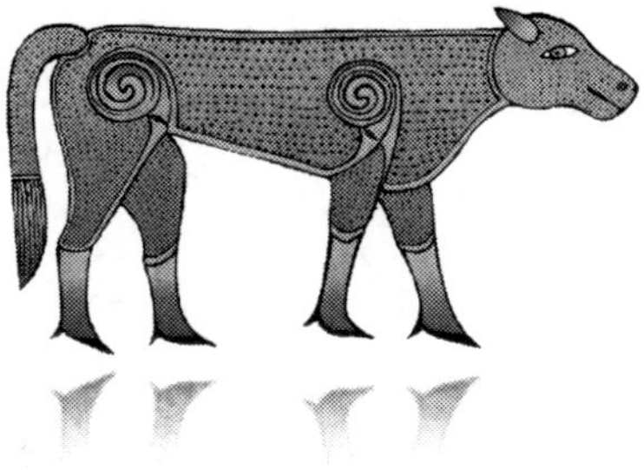

Caesar
Et tu, Brute?

***Julius Caesar* 3.1.77**

As he is being assassinated, Caesar says this to his trusted friend Brutus who is the last of the conspirators to plunge a sword into Caesar's body.

Caesar: *And you too, Brutus?*

False Comfort

SEPTEMBER 30

Gonzalo

You rub the sore
When you should bring the plaster.

The Tempest 2.1.139-40

Gonzalo says this to Sebastian who is berating the King of Naples for his foolishness in marrying his daughter off to a foreign prince and then losing his son in a shipwreck on the way back from Tunisia.

Gonzalo: *You are scrubbing the wound when you should be applying an anesthetic.*

Nature's Raging Storms

OCTOBER 1

Caska
I have seen tempests when the scolding winds
Have rived the knotty oaks, and I have seen
Th'ambitious ocean swell, and rage, and foam,
To be exalted with the threatening clouds:
But never till tonight, never till now,
Did I go through a tempest dropping fire.

Julius Caesar 1.3.5-10

After following Caesar's procession through the streets of Rome, Caska meets Cicero and breathlessly tells him of the strange natural events that Caska has just witnessed.

Caska: *I have seen storms in which brawling winds have split gnarled oak trees. And I have observed the towering ocean rise, spout foam, toss vehemently to and fro, and then rise even more because of the dark clouds. But not until this very moment have I experienced a storm which discharged fire itself.*

Dangers of Meddling

OCTOBER 2

Hamlet

Thou find'st to be too busy is some danger.

Hamlet 3.4.33

Hamlet says this to the dead Polonius whom Prince Hamlet has just accidentally killed, mistaking Polonius for Hamlet's uncle Claudius.

Hamlet: *You are discovering that being too much of a busybody is hazardous.*

Bewilderment

OCTOBER 3

Alonso
This is as strange a maze as e'er men trod. . . .
The Tempest 5.1.243

Alonso says this after hearing his Boatswain's tale of being shipwrecked, falling asleep in the hatches of the boat, and being awakened. His garments are now fresh, and the boat has been returned to the condition it was in when the crew and passengers set sail.

Alonso: *This is as astonishing a winding path as ever people have trudged.*

Imagination's Nocturnal Journey

OCTOBER 4

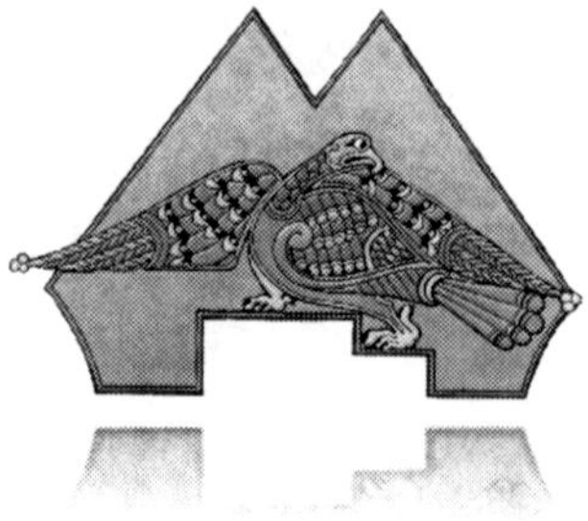

Sonnet 27

Weary with toil, I haste me to my bed,
The dear repose for limbs with travail tired;
But then begins a journey in my head
To work my mind, when body's work's expired:
For then my thoughts, from far where I abide,
Intend a zealous pilgrimage to thee,
And keep my drooping eyelids open wide. . . .

Lines 1-7

Sonnet 27: *Exhausted by hard work, I hurry to bed, the precious relief for my arms and legs worn out with traveling. But now another inner expedition takes place that wears out my mind long after my physical labor ends. At this time, my thoughts, like pilgrims far away from where I dwell, ardently journey to you and keep me from falling asleep.*

Arrogance
OCTOBER 5

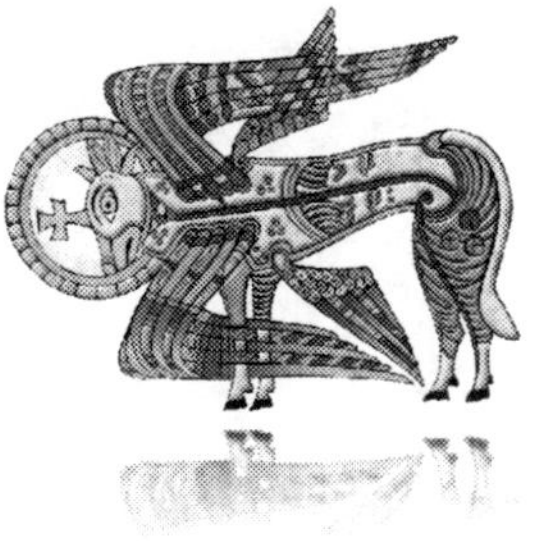

Caesar

Danger knows full well
That Caesar is more dangerous than he.
We are two lions littered in one day,
And I the elder and more terrible,
And Caesar shall go forth.

Julius Caesar 2.2.44-48

Caesar says this to his wife Calpurnia when Caesar decides to disregard Calpurnia's dreadful premonitions and to go to the Capitol where he will be assassinated.

Caesar: *My opponent, Danger, readily acknowledges that I am more fearsome than he is. He and I are two kings of beasts born on the same day, but I was born first--and also more terrible. I will go to the Capitol today.*

Witty Retorts

OCTOBER 6

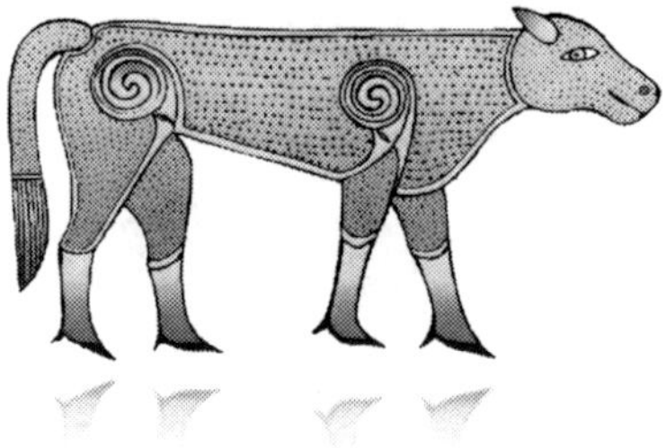

Chief Justice
Well, the truth is, Sir John, you live in
great infamy. . . . Your means are very slender and your
waste is great.
Falstaff
I would it were otherwise, I would my means
were greater and my waist slenderer.

King Henry IV, Part 2 1.2.136-37; 140-43

The Chief Justice has come in person to chide Falstaff for refusing to answer the official summons to fight in the Battle of Shrewsbury. Falstaff makes light of the matter.

Chief Justice: *The truth of the matter, Sir John, is that you continue to spend your days in utter disrepute. Your personal riches are very slim, yet your waste is tremendous.*
Falstaff: *I wish it were the other way around: I wish my wealth were greater and my waist thinner.*

Caution in Love

OCTOBER 7

Laertes

best safety lies in fear.

Hamlet 1.3.43

Laertes says this to his sister Ophelia when he advises her not to take Hamlet's attention to her too seriously. Since Hamlet is of royal birth, he cannot choose his mate for himself.

Laertes: *The best way to protect yourself is to be wary.*

Self-denigration

OCTOBER 8

Sonnet 103

Alack, what poverty my muse brings forth,
That, having such a scope to show her pride,
The argument all bare is of more worth
Than when it hath my added praise beside.

Lines 1-4

Sonnet 103: *Overwhelmed by you, my creativity and inspiration produce such barren language that your naked perfection and indescribable beauty communicate their quality more powerfully than my poor words can.*

Wasted Compassion

OCTOBER 9

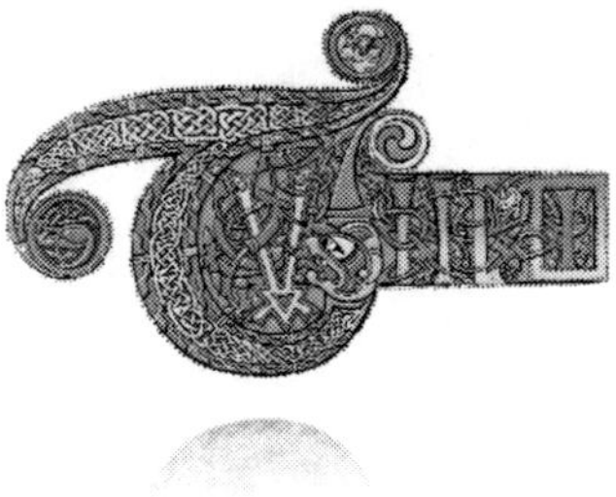

Prospero
A devil, a born devil, on whose nature
Nurture can never stick; on whom my pains
Humanely taken - all, all lost, quite lost!
The Tempest 4.1.188-90

Speaking to himself, Prospero says this about Caliban after the spirit Ariel has described how Caliban has goaded Stephano and Trinculo into attempting to assassinate Prospero. When Prospero first fled to the island after being deposed as Duke of Milan, Caliban was a pitiful creature that Prospero willingly helped--until Caliban tried to rape Prospero's daughter Miranda.

Prospero: *He is a demon, an inherent demon, whose constitution cannot retain cultivation. The trouble I have kindly taken with him is all in vain, entirely wasted!*

Adulation of Virtue

OCTOBER 10

Lucio
I hold you as a thing enskied and sainted
By your renouncement, an immortal spirit,
And to be talk'd with in sincerity,
As with a saint.

Measure for Measure 1.4.34-37

The fop Lucio brings a message from the imprisoned Claudio to his sister Isabella, a novice in the convent. Jesting about the cause of Claudio's plight (impregnating his fiancée), Lucio nevertheless balks when Isabella suggests that she is the object of Lucio's mirth.

***Lucio:** Because of your renunciation of secular life, I regard you as a heavenly and an angelic creature, an eternal soul, who must be addressed genuinely as one would a saint.*

Patriotic Sorrow

OCTOBER 11

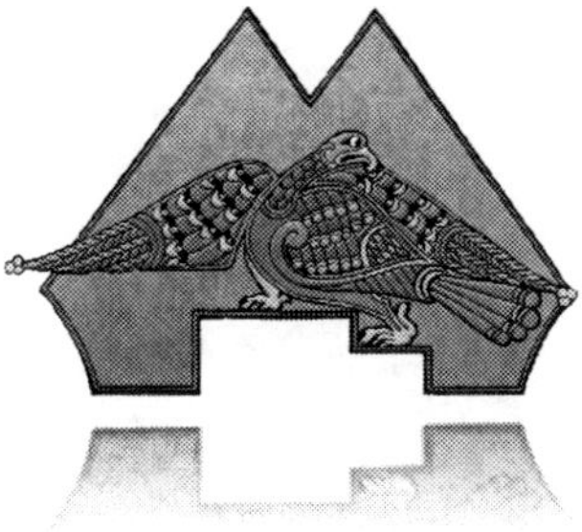

Malcolm
I think our country sinks beneath the yoke;
It weeps, it bleeds; and each new day a gash
Is added to her wounds. . . .

Macbeth 4.3.39-41

Malcolm, heir to the Scottish throne before Macbeth usurped it, says this to Macduff, a virtuous Scottish noble. Malcolm describes the country as suffering under Macbeth's cruel reign.

Malcolm: *I believe our nation perishes under Macbeth's tyranny. Scotland cries out, sheds blood, and every single day a new knife wound is inflicted upon the country's flesh.*

Necessity of Truthfulness

OCTOBER 12

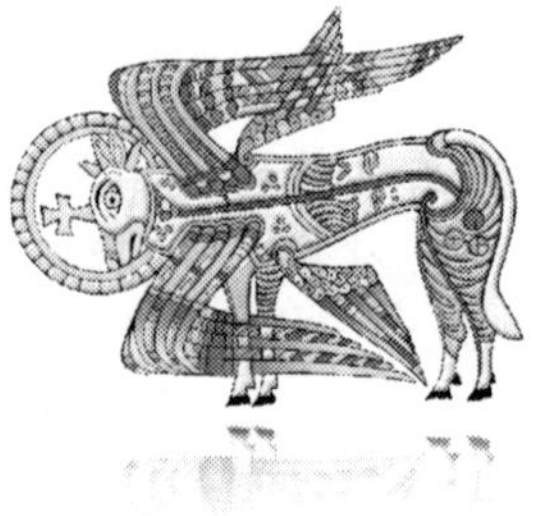

Portia

Am I your self
But as it were in sort or limitation,
To keep with you at meals, comfort your bed
And talk to you sometimes? Dwell I but in the suburbs
Of your good pleasure? If it be no more,
Portia is Brutus' harlot, not his wife.

***Julius Caesar* 2.1.281-86**

Portia says this to her husband Brutus when she finds him awake and alone one night. Brutus is preparing himself for the assassination of Caesar that day. However, he tells her only that he is up because he is sick. Portia doesn't believe him.

____

____

____

____

____

____

Portia: *Am I your other half for limited periods of time to keep you company at meals and in bed and to converse with you only on occasion? Do I inhabit only the outlying reaches of your thoughts and desires? If this is the case, Portia is Brutus' whore, not his wife.*

Irony of Good Fortune

OCTOBER 13

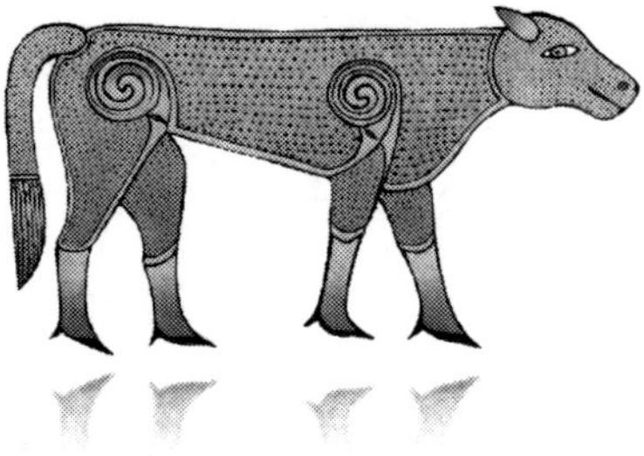

King

[Fortune] either gives a stomach, and no food -
Such are the poor, in health; or else a feast
And takes away the stomach - such are the rich
That have abundance and enjoy it not.

***King Henry IV, Part 2* 4.4.105-08**

Hearing news that the rebels Mowbray, Scroop, and Hastings have been executed and that Northumberland's rebellion has been defeated, the dying King Henry IV suddenly feels ill.

King: *Fortune either gives a hearty appetite but no daily provisions, for example, to the penniless who are not ill or else dangles a feast in front of the rich who already have plenty but cannot enjoy the meal.*

Reconciliation

OCTOBER 14

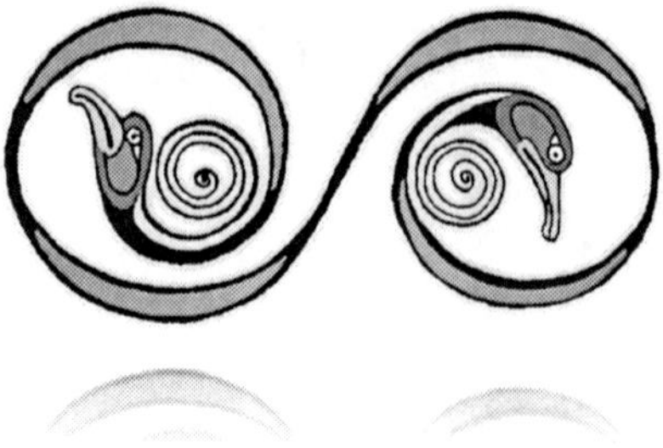

Lear

Come, let's away to prison;
We two alone will sing like birds i'the cage.
When thou dost ask me blessing I'll kneel down
And ask of thee forgiveness.

King Lear 5.3.8-11

Captured as a prisoner of war by his own family members, King Lear is united with his daughter Cordelia who is also a prisoner of war.

Lear: *Come, let's go to prison. We two will sing by ourselves like caged birds. When you ask me to bless you, I'll fall on my knees and beg for your pardon.*

Mercy

OCTOBER 15

Portia
And earthly power doth then show likest God's
When mercy seasons justice. . . .
The Merchant of Venice 4.1.194-95

Still trying to persuade the moneylender Shylock to be merciful to the merchant Antonio who has forfeited his bond to Shylock, Portia (who is disguised a a doctor of law) elaborates on the nature of mercy.

Portia: *Human power is closest to divine power when compassion tempers strict judgment.*

Traveling at the Speed of Thought

OCTOBER 16

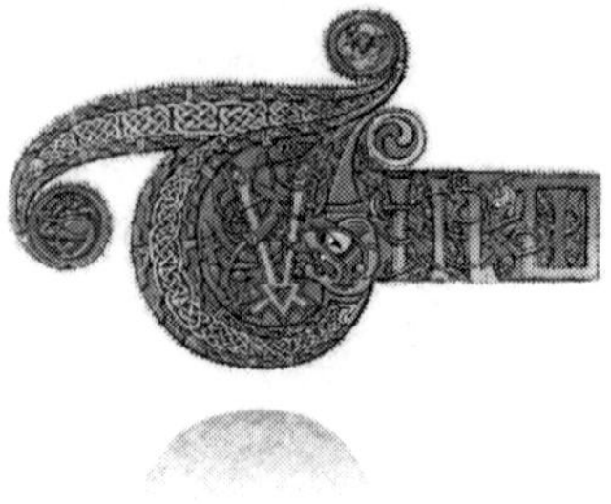

Ariel
I drink the air before me and return
Or ere your pulse twice beat.

The Tempest 5.1.102-103

Prospero, the dispossessed Duke of Milan, commands the spirit Ariel to awaken members of a shipwrecked boat and bring them to Prospero. Ariel responds.

Ariel: *I will inhale the wind in front of me and be back here before your heart strikes two beats.*

Impermanence

OCTOBER 17

Gloucester
O ruined piece of nature, this great world
Shall so wear out to naught.

King Lear 4.6.130-31

Gloucester says this to the mad King Lear who is running around on the heath wearing not much more than a crown of wild flowers.

***Gloucester:** Oh, destroyed specimen of nature! This vast world will deteriorate into ruin, just as you have.*

Lingering Stain of Betrayal

OCTOBER 18

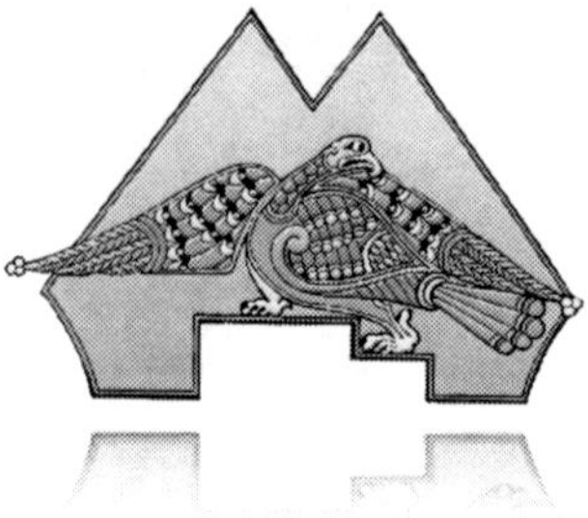

Worchester

For treason is but trusted like the fox,
Who, never so tame, so cherish'd and lock'd up,
Will have a wild trick of his ancestors.

King Henry IV, Part 1 5.2.9-11

Worchester says this to Vernon after the two rebels have just returned from a negotiating session with King Henry and Prince Hal. Henry has offered to forgive all the rebels if they surrender. However, Worchester argues that they must not even communicate the King's peace offer to Hotspur since the rebels will never be free from suspicion.

Worchester: *The person who commits treason is only believed as far as the fox is: however domesticated the fox is, however kindly he is cared for and securely kept under lock and key, he will nonetheless still possess the fierce traits of his ancestors.*

Experience Beyond Words

OCTOBER 19

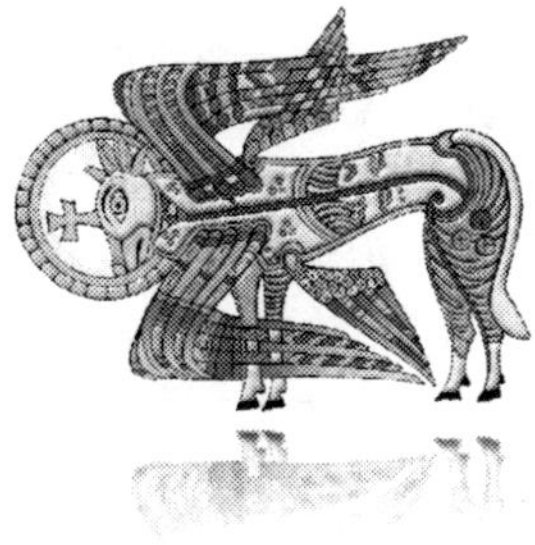

3 Gentleman

Did you see the meeting of the
two kings?. . .
Then you have lost a sight which was to
be seen, cannot be spoken of.

***The Winter's Tale* 5.2.40-41; 43-44**

A Gentleman in Leontes' court is narrating the profound joy that occurs when Leontes is reunited with his long estranged friend Polixenes. Polixenes reveals to Leontes that his daughter Perdita, who was thought dead, is alive.

____

____

____

____

____

____

3 Gentleman: *Did you see the two Kings reunited? Then you have missed a sight which had to have been witnessed and which cannot adequately be reported.*

Friendship

OCTOBER 20

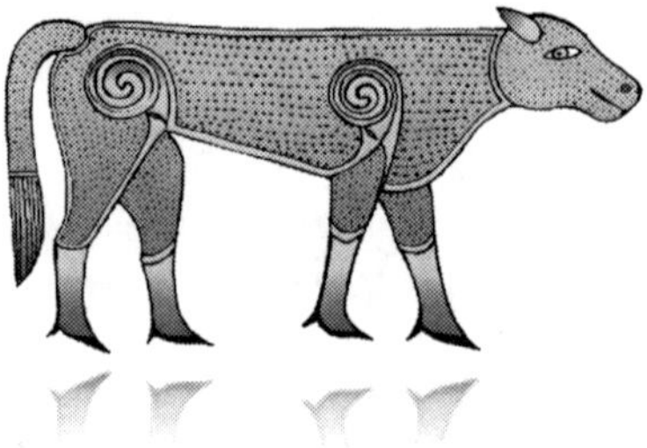

Helena

So we grew together,
Like to a double cherry, seeming parted,
But yet an union in partition,
Two lovely berries moulded on one stem. . . .

A Midsummer Night's Dream 3.2.208-11

Thinking that Hermia is mocking Helena's unrequited love of Demetrius, Helena reminds Hermia of their childhood bonds.

Helena: *Thus we grew up together like a double cherry that appears to be separate yet is one whole, albeit divided. We were like two beautiful berries formed on a single stem.*

Unworthiness in Love

OCTOBER 21

Sonnet 87

Farewell, thou art too dear for my possessing,
And like enough thou know'st thy estimate. . . .
For how do I hold thee but by thy granting,
And for that riches where is my deserving?
The cause of this fair gift in me is wanting,
And so my patent back again is swerving.

Lines 1-2, 5-8

Sonnet 87: *Goodbye. You are too precious for me to have, and you probably know your own worth. Only by your consent do I have any claim to you. But how have I merited such a treasure? I lack any justification for your gift of love, so my right to your love reverts back to your hands.*

Curse

OCTOBER 22

Caliban

As wicked dew as ere my mother brushed
With raven's feather from unwholesome fen
Drop on you both. A southwest blow on ye
And blister you all o'er.

***The Tempest* 1.2.322-25**

Caliban, the son of the witch Sycorax, says this to Prospero, the deposed Duke of Milan, who has enslaved Caliban after Caliban tries to assault Prospero's daughter Miranda.

Caliban: *On both of you may dewdrops fall that are as poisonous as any my mother ever scooped up from a decaying marsh, using the feather of a raven. May a fierce southwest wind blast you and whip you from head to foot.*

Power of Brevity

OCTOBER 23

Gaunt

Where words are scarce they are seldom spent in vain. . . .

King Richard II 2.1.7

The dying Gaunt says this to his brother Duke of York as Gaunt expresses his wish to give final advice to his irresponsible nephew, King Richard II.

Gaunt: *When a person utters only a few words, they are rarely wasted.*

Biting Words

OCTOBER 24

Benedick

She speaks poniards, and every word stabs: if her breath were as terrible as her terminations, there were no living near her, she would infect to the North Star.

Much Ado About Nothing 2.1.232-35

Benedick says this about Beatrice, the woman he loves to hate. At a masked ball, Benedick pretends to be someone else and reports to Beatrice that some unnamed person has accused her of being scornful and of having worn-out wit. Beatrice gets even by referring to Benedick as the prince's jester.

Benedick: *She talks as if she were hurling daggers, and every word stabs. If her breath were as terrible as her words, it would be impossible to live around her because she would poison the entire universe.*

Inspiration of Children

OCTOBER 25

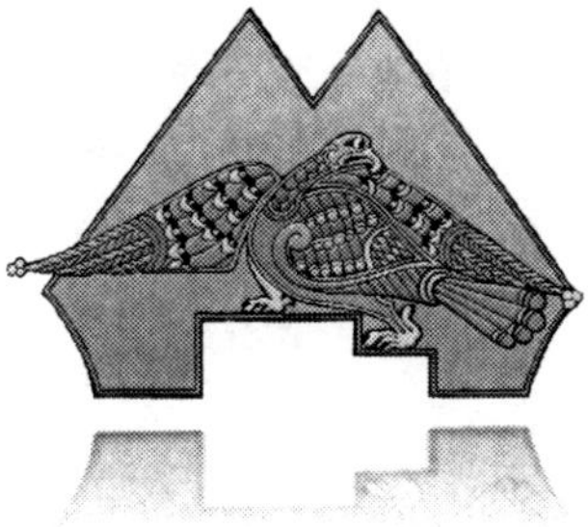

Prospero

O, cherubin
Thou wast that did preserve me. Thou didst smile,
Infused with a fortitude from heaven,
When I have decked the sea with drops full salt. . . .

The Tempest 1.2.152-55

Prospero says this to his daughter Miranda after he tells her for the first time about the dangerous journey the two of them were forced to take aboard a ship unfit to be on the seas when she was a babe.

Prospero: *Oh! You were an angel that kept me alive. You smiled, inspired by a heavenly strength, when I covered the ocean with my salty tears.*

Manufacturing Courage

OCTOBER 26

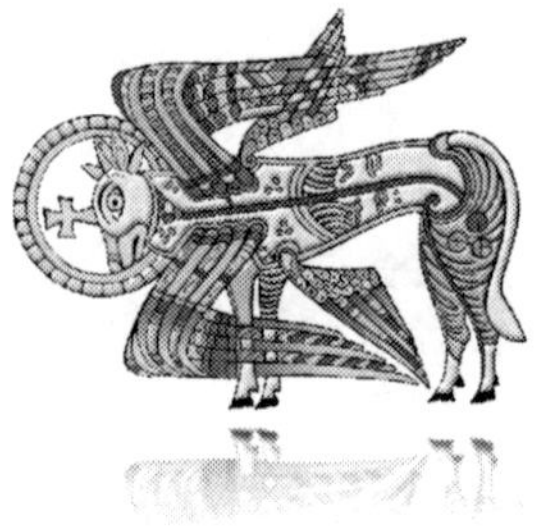

Hotspur

Let them come!
They come like sacrifices in their trim,
And to the fire-ey'd maid of smoky war
All hot and bleeding will we offer them:
The mailed Mars shall on his altar sit
Up to the ears in blood.

King Henry IV, Part 1 4.1.112-17

Hotspur says this to one of his rebel troops, Sir Richard Vernon, who has just delivered an epic-like tribute about the transformed Prince Hal and his fully bedecked soldiers heading towards the Battle of Shrewsbury. Admitting that Vernon's praise makes him sick, Hotspur nonetheless tries to pump up his courage with brazen predictions.

Hotspur: *Let them advance! They approach like sacrificial offerings in all their fine attire, and we will offer them up, sweaty and bloody, to the glowing-eyed goddess of grimy war. Mars in his chain mail will preside on his altar--in blood up to his ears.*

Ephemeral Nature of Power

OCTOBER 27

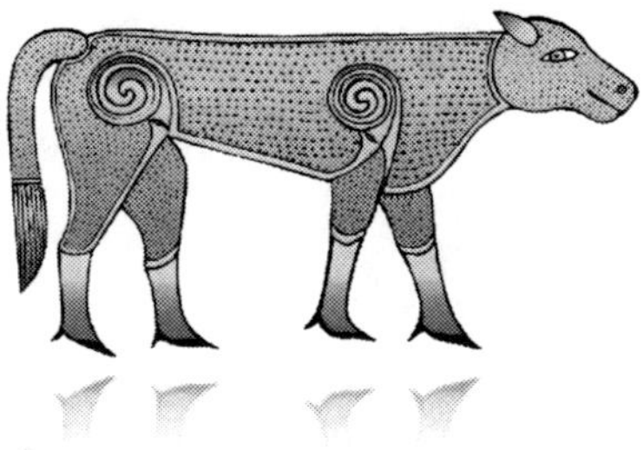

Antony
O mighty Caesar! Dost thou lie so low?
Are all thy conquests, glories, triumphs, spoils,
Shrunk to this little measure?

Julius Caesar 3.1.148-50

Although Antony will later seize the opportunity of Caesar's death to launch himself into power, here Antony comes upon the dead Caesar for the first time and is genuinely overcome with sorrow. Antony addresses Caesar's body which is virtually perforated with stab wounds.

Antony: *Oh all-powerful Caesar, have you fallen so far from your former glory? Are all your military victories, honors, great achievements, and captured plunder reduced to this minuscule quantity?*

Emptiness of False Praise

OCTOBER 28

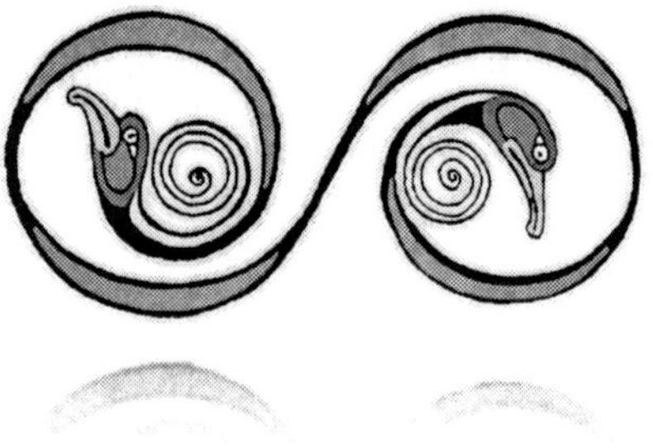

Horatio
His purse is empty already, all's golden words
are spent.

Hamlet 5.2.132-33

Horatio says this about the courtier Osric who is tripping over himself with strained politeness and inflated verbage while praising Laertes' skill and character. Osric has been sent by the King to persuade Hamlet, Prince of Denmark, to engage in a duel with Laertes.

Horatio: *Osric's wallet is already bare. All the golden coins of his vocabulary have been squandered.*

Cultivating Duplicity

OCTOBER 29

Lady Macbeth

To beguile the time,
Look like the time; bear welcome in your eye,
Your hand, your tongue: look like th'innocent flower,
But be the serpent under't.

Macbeth 1.5.62-65

Lady Macbeth says this to her husband who has just announced that King Duncan will be arriving at their castle that day. Lady Macbeth has just read her husband's letter detailing the two prophecies of the witches, including the final one that states that Macbeth shall be king. Lady Macbeth advises her husband to seize the opportunity of the King's arrival to dispatch Duncan.

Lady Macbeth: *In order to deceive the world, act as people in society do: convey openness and warmth in your eyes, your speech, and your gesture. Appear like a pure blossom but underneath be cunning and treacherous like a snake.*

On Destiny

OCTOBER 30

Hamlet

My fate cries out
And makes each petty artire in this body
As hardy as the Nemean lion's nerve.

Hamlet 1.4.81-83

Hamlet says this to Horatio when the ghost of King Hamlet beckons the Prince to follow. Horatio tries to plead with Hamlet not to follow the apparition and possibly court disaster.

Hamlet: *My fate beckons me and makes every fiber in my nervous system as taut as the nerves of the fearless lion Nemea [which Hercules slew as one of his twelve labors].*

Spine-tingling Moments

OCTOBER 31

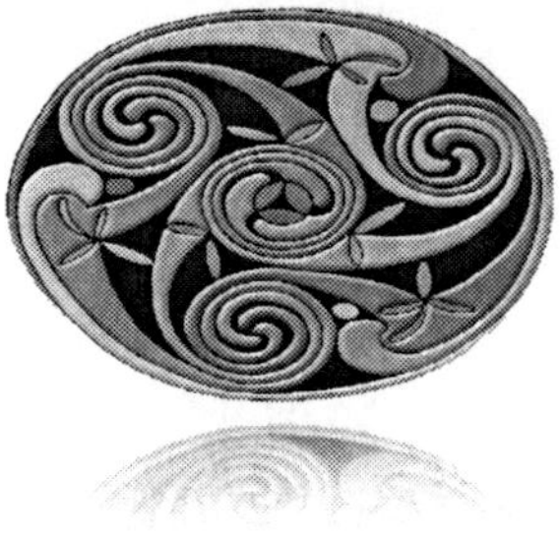

Hamlet
'Tis now the very witching time of night,
When churchyards yawn and hell itself breathes out
Contagion to this world.

Hamlet 3.2.390-92

Prince Hamlet, alone late at night, says this as he contemplates going to see his mother Gertrude in her chamber. Queen Gertrude has summoned him to see her after witnessing the play-within-the-play that has shocked Claudius into abruptly leaving the theatre. Hamlet, who has deliberately altered the play, is convinced that Claudius' actions prove that the King is guilty of Hamlet's father's death.

***Hamlet:** It is now the time of night when the supernatural prevails, when graveyards open wide, and when hell itself exhales pestilence into the world.*

Prayer

NOVEMBER 1

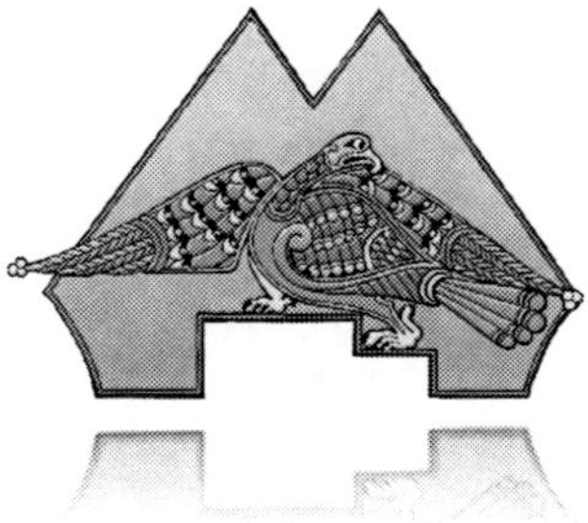

Horatio

Good night, sweet prince,
And flights of angels sing thee to thy rest.

Hamlet 5.2.365-66

Just after Hamlet, Prince of Denmark, dies from the poison-tipped sword in his duel with Laertes, the faithful Horatio blesses the passage of his dear friend's soul into heaven.

Horatio: *Farewell, gentle sovereign, may entire flocks of ministering spirits accompany you with song to your final resting place.*

Lovers' Battles of Wit

NOVEMBER 2

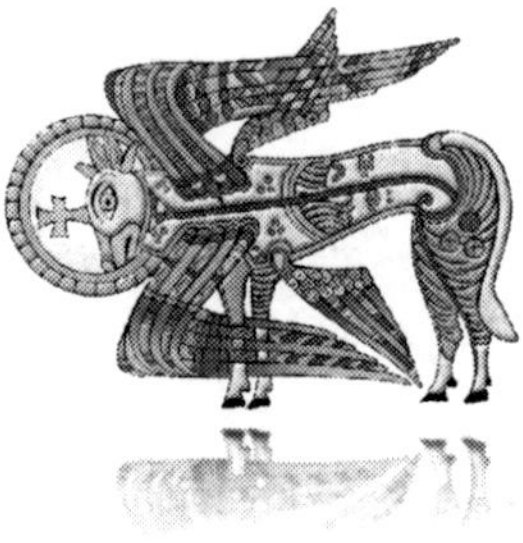

Beatrice
Thou and I are too wise to woo peaceably.
Benedick
It appears not in this confession; there's not
one wise man among twenty that will praise himself.
Much Ado About Nothing 5.2.69-71

Benedick says this to his beloved Beatrice as the two of them try to express their love for one another but keep getting sidetracked into battles of wit. When Beatrice tries to make a serious comment, Benedick fires back.

Beatrice: *You and I are too sophisticated to court without quarreling.*
Benedick: *Your statement doesn't indicate such wisdom: you can't find one wise person in a group of twenty who will dare to engage in self-praise.*

Incomprehension

NOVEMBER 3

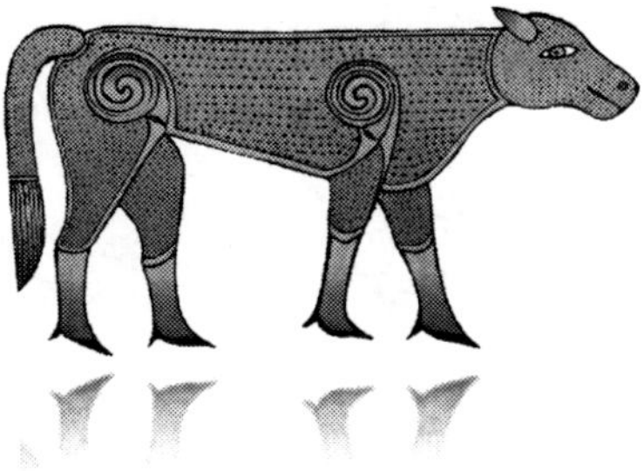

Casca

those that understood him, smiled at one another, and shook their heads; but for mine own part, it was Greek to me.

Julius Caesar 1.2.281-83

Speaking disdainfully about the crowd's adulation when the politic Caesar three times refuses the crown, Casca reports that Cicero also spoke on this occasion--but in Greek.

Casca: *Crowd members who could comprehend Cicero's language grinned and nodded at each other. As far as I'm concerned, however, his speech was simply an unintelligible foreign language.*

Love of Honor

NOVEMBER 4

Brutus
What is it that you would impart to me?
If it be aught toward the general good,
Set honour in one eye, and death i'th' other,
And I will look on both indifferently.
For let the gods so speed me as I love
The name of honour more than I fear death.

Julius Caesar 1.2.84-89

Brutus says this as Cassius plies Brutus with compliments in an effort to win him over to Cassius' plot to assassinate Caesar. Brutus sees through Cassius' ploy.

____

____

____

____

____

____

Brutus: *What is it you want to tell me? If it is for the good of the whole commonwealth, then, if both honor and death are placed within my view, I will look upon both impartially. Let the gods advance me only so far as I love an honorable reputation more than I fear death.*

Accepting Death

NOVEMBER 5

Edgar
What, in ill thoughts again? Men must endure
Their going hence even as their coming hither.
Ripeness is all.

King Lear 5.2.9-11

The disguised Edgar says this to his blind father, Gloucester. Edgar has just told his father that King Lear and his daughter Cordelia have been taken prisoner by English forces commanded by Lear's vicious daughters. Gloucester expresses his despair.

Edgar: *Are you engulfed in gloomy melancholy again? Human beings must accept their death just as they accept their birth. Readiness is everything.*

Love's Extremes

NOVEMBER 6

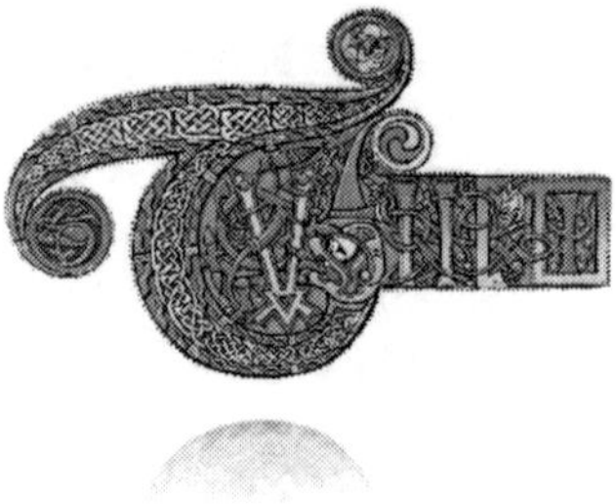

Sonnet 88

And I by this will be a gainer too,
For bending all my loving thoughts on thee,
The injuries that to myself I do,
Doing thee vantage, double vantage me,
  Such is my love, to thee I so belong,
  That for thy right myself will bear all wrong.

Lines 9-14

____

____

____

____

____

____

Sonnet 88: *When I side with you in condemning my own faults (actual or nonexistent) and focus all my love on you, my devaluing of myself and honoring of your viewpoint actually bring me a double reward because they bring merit to you. My love for you makes me identify completely with you so that for your sake I will accept all blame.*

Curse

NOVEMBER 7

Caliban
The dropsy drown this fool!

The Tempest 4.1.231

On his way to attempt to assassinate Prospero, the deposed Duke of Milan exiled on this island, the jester Trinculo spots some sparkling clothing that is really only an apparition created by the spirit Ariel to distract the rebels from their task. The mastermind of this operation, Caliban, the son of the witch Sycorax, is angry with Trinculo for straying from Caliban's designated mission.

Caliban: *May excessive fluid in his lungs choke this idiot!*

Self-examination

NOVEMBER 8

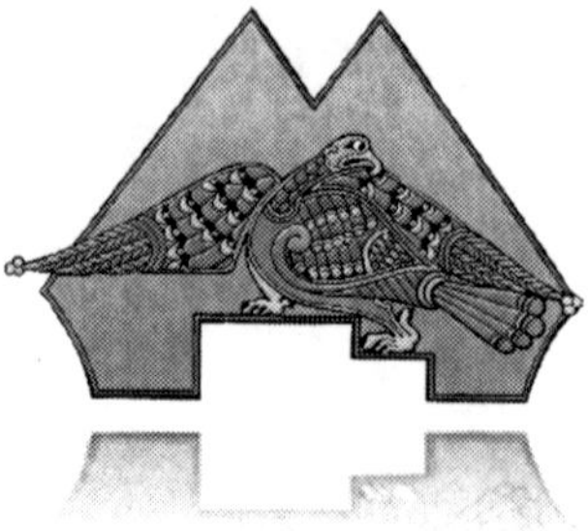

Lear

Let the great gods
That keep this dreadful pudder o'er our heads
Find out their enemies now. . . . I am a man
More sinned against than sinning.

King Lear 3.2.49-51; 59-60

Insulted and enraged by his daughters' treatment of him, King Lear is wandering mad on the heath in the midst of a dreadful storm. Slipping in and out of sanity, Lear says this as he imagines that the raging thunderstorm is actually the gods overhead summoning those guilty of hidden crimes.

Lear: *May the gods on high who hold this frightful commotion above us discover their true enemies immediately! I am a person more wronged than guilty of wronging others.*

Valuing What We Have Lost

NOVEMBER 9

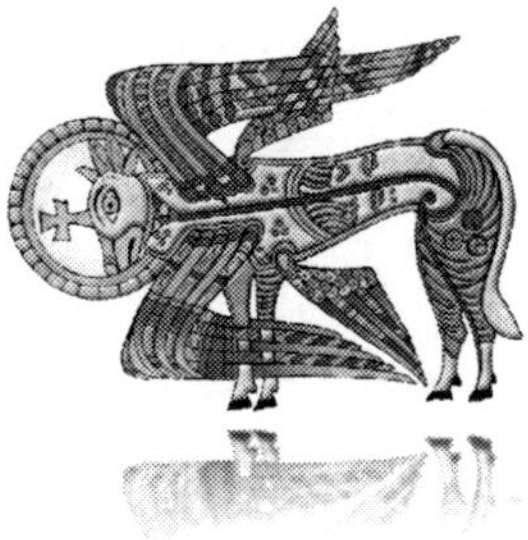

Friar

what we have we prize not to the worth
Whiles we enjoy it, but being lack'd and lost,
Why then we rack the value, then we find
The virtue that possession would not show us
Whiles it was ours. . . .

Much Ado About Nothing 4.1.217-21

On her wedding day Hero has unjustly been accused by her groom-to-be of repeatedly making love to another man. When Hero faints and is left alone with her father, with her friend Beatrice, and with Benedick, the Friar suggests that they report Hero's death so that her reputation may be restored in the eyes of society and of her fiancé.

Friar: *What we possess, we don't value according to its true worth while we have it. But when we lose something or are without it, then we stretch its worth and discover the true quality that we could not see when we had it.*

Inspiration

NOVEMBER 10

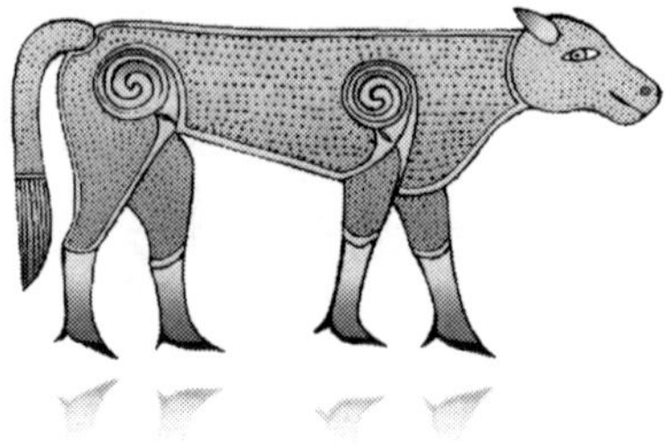

Chorus
O for a muse of fire, that would ascend
The brightest heaven of invention,
A kingdom for a stage, princes to act,
And monarchs to behold the swelling scene!

King Henry V 1.Prologue.1-4

The Chorus that opens the play asks for the most brilliant production possible to present the tale of one of England's greatest kings, Henry V, and one of England's greatest battles in the war against the French, the Battle of Agincourt.

Chorus: *Oh, I wish that there were a goddess of inspiration that could reach the very top of the heavens with her creative imagination. I wish the entire length of the realm could serve as the acting area, that princes could be the actors, and that kings and queens themselves could observe this captivating, grand performance.*

Steadfast in Purpose

NOVEMBER 11

King
We are but warriors for the working-day;
Our gayness and our gilt are all besmirched
With rainy marching in the painful field. . . .
But by the mass, our hearts are in the trim. . . .

***King Henry V* 4.3.109-111; 115**

King Henry says this to Montjoy, the French herald, just before the Battle of Agincourt. Montjoy has come, for the last time, to ask King Henry to ransom himself before what the French mistakenly believe will be the English army's inevitable defeat. Henry responds.

King Henry V: *We (the English) are only soldiers for the work week. Our bright spirits and our dazzling attire are soiled by laborious progress through the rain over difficult fields. But, by God, our hearts are exquisitely adorned!*

Seizing the Moment

NOVEMBER 12

Prospero
I find my zenith doth depend upon
A most auspicious star, whose influence
If now I court not, but omit, my fortunes
Will ever after droop.

The Tempest 1.2.181-84

Prospero, the deposed Duke of Milan, says this to his daughter Miranda as he explains to her why he has raised a storm to detain his enemies, who have been brought by chance to the shore of the island on which he and Miranda live.

Prospero: *Attaining the peak of my fortunes now rests on a highly favorable star whose influence I must presently woo. If I don't, my destiny will forever decline.*

Shared Humanity

NOVEMBER 13

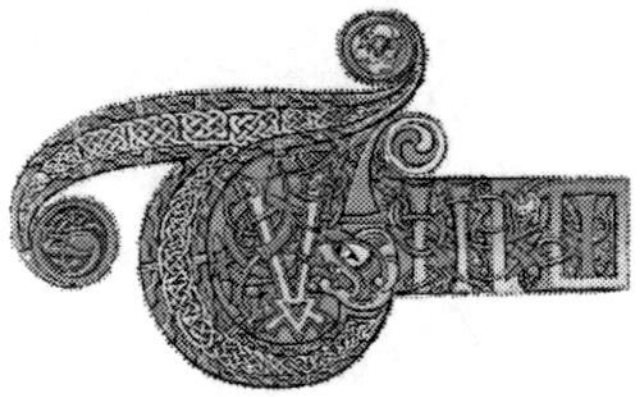

Shylock

I am a Jew. Hath not a Jew eyes?
hath not a Jew hands, organs, dimensions, senses,
affections, passions? fed with the same food, hurt with
the same weapons, subject to the same diseases, healed
by the same means, warmed and cooled by the same
winter and summer as a Christian is?

The Merchant of Venice 3.1.54-59

The merchant Shylock says this to Salerio and Solano, who have come to ask Shylock what news he hears of late about the fortune of ships on the sea. Salerio and Solanio have also come to taunt Shylock, who is Jewish, about the loss of his daughter Jessica who has run away to marry a Christian.

Shylock: *I am a Jew. Doesn't a Jew have eyes, hands, organs, proportions, perceptions, emotions, desires? Isn't a Jew nourished by the same types of food, injured by the same kinds of weapons, heated and chilled by the same seasons of winter and summer as a Christian is?*

Untrustworthy Individuals

NOVEMBER 14

Richard
The love of wicked men converts to fear,
That fear to hate, and hate turns one or both
To worthy danger and deserved death.

King Richard II 5.1.66-68

The deposed King Richard says this to Northumberland, the nobleman to whom Richard refers as the ladder by which the ambitious Henry Bolingbroke ascended the throne of England as Henry IV. Richard warns Northumberland that because he helped unseat one rightful King, the new King Henry may soon suspect Northumberland of repeating his betrayal.

Richard: *The affection of corrupt individuals easily transforms into distrust and then to hatred. Then either of these states mutates into life-threatening risk and death, which are well-deserved (by those who fawned over the usurping ruler).*

Experience of Chaos

NOVEMBER 15

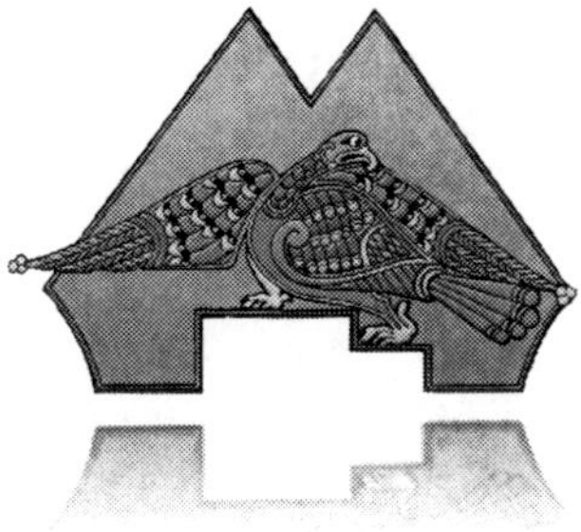

Ariel

'Hell is empty,
And all the devils are here'.

The Tempest 1.2.214-15

The spirit Ariel tells Prospero that Ferdinand, the son of the King of Naples, shouts this in the midst of the terrible storm that Prospero has manufactured as an illusion in order to take revenge against his enemies.

Ariel: *"Hell is vacant. Every last devil inhabits this place."*

Power of Illusion

NOVEMBER 16

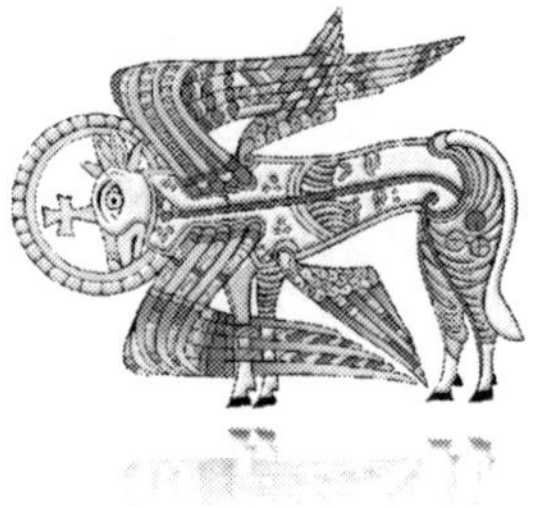

Hamlet

The play's the thing
Wherein I'll catch the conscience of the King.

Hamlet 2.2.606-07

Having just greeted a troupe of traveling actors, Prince Hamlet hatches a plan to use their dramatic performance as a means to test whether or not his uncle, King Claudius, is guilty of Hamlet's father's murder.

Hamlet: *The play is the means by which I'll trap the guilt of the King.*

Submissiveness and Tyranny

NOVEMBER 17

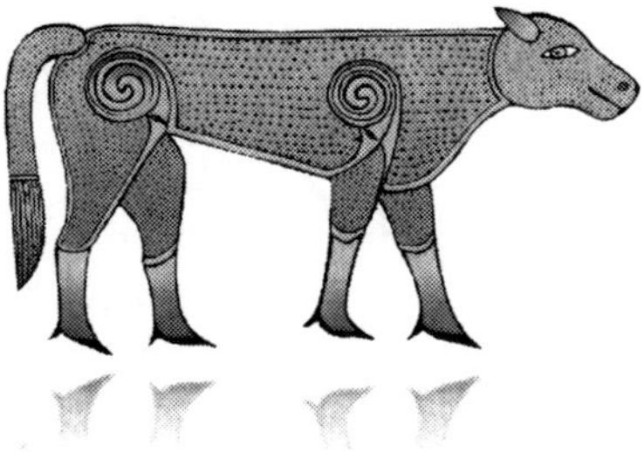

Cassius
Why, man, he doth bestride the narrow world
Like a colossus, and we petty men
Walk under his huge legs and peep about
To find ourselves dishonourable graves.

Julius Caesar 1.2.134-37

Cassius says this to Brutus when they hear a shout offstage, signaling that the citizens want to proclaim Caesar as King. Upset by the news, Cassius responds.

Cassius: *Look it, man, Caesar towers over the tiny world like the statue of Apollo astride the entrance to the harbor at Rhodes. We puny individuals slink under his massive legs and skulk around to find ourselves an ignominious place to die.*

Effective Threats

NOVEMBER 18

Prospero

If thou more murmur'st, I will rend an oak
And peg thee in his knotty entrails till
Thou hast howled away twelve winters.

The Tempest 1.2.294-96

Prospero says this to the spirit Ariel who was once confined to a pine tree by the curse that Sycorax, the witch, laid upon Ariel. Now in service to Prospero, Ariel wants complete freedom and reminds Prospero of this fact.

Prospero: *If you so much as open your mouth, I will rip an oak tree to pieces and pound you into the gnarled insides until you have screamed your lungs out for twelve years.*

Meeting Fate

NOVEMBER 19

King
The sum of all our answer is but this:
We would not seek a battle as we are,
Nor as we are, we say, we will not shun it:
So tell your master.

King Henry V 3.6.164-67

King Henry says this to the French herald Montjoy who, because the French outnumber the English twenty to one, has come to ask Henry to name a ransom price in lieu of going ahead with the battle against the French. Henry refuses this proposal.

King Henry V: *The sum total of our response is simply this: we would not look for a battle in our present beleaguered condition. On the other hand, being who we are, we tell you, we will not shrink from it. Communicate this to your sovereign.*

Harmony in Music and Love

NOVEMBER 20

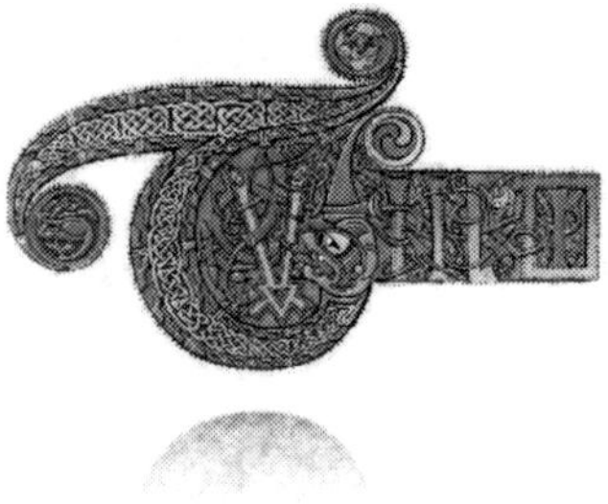

Sonnet 8

Mark how one string, sweet husband to another,
Strikes each in each by mutual ordering,
Resembling sire, and child, and happy mother,
Who all in one, one pleasing note do sing. . . .

Lines 9-12

Sonnet 8: *Notice the way that one string of a lute tuned to another causes the other to vibrate. In this way, the strings imitate a father, a child, and a delighted mother who, united as one family, produce a single harmonious note.*

Anguish of Leadership

NOVEMBER 21

King
What kind of god art thou that suffer'st more
Of mortal griefs than do thy worshippers?

King Henry V 4.1.237-38

Disguised and walking alone through the English camp the night before a hugely important battle with the French at Agincourt, King Henry tries to discern his men's true state of mind as they face this horrendous battle. Henry also laments his dual nature as both a vulnerable mortal and a representative of God in his role as King of England.

King Henry V: *What sort of divine creature am I that endures more of the sufferings of being human than do those individuals who bow down to me?*

Cowardice and Courage

NOVEMBER 22

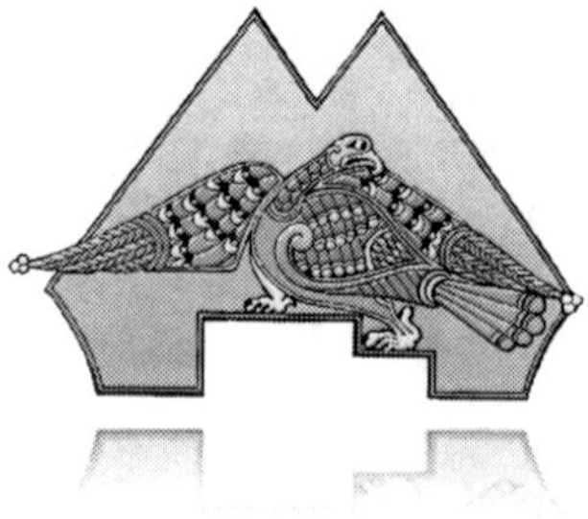

Caesar
Cowards die many times before their deaths;
The valiant never taste of death but once.

Julius Caesar 2.2.32-33

Caesar says this to his wife Calphurnia who, fearing for her husband's life, is trying to persuade him not to go to the Capitol that day because of the horrendous natural portents reported all around Rome. Calphurnia reminds Caesar that no comets appear when a lowly person dies, but the heavens themselves shout the death of a leader.

Caesar: *Those who lack courage give up their lives over and over before they actually perish. The courageous die only once.*

Healing Oneself

NOVEMBER 23

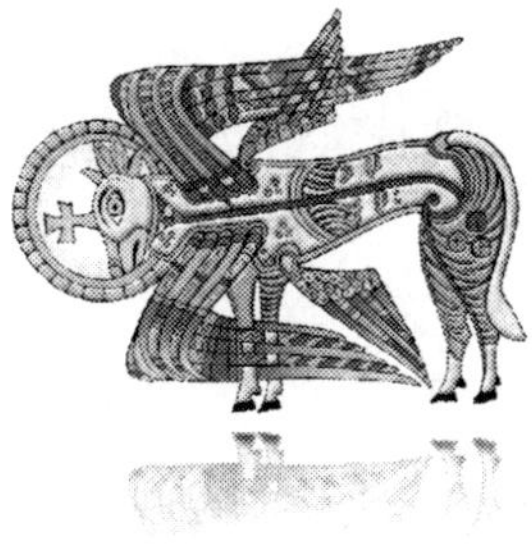

Macbeth
Canst thou not minister to a mind diseas'd,
Pluck from the memory a rooted sorrow,
Raze out the written troubles of the brain,
And with some sweet oblivious antidote
Cleanse the stuff 'd bosom of that perilous stuff
Which weighs upon the heart?
Doctor
Therein the patient
Must minister to himself.

Macbeth 5.3.40-46

While Macbeth is arming for battle, the Doctor observes Lady Macbeth sleepwalking and enacting her guilty ritual of washing her hands of blood. When the Doctor says it is her own disturbed fantasies that keep her from sleeping, Macbeth responds.

____

____

____

____

____

____

Macbeth: *Can you not apply remedies to a sick mind, remove from memory a deeply ingrained suffering, erase difficulties recorded there, and with a pleasing, mindnumbing medicine rinse clean the overcharged thoughts and feelings of the dangerous matter that burdens her heart?*
Doctor: *In such a case the patient must doctor herself.*

Inner Music

NOVEMBER 24

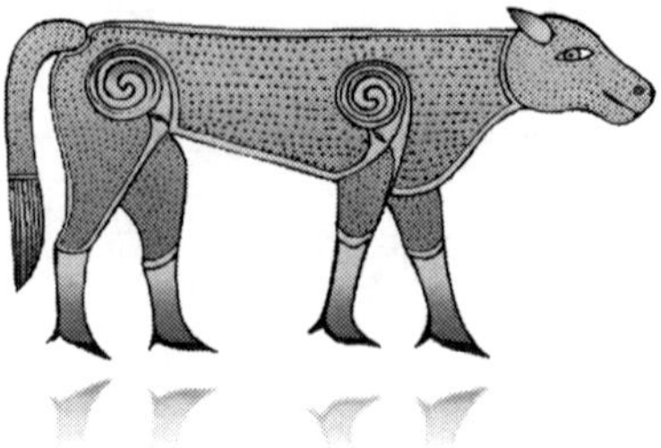

Lorenzo
The man that hath no music in himself,
Nor is not moved with concord of sweet sounds,
Is fit for treasons, strategems, and spoils,
The motions of his spirit are dull as night,
And his affections dark as Erebus:
Let no such man be trusted. . . .

The Merchant of Venice 5.1.83-88

When his wife Jessica remarks that music makes her sad, the newly wed Lorenzo observes the cause of his wife's intense spirit. Lesser mortals, he says, are not thus affected. He goes on to elaborate.

____

____

____

____

____

____

Lorenzo: *The person whose soul does not contain music and is not deeply touched by the agreeable nature of its harmony is suited only for treachery, violent acts, and brutal plundering. The life force of such an individual is as gloomy as night, and this person's emotions are as black as the underground passageway to Hades.*

Pandora's Box

NOVEMBER 25

Portia

How all the other passions fleet to air:
As doubtful thoughts, and rash-embrac'd despair,
And shudd'ring fear, and green-eyed jealousy.

The Merchant of Venice 3.2.108-10

Portia says this as Bassanio, the man who has captured her heart, is about to choose among three caskets for Portia's hand in marriage. Only one contains Portia's portrait, and any suitor who fails to pick the correct casket must leave and promise never to marry.

***Portia:** Isn't it amazing that all of these other feelings besides love escape into the air, such as suspicious thoughts, hastily-adopted despair, trembling fear, and fierce possessiveness!*

Self-disgust

NOVEMBER 26

Hamlet

Why, what an ass am I! This is most brave,
That I, the son of a dear father murder'd,
Prompted to my revenge by heaven and hell,
Must like a whore unpack my heart with words
And fall a-cursing like a very drab,
A scullion!

***Hamlet* 2.2.584-89**

Hamlet says this to himself after he has just witnessed a traveling actor exquisitely recite a speech describing the revenge killing of old King Priam as his desperate wife Hecuba watched. Prince Hamlet lacerates himself for his failure to avenge his own father's murder.

Hamlet: *What a jackass I am! This is a fine show that I, a son whose precious father has been murdered, who has been spurred by rightful justice and by hellish hatred, must bare my soul like a harlot and resort to cussing like a prostitute or a kitchen maid.*

Desire as Impetuous

NOVEMBER 27

Portia

I can easier teach twenty what were good to be done, than be one of the twenty to follow mine own teaching: the brain may devise laws for the blood, but a hot temper leaps o'er a cold decree. . . .

The Merchant of Venice 1.2.15-19

Waiting nervously for suitors to arrive to seek her hand in marriage according to a system of chance set up by her dead father, Portia exchanges banter with her waiting woman, Nerissa.

Portia: *I can more readily tell twenty people what ought to be done than be one of those to follow what I say. Reason may invent commands to govern feeling, but fiery passion simply jumps over the hurdle of an abstract edict.*

Nature's Tempest

NOVEMBER 28

Miranda
The sky, it seems, would pour down stinking pitch
But that the sea, mounting to th' welkin's cheek,
Dashes the fire out.

The Tempest 1.2.3-5

Having been betrayed by his brother Antonio who is the usurping Duke of Milan, Prospero, the deposed Duke, creates a storm to lure the right people to his island in order to work out the details of his revenge plot. His innocent daughter Miranda, completely unaware of her father's past beyond their life together on the island, believes the storm is real.

Miranda: *The heavens would toss down boiling tar, or so it seems, except that the ocean, rising as high as the cloud's cheek, drowns out the fire.*

Respecting Others

NOVEMBER 29

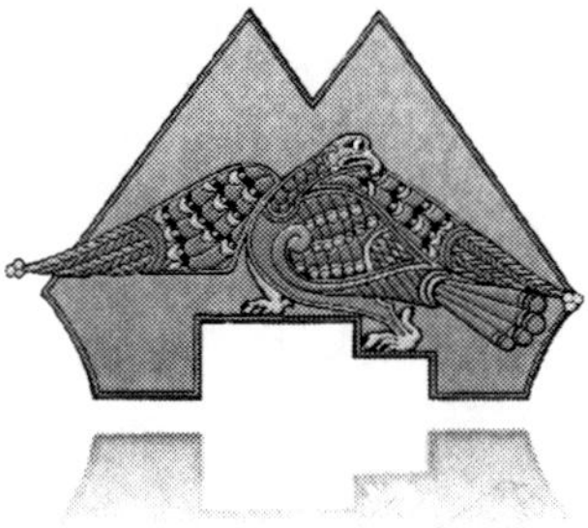

Hamlet

Good, my lord, will you see the players
well bestowed? . . . . Use every
man after his desert, and who shall scape whipping?
Use them after your own honour and dignity: the less
they deserve, the more merit is in your bounty.

Hamlet 2.2.523-24; 530-33

Just as the itinerant actors arrive at Elsinore, Prince Hamlet instructs Polonius to take care of them and gives Polonius a lecture on respect.

Hamlet: *My good man, will you see that the players are well taken care of? If you treat all people according to what they deserve, who among us will escape being punished? Treat them according to your own dignity and worth. The less honor they deserve, the more reward your goodness justifies.*

Irreverence Towards Death

NOVEMBER 30

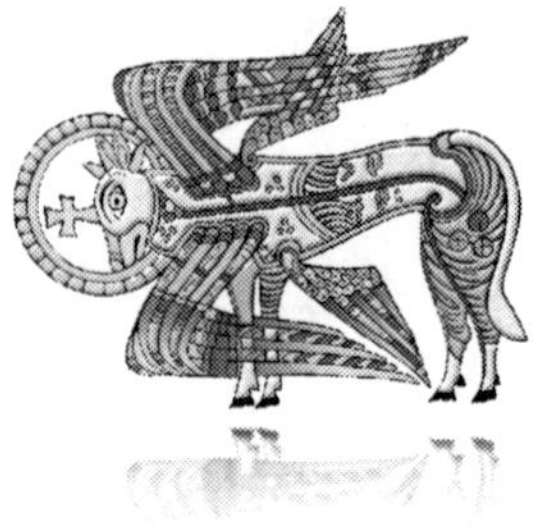

Hamlet

Did these bones cost no more the breeding but to play at loggets with 'em? Mine ache to think on't.

Hamlet 5.1.91-93

Hamlet says this to Horatio as the two watch the gravedigger merrily singing while tossing up skulls from the earth in the process of digging a new grave.

***Hamlet:** Did these bones require so little expense in their nurturing that it is acceptable to toss them around like sticks tossed at a stake in a game of loggets? My own body quivers just imagining this irreverence.*

Dawn's Herald

DECEMBER 1

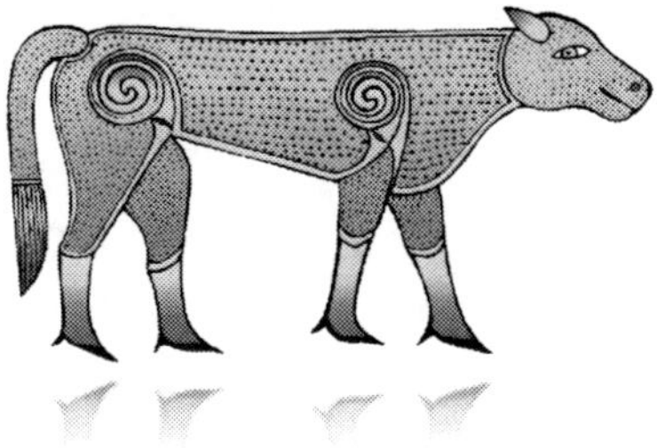

Horatio

I have heard
The cock, that is the trumpet to the morn,
Doth with his lofty and shrill-sounding throat
Awake the god of day, and at his warning,
Whether in sea or fire, in earth or air,
Th'extravagant and erring spirit hies
To his confine. . . .

Hamlet 1.1.154-60

Horatio, Hamlet's dear friend, recounts this tale to Marcellus and Barnardo, the soldiers of the watch, after the three of them have witnessed the appearance of King Hamlet's ghost.

Horatio: *I've been told that the rooster, herald to the morning, arouses the sun by means of his imposing, piercing cry. Hearing his alarm, whether dwelling in the ocean, in the air, on the ground, or even in fire, the wandering, vagrant ghost flees to its prison cell.*

Innocence

DECEMBER 2

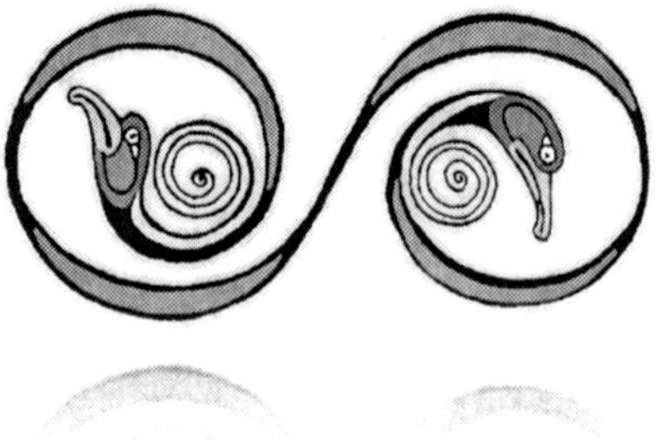

Miranda
There's nothing ill can dwell in such a temple.
If the ill spirit have so fair a house,
Good things will strive to dwell with't.

The Tempest 1.2.458-60

Trying to test the character of the man that Prospero has devised his daughter Miranda to fall in love with, Prospero is sharp with Ferdinand. Miranda defends him.

Miranda: *Nothing bad can live in such a divine house. If the devil's home were this beautiful, only virtuous creatures would want to live in it.*

Reunion

DECEMBER 3

Abbess
After so long grief, such felicity!

Comedy of Errors 5.1.407

The Abbess says this in the climactic reunion scene when, after thirty-three years have passed, husband and wife, twin sons, and twin servants are reunited by accident in Ephesus.

***Abbess:** After such prolonged sorrow, what happiness!*

Fragile Promises

DECEMBER 4

Queen
The lady doth protest too much, methinks.

Hamlet 3.2.232

Hamlet's mother, Gertrude, says this to Prince Hamlet when he asks her how she likes the play that the visiting actors are performing at Elsinore. The "lady" Gertrude refers to is the Player Queen who has just protested to her husband that if he should die before she does, she would mourn perpetually and never remarry. Gertrude, on the other hand, has just married her dead husband's brother.

Queen: *The lady promises too much, I believe.*

Newly Found Courage

DECEMBER 5

Stephano

Ha! I have not 'scaped drowning to be afeard now of
your four legs. . . .

The Tempest 2.2.59-60

The drunk sailor Stephano says this when he encounters what he believes to be a four-legged speaking creature lying on the ground, covered by a cloth. It is, in fact, two creatures: Caliban, the son of the witch Sycorax who is hiding on the ground, and the jester Trinculo who has hidden under Caliban's garments to take refuge from the storm, mistakenly believing that Caliban is dead.

***Stephano:** Oh, no! I haven't survived a shipwreck only to be terrified by a four-legged creature.*

Avoiding Awareness

DECEMBER 6

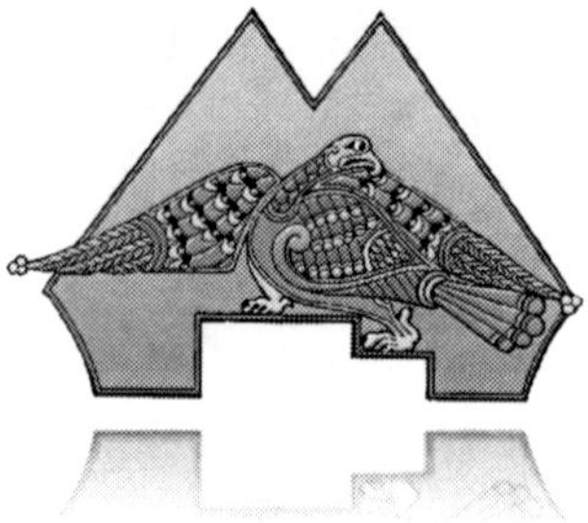

Macbeth
I am afraid to think what I have done;
Look on't again I dare not.

Macbeth 2.2.50-51

Macbeth reveals to his wife that he hears voices cry out "Sleep no more" after he has murdered King Duncan. Lady Macbeth tells her husband to go incriminate the grooms by smearing their hands with blood from the daggers that Macbeth has used to murder the King. Macbeth refuses.

***Macbeth:** Fear prevents me from contemplating my deed. I do not have the courage to examine it again.*

Respect for the Dead

DECEMBER 7

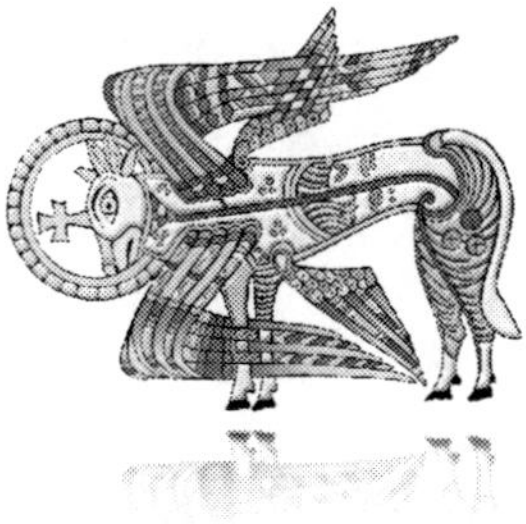

Montjoy
I come to thee for charitable licence
That we may wander o'er this bloody field
To look our dead and then to bury them. . . .

King Henry V 4.7.70-72

Montjoy, the gentle French herald, says this to King Henry after the Battle of Agincourt. In this battle the French outnumbered the English twenty to one but still faced a bloody defeat at the hands of the English.

Montjoy: *I came to ask your gracious permission to scour this bloodstained battlefield so that we may find our dead soldiers and bury them.*

World Weariness

DECEMBER 8

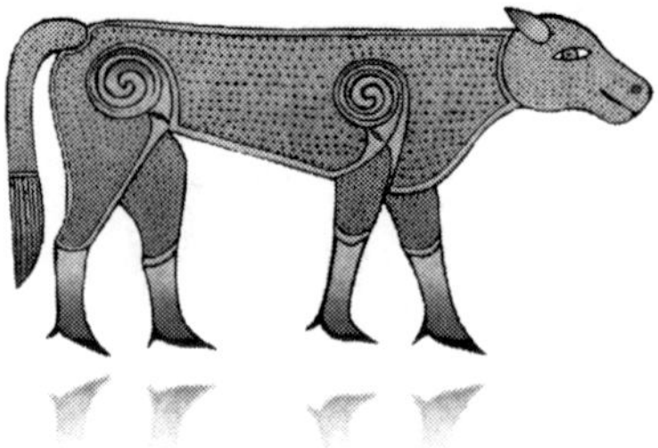

Hamlet

I have of late, but
wherefore I know not, lost all my mirth, forgone all
custom of exercises; and indeed it goes so heavily with
my disposition that this goodly frame the earth seems
to me a sterile promontory. . . .

***Hamlet* 2.2.297-301**

Hamlet, Prince of Denmark, says this to his childhood acquaintances, Rosencrantz and Guildenstern, who have been sent by the King and Queen to try to decipher the cause of Hamlet's recent melancholy.

____

____

____

____

____

____

Hamlet: *I don't understand why, but I have recently lost all my joy and even stopped exercising. Honestly, I am in such despair that this lovely structure, the earth, seems no more to me than a barren cliff.*

Rationalization

DECEMBER 9

Brutus

Let's be sacrificers but not butchers, Caius.
We all stand up against the spirit of Caesar,
And in the spirit of men there is no blood. . . .
Let's carve him as a dish fit for the gods,
Not hew him as a carcass fit for hounds.

Julius Caesar 2.1.165-67; 172-73

Brutus says this as he addresses the conspirators, trying to persuade them of the necessity to assassinate Julius Caesar.

Brutus: *Let us be celebrants of sacrifices but not slaughterers, Caius. We all rise up against the animating principle of Caesar, and such insubstantial matter contains no blood. Let us sculpt Caesar as a banquet meal worthy of the gods and not butcher him as if he were the remains of a dead animal to be tossed to the hounds.*

Asking Forgiveness

DECEMBER 10

Hamlet

Give me your pardon, sir. I have done you wrong. . . .
Let my disclaiming from a purpos'd evil
Free me so far in your most generous thoughts
That I have shot my arrow o'er the house
And hurt my brother.

Hamlet 5.2.225; 240-43

About to engage in a duel that will kill both of them, Hamlet apologizes to Laertes for accidentally killing his father Polonius.

Hamlet: *Please forgive me, sir. I have injured you. But forgive me, being the gentleman that you are. May my repudiation of any intended evil clear me from blame in your most magnanimous thoughts. For I have blindly shot an arrow and unintentionally injured my brother.*

Curse

DECEMBER 11

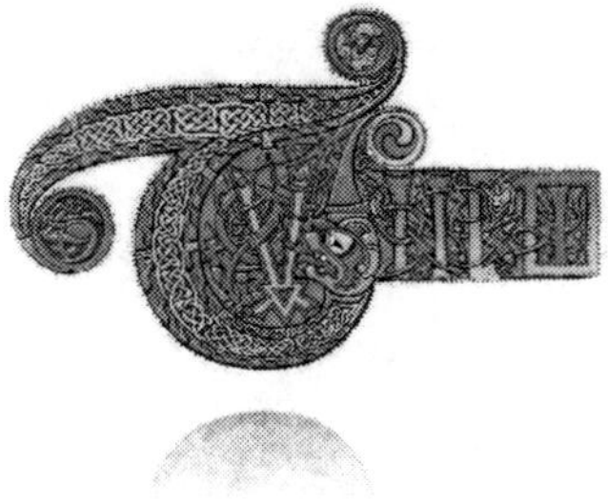

Caliban
All the infections that the sun sucks up
From bogs, fens, flats, on Prosper fall, and make him
By inchmeal a disease!

The Tempest 2.2.1-3

Forced to be Prospero's slave because of Caliban's attempted act of violence against Prospero's daughter, Caliban is gathering wood for Prospero--and cursing him the whole while.

Caliban: *Let Prospero be infected with every possible bacteria that the sun's rays dry up in marshes, swamps, and plains. Bit by bit, turn him into an illness.*

Difficulty of Following Advice

DECEMBER 12

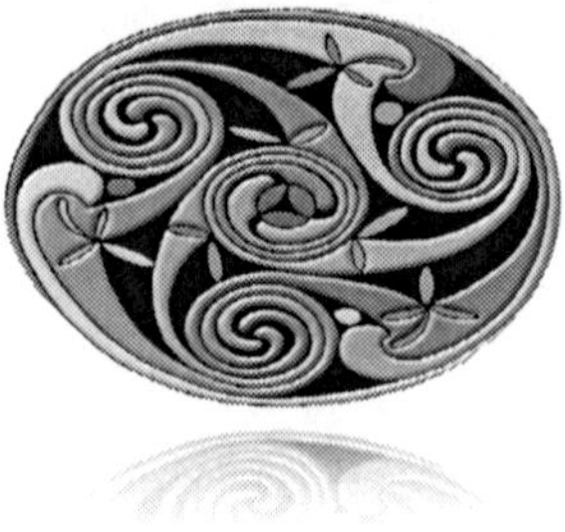

Portia

If to do were as easy as to know what were good
to do, chapels had been churches, and poor men's
cottages princes' palaces, - it is a good divine that
follows his own instructions. . . .

The Merchant of Venice 1.2.12-15

When Portia praises the good advice of her waiting woman, Nerissa, on the subject of moderation, Nerissa remarks that it would be even better if she herself actually followed it. Portia comments.

Portia: *If performing a deed were as simple a matter as discerning which action were best, small places of worship would have been expensive churches and the humble dwellings of the poor would have been palatial mansions of rulers. Only an exceptionally virtuous priest follows his/her own advice.*

Lover's Struggle for Words

DECEMBER 13

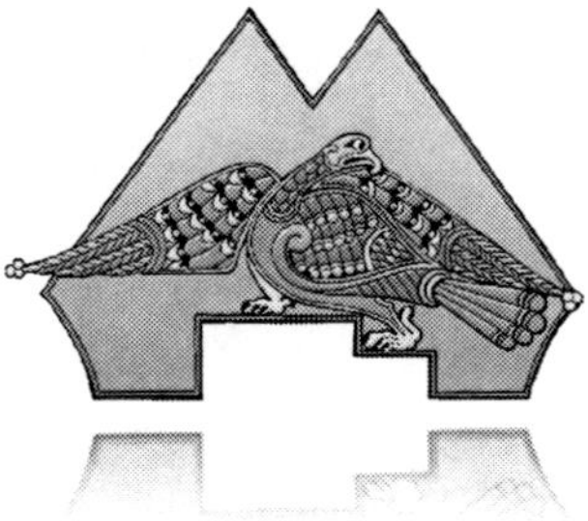

Benedick

No, I was not
born under a rhyming planet, nor I cannot woo in
festival terms.

Much Ado About Nothing 5.2.39-41

Benedick says this to himself while waiting to speak with his adored Beatrice. He laments he cannot put his love into verse form even though his love is as great as some of the great lovers in classical literature.

Benedick: *I was not born under an astrological sign favoring poetry, nor am I capable of jubilant language.*

Resoluteness

DECEMBER 14

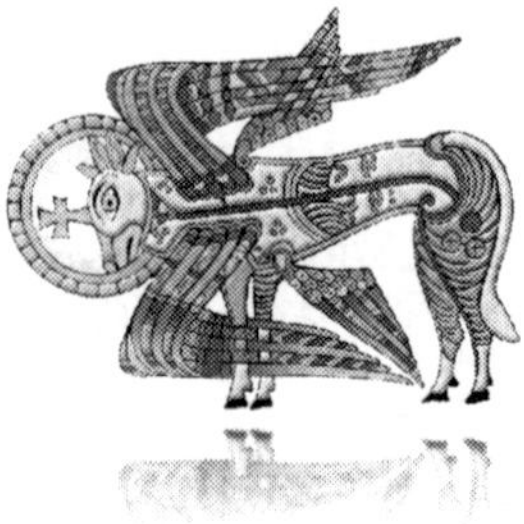

Claudio

Why give you me this shame?
Think you I can a resolution fetch
From flowery tenderness? If I must die,
I will encounter darkness as a bride
And hug it in mine arms.

Measure for Measure 3.1.80-84

Sentenced to die for impregnating his fiancée contrary to the laws of Vienna, Claudio rejects the advice of his sister Isabella that the fear of death is mostly in one's imagination.

Claudio: *Why do you disgrace me this way? Do you think I can derive the conviction to die from sugary sentiments? If I must die, I will meet the dark void like a bride and embrace it.*

Dawn
DECEMBER 15

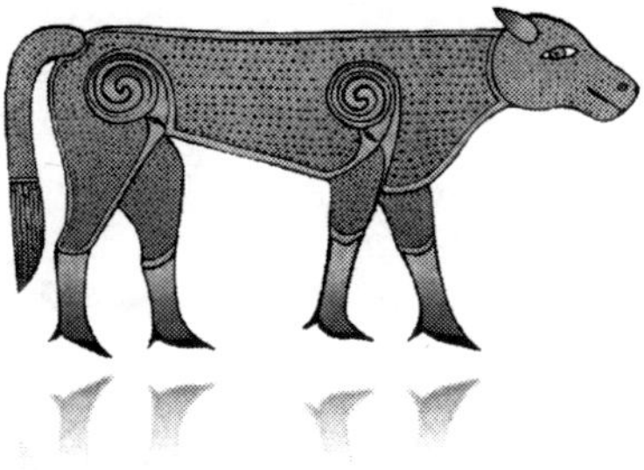

Prospero

the morning steals upon the night,
Melting the darkness. . . .

The Tempest 5.1.65-66

Prospero says this to Ariel, using the sunrise as an analogy to describe the way in which the charm that he has used to ensnare his enemies is now melting away.

Prospero: *The morning creeps softly upon the night, dissolving the blackness.*

Uneasiness

DECEMBER 16

Horatio
A mote it is to trouble the mind's eye.

Hamlet 1.1.115

Barnardo, one of the soldiers on watch at the castle's battlements, and Horatio, Prince Hamlet's dear friend, are discussing recent appearances of the ghost of King Hamlet.

Horatio: *It disturbs one's soul like a particle of dust disturbs the eye.*

Currying Favor

DECEMBER 17

Metellus

O let us have him, for his silver hairs
Will purchase us a good opinion,
And buy men's voices to commend our deeds.
It shall be said his judgement ruled our hands.
Our youths and wildness shall no whit appear,
But all be buried in his gravity.

Julius Caesar 2.1.143-48

Although Brutus eventually convinces the group of conspirators that Cicero won't follow anything that someone else started, one of the conspirators, Metellus, suggests that the support of the elder statesman Cicero will help them in their planned assassination of Caesar.

Metellus: *Oh, let us include him since his lustrous grey hairs will win us public commendation and also gain the approval of others. If Cicero joins us, it will be claimed that Cicero's good sense guided our actions. Therefore, our youth and rashness will disappear under the weight of Cicero's seriousness and importance.*

Prayer

DECEMBER 18

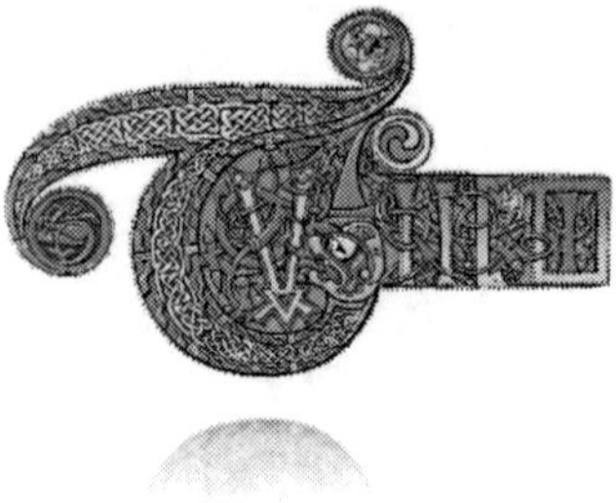

King
O wretched state! O bosom black as death!
O limed soul, that struggling to be free
Art more engag'd! Help, angels!

***Hamlet* 3.3.67-69**

Claudius, alone at prayer, acknowledges the darkness of his soul which is burdened with the murder of his brother, King Hamlet. Unwilling to give up the fruits of his sin, namely the crown and his brother's former wife, King Claudius admits the paralysis of his soul.

Claudius: *Oh, loathsome condition! Oh, passions as moonless as eternal night! Oh, trapped spirit that fighting to release itself is even more deeply ensnared! Assist me, ministering spirits!*

Novelty of the Macabre

DECEMBER 19

Trinculo

A strange fish! Were I in England
now (as once I was) and had but this fish painted, not
a holiday fool there but would give a piece of silver. . . .
When they will not give a
doit to relieve a lame beggar, they will lay out ten to
see a dead Indian.

The Tempest 2.2.27-29; 31-33

The jester Trinculo says this to himself as he tries to figure out what form of beast or man Caliban is. Caliban, the primitive son of the witch Sycorax, is trying to hide because he thinks the magician Prospero has sent a spirit, i.e. Trinculo, to plague him for working too slowly.

Trinculo: *A bizarre specimen! If I were in England as I once was and simply displayed this fish in public, every tourist there would pay me money. Even though such people refuse to contribute pennies to help a lame homeless person, they won't hesitate to give away ten times as much to view a dead exotic foreigner.*

Responding to a Crisis
DECEMBER 20

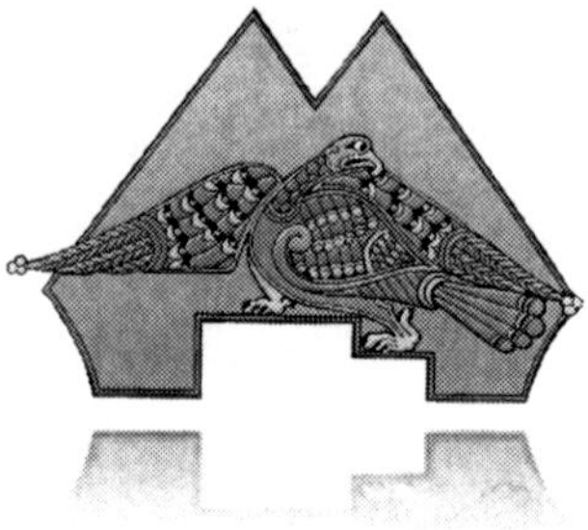

King Claudius

Diseases desperate grown
By desperate appliance are reliev'd,
Or not at all.

Hamlet 4.3.9-11

Claudius says this to a small coterie of his lords after Prince Hamlet has accidentally killed Polonius (Hamlet believed it was King Claudius himself). Claudius, fearing Hamlet's next action if the Prince were to remain in Denmark, decides to send Hamlet away to England.

King Claudius: *Illnesses that have advanced to a drastic stage must with a drastic remedy be cured--or never at all.*

Pain of Separation

DECEMBER 21

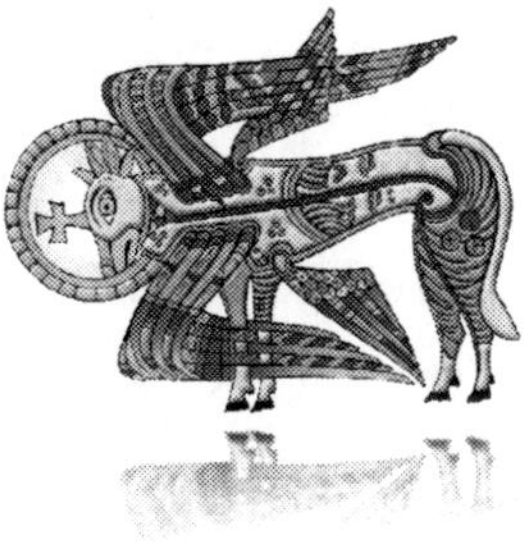

Sonnet 97
How like a winter hath my absence been
From thee, the pleasure of the fleeting year!
What freezings have I felt, what dark days seen,
What old December's bareness everywhere!

Lines 1-4

Sonnet 97: *How much like the season of winter has my separation from you seemed, who is the delight of the swiftly passing year. What stinging cold have I felt, what gloomy days have I seen, what evidence of old man December's destitution have I witnessed all around me!*

Lively Temperaments

DECEMBER 22

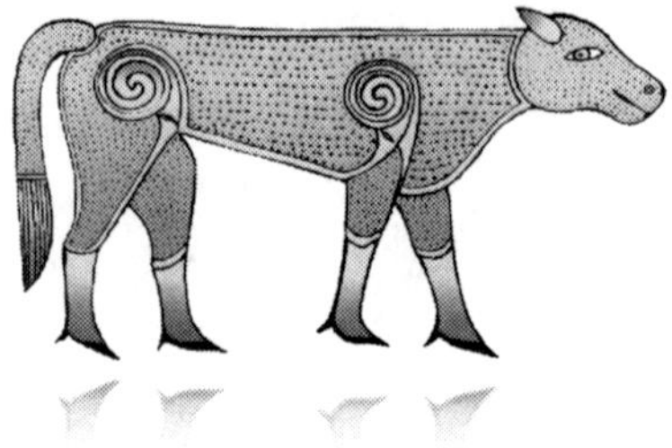

Gonzalo
You are gentlemen of brave mettle. You
would lift the moon out of her sphere, if she would
continue in it five weeks without changing.

The Tempest 2.1.183-85

Gonzalo, the faithful councilor, says this to Alonso, King of Naples, and Sebastian, his brother, who have been teasing Gonzalo. Gonzalo has been attempting to describe a utopian kingdom in order to distract Alonso who believes his son has drowned.

____

____

____

____

____

____

Gonzalo: *You are men who possess spirited temperaments. You would yank the moon out of her orbit if she would only manage to stay in it for five weeks without varying.*

Limited Perspective

DECEMBER 23

Prospero

Foolish wench,
To th' most of men, this is a Caliban,
And they to him are angels.

The Tempest 1.2.480-82

Having fallen in love at first sight with the third man she's ever seen, Miranda tells her father not to speak unkindly to Ferdinand. Her father berates her.

Prospero: *Silly girl! In the eyes of most men, this creature is a savage, and such a man views other men as divine beings.*

Love's Riches

DECEMBER 24

Sonnet 29

When in disgrace with fortune and men's eyes
I all alone beweep my outcast state. . . .
  thy sweet love rememb'red such wealth brings
 That then I scorn to change my state with kings.

Lines 1-2; 13-14

Sonnet 29: *When I suffer misfortune in the world and in society's eyes, in isolation I weep over my despised existence. Yet when I recall your precious love, it produces such riches that I disdain the prospect of exchanging places with kings.*

Legends of the Christmas Season

DECEMBER 25

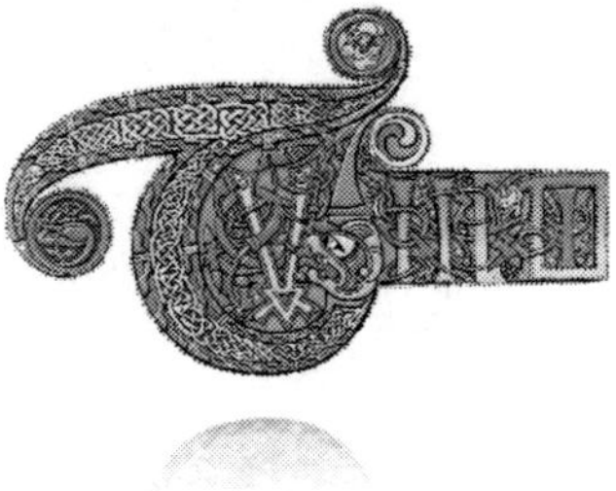

Marcellus

Some say that ever 'gainst that season comes
Wherein our Saviour's birth is celebrated,
This bird of dawning singeth all night long;
And then, they say, no spirit dare stir abroad,
The nights are wholesome, then no planets strike,
No fairy takes, nor witch hath power to charm,
So hallow'd and so gracious is that time.

Hamlet 1.1.163-69

The soldier on watch, Marcellus, says this to Horatio, Prince Hamlet's friend, and to Barnardo as the three recount the appearance of King Hamlet's ghost. The ghost flees when the cock crows.

Marcellus: *It is said that just before the season of Christ's birth is observed, the cock, the morning bird, crows all throughout the night. When this happens, the story goes, not a single spirit braves moving throughout the land, and the nights are beneficial. During this period, no planets cast an unhealthy influence, fairies don't steal, and no witch casts a spell because this time is so blessed and favorable.*

Contentment

DECEMBER 26

Sonnet 8
Sweets with sweets war not, joy delights in joy. . . .

Line 2

Sonnet 8: *Pleasantly perfumed flowers don't compete with one another. Happiness celebrates happiness.*

Questions of Existence

DECEMBER 27

Hamlet

What is a man
If his chief good and market of his time
Be but to sleep and feed? A beast, no more.

Hamlet 4.4.33-35

Hamlet has just witnessed the Norwegian Prince Fortinbras march through Denmark in order to fight the Poles over what Hamlet considers to be a worthless piece of land. Seeing Fortinbras' aggressive action, Prince Hamlet condemns his own inaction.

Hamlet: *What is a human being if the main purpose and use of his time is sleeping and eating? An animal, nothing more.*

Nature’s Fierce Wrath

DECEMBER 28

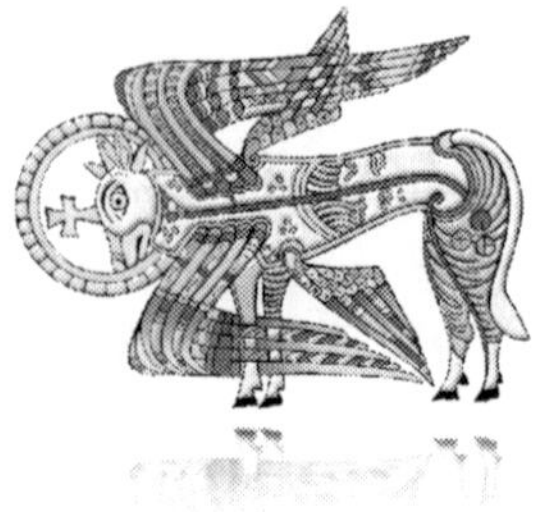

Prospero

I have bedimmed
The noontide sun, called forth the mutinous winds,
And ‘twixt the green sea and the azured vault
Set roaring war. . . .

***The Tempest* 5.1.41-44**

The deposed Duke of Milan, Prospero (who has taught himself magic), speaks to himself about the tempest he created earlier in the play to bring his enemies to his island. Prospero engineered a shipwreck so that he might exact revenge and force the repentance of his enemies.

____

____

____

____

____

____

Prospero: *I have clouded over the noonday sun, stirred up the turbulent winds, and caused a riotous tumult between the green sea and the sky’s blue ceiling.*

Importance of Wit

DECEMBER 29

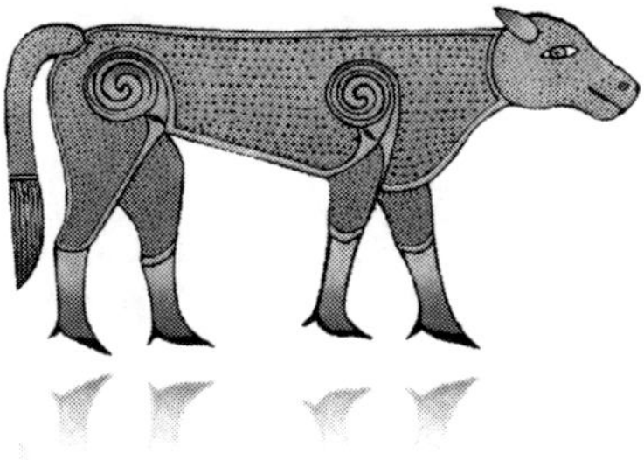

Stephano

Wit shall not go unrewarded while I am king of this country.

The Tempest 4.1.243-44

Imagining falsely that he is going to assassinate Prospero, the deposed Duke of Milan, and rule over the island that Prospero governs, the drunken sailor Stephano compliments the jester Trinculo for his witty remark.

Stephano: *Humor will not exist without being rewarded when I rule this land!*

DECEMBER 30

Prospero

this thing of darkness I
Acknowledge mine.

***The Tempest* 5.1.276-77**

Prospero, the newly reinstated Duke of Milan, says this to Alonso, King of Naples, concerning Caliban, the son of the witch Sycorax, who has masterminded a failed plot to assassinate Prospero.

Prospero: *This tainted creature I claim as a part of me.*

Recalling Wilder Days

DECEMBER 31

Falstaff
We have heard the chimes at midnight,
Master Shallow.
Shallow
That we have, that we have, that we have; in
faith, Sir John, we have; our watchword was 'Hem,
boys!'. . . .
Jesus, the days that we have seen!

King Henry IV, Part 2 3.2.214-19

Falstaff is speaking with Shallow, one of the justices of the peace who has been ordered to help Falstaff recruit soldiers to squelch the rebellion against King Henry IV. Not having seen Falstaff in many decades, Shallow and Falstaff eagerly reminisce about some of their more raucous youthful escapades.

Falstaff: *Many times we heard the music blasting at midnight, Master Shallow.*
Shallow: *Yes, we have, yes we have, yes we have; for sure, Sir John, we have. Our warning call then was "Let's get out of here!" Geez, the times we have had!*

2014

January

S	M	T	W	T	F	S
			1	2	3	4
5	6	7	8	9	10	11
12	13	14	15	16	17	18
19	20	21	22	23	24	25
26	27	28	29	30	31	

February

S	M	T	W	T	F	S
						1
2	3	4	5	6	7	8
9	10	11	12	13	14	15
16	17	18	19	20	21	22
23	24	25	26	27	28	

March

S	M	T	W	T	F	S
						1
2	3	4	5	6	7	8
9	10	11	12	13	14	15
16	17	18	19	20	21	22
23	24	25	26	27	28	29
30	31					

April

S	M	T	W	T	F	S
		1	2	3	4	5
6	7	8	9	10	11	12
13	14	15	16	17	18	19
20	21	22	23	24	25	26
27	28	29	30			

May

S	M	T	W	T	F	S
				1	2	3
4	5	6	7	8	9	10
11	12	13	14	15	16	17
18	19	20	21	22	23	24
25	26	27	28	29	30	31

June

S	M	T	W	T	F	S
1	2	3	4	5	6	7
8	9	10	11	12	13	14
15	16	17	18	19	20	21
22	23	24	25	26	27	28
29	30					

July

S	M	T	W	T	F	S
		1	2	3	4	5
6	7	8	9	10	11	12
13	14	15	16	17	18	19
20	21	22	23	24	25	26
27	28	29	30	31		

August

S	M	T	W	T	F	S
					1	2
3	4	5	6	7	8	9
10	11	12	13	14	15	16
17	18	19	20	21	22	23
24	25	26	27	28	29	30
31						

September

S	M	T	W	T	F	S
	1	2	3	4	5	6
7	8	9	10	11	12	13
14	15	16	17	18	19	20
21	22	23	24	25	26	27
28	29	30				

October

S	M	T	W	T	F	S
			1	2	3	4
5	6	7	8	9	10	11
12	13	14	15	16	17	18
19	20	21	22	23	24	25
26	27	28	29	30	31	

November

S	M	T	W	T	F	S
						1
2	3	4	5	6	7	8
9	10	11	12	13	14	15
16	17	18	19	20	21	22
23	24	25	26	27	28	29
30						

December

S	M	T	W	T	F	S
	1	2	3	4	5	6
7	8	9	10	11	12	13
14	15	16	17	18	19	20
21	22	23	24	25	26	27
28	29	30	31			

2015

January

S	M	T	W	T	F	S
				1	2	3
4	5	6	7	8	9	10
11	12	13	14	15	16	17
18	19	20	21	22	23	24
25	26	27	28	29	30	31

February

S	M	T	W	T	F	S
1	2	3	4	5	6	7
8	9	10	11	12	13	14
15	16	17	18	19	20	21
22	23	24	25	26	27	28

March

S	M	T	W	T	F	S
1	2	3	4	5	6	7
8	9	10	11	12	13	14
15	16	17	18	19	20	21
22	23	24	25	26	27	28
29	30	31				

April

S	M	T	W	T	F	S
			1	2	3	4
5	6	7	8	9	10	11
12	13	14	15	16	17	18
19	20	21	22	23	24	25
26	27	28	29	30		

May

S	M	T	W	T	F	S
					1	2
3	4	5	6	7	8	9
10	11	12	13	14	15	16
17	18	19	20	21	22	23
24	25	26	27	28	29	30
31						

June

S	M	T	W	T	F	S
	1	2	3	4	5	6
7	8	9	10	11	12	13
14	15	16	17	18	19	20
21	22	23	24	25	26	27
28	29	30				

July

S	M	T	W	T	F	S
			1	2	3	4
5	6	7	8	9	10	11
12	13	14	15	16	17	18
19	20	21	22	23	24	25
26	27	28	29	30	31	

August

S	M	T	W	T	F	S
						1
2	3	4	5	6	7	8
9	10	11	12	13	14	15
16	17	18	19	20	21	22
23	24	25	26	27	28	29
30	31					

September

S	M	T	W	T	F	S
		1	2	3	4	5
6	7	8	9	10	11	12
13	14	15	16	17	18	19
20	21	22	23	24	25	26
27	28	29	30			

October

S	M	T	W	T	F	S
				1	2	3
4	5	6	7	8	9	10
11	12	13	14	15	16	17
18	19	20	21	22	23	24
25	26	27	28	29	30	31

November

S	M	T	W	T	F	S
1	2	3	4	5	6	7
8	9	10	11	12	13	14
15	16	17	18	19	20	21
22	23	24	25	26	27	28
29	30					

December

S	M	T	W	T	F	S
		1	2	3	4	5
6	7	8	9	10	11	12
13	14	15	16	17	18	19
20	21	22	23	24	25	26
27	28	29	30	31		

2016

January

S	M	T	W	T	F	S
					1	2
3	4	5	6	7	8	9
10	11	12	13	14	15	16
17	18	19	20	21	22	23
24	25	26	27	28	29	30
31						

February

S	M	T	W	T	F	S
	1	2	3	4	5	6
7	8	9	10	11	12	13
14	15	16	17	18	19	20
21	22	23	24	25	26	27
28	29					

March

S	M	T	W	T	F	S
		1	2	3	4	5
6	7	8	9	10	11	12
13	14	15	16	17	18	19
20	21	22	23	24	25	26
27	28	29	30	31		

April

S	M	T	W	T	F	S
					1	2
3	4	5	6	7	8	9
10	11	12	13	14	15	16
17	18	19	20	21	22	23
24	25	26	27	28	29	30

May

S	M	T	W	T	F	S
1	2	3	4	5	6	7
8	9	10	11	12	13	14
15	16	17	18	19	20	21
22	23	24	25	26	27	28
29	30	31				

June

S	M	T	W	T	F	S
			1	2	3	4
5	6	7	8	9	10	11
12	13	14	15	16	17	18
19	20	21	22	23	24	25
26	27	28	29	30		

July

S	M	T	W	T	F	S
					1	2
3	4	5	6	7	8	9
10	11	12	13	14	15	16
17	18	19	20	21	22	23
24	25	26	27	28	29	30
31						

August

S	M	T	W	T	F	S
	1	2	3	4	5	6
7	8	9	10	11	12	13
14	15	16	17	18	19	20
21	22	23	24	25	26	27
28	29	30	31			

September

S	M	T	W	T	F	S
				1	2	3
4	5	6	7	8	9	10
11	12	13	14	15	16	17
18	19	20	21	22	23	24
25	26	27	28	29	30	

October

S	M	T	W	T	F	S
						1
2	3	4	5	6	7	8
9	10	11	12	13	14	15
16	17	18	19	20	21	22
23	24	25	26	27	28	29
30	31					

November

S	M	T	W	T	F	S
		1	2	3	4	5
6	7	8	9	10	11	12
13	14	15	16	17	18	19
20	21	22	23	24	25	26
27	28	29	30			

December

S	M	T	W	T	F	S
				1	2	3
4	5	6	7	8	9	10
11	12	13	14	15	16	17
18	19	20	21	22	23	24
25	26	27	28	29	30	31

2017

January

S	M	T	W	T	F	S
1	2	3	4	5	6	7
8	9	10	11	12	13	14
15	16	17	18	19	20	21
22	23	24	25	26	27	28
29	30	31				

February

S	M	T	W	T	F	S
			1	2	3	4
5	6	7	8	9	10	11
12	13	14	15	16	17	18
19	20	21	22	23	24	25
26	27	28				

March

S	M	T	W	T	F	S
			1	2	3	4
5	6	7	8	9	10	11
12	13	14	15	16	17	18
19	20	21	22	23	24	25
26	27	28	29	30	31	

April

S	M	T	W	T	F	S
						1
2	3	4	5	6	7	8
9	10	11	12	13	14	15
16	17	18	19	20	21	22
23	24	25	26	27	28	29
30						

May

S	M	T	W	T	F	S
	1	2	3	4	5	6
7	8	9	10	11	12	13
14	15	16	17	18	19	20
21	22	23	24	25	26	27
28	29	30	31			

June

S	M	T	W	T	F	S
				1	2	3
4	5	6	7	8	9	10
11	12	13	14	15	16	17
18	19	20	21	22	23	24
25	26	27	28	29	30	

July

S	M	T	W	T	F	S
						1
2	3	4	5	6	7	8
9	10	11	12	13	14	15
16	17	18	19	20	21	22
23	24	25	26	27	28	29
30	31					

August

S	M	T	W	T	F	S
		1	2	3	4	5
6	7	8	9	10	11	12
13	14	15	16	17	18	19
20	21	22	23	24	25	26
27	28	29	30	31		

September

S	M	T	W	T	F	S
					1	2
3	4	5	6	7	8	9
10	11	12	13	14	15	16
17	18	19	20	21	22	23
24	25	26	27	28	29	30

October

S	M	T	W	T	F	S
1	2	3	4	5	6	7
8	9	10	11	12	13	14
15	16	17	18	19	20	21
22	23	24	25	26	27	28
29	30	31				

November

S	M	T	W	T	F	S
			1	2	3	4
5	6	7	8	9	10	11
12	13	14	15	16	17	18
19	20	21	22	23	24	25
26	27	28	29	30		

December

S	M	T	W	T	F	S
					1	2
3	4	5	6	7	8	9
10	11	12	13	14	15	16
17	18	19	20	21	22	23
24	25	26	27	28	29	30
31						

Acknowledgments

I owe a debt of thanks to my twin sister Judy, Pat Rose, my sister Colleen, Judith Branzburg, Manny Perea, Pat Shapiro, and my sons Ben and Nate for their invaluable help at various stages of this project. Without their assistance, this book would have been immeasurably poorer.

CPSIA information can be obtained at www.ICGtesting.com
Printed in the USA
LVOW12s1657311013

359332LV00007B/25/P

9 781457 523045